Dispatches from an Unofficial War Artist

Dispatches from an

Text and images: Peter Kennard

Unofficial War Artist

Foreword: Ken Livingstone MP,
Mayor of London

Introduction: Amanda Hopkinson

Design: Peter Brawne

Lund Humphries

First published in 2000 by
Lund Humphries
Gower House
Croft Road
Aldershot
Hampshire GU11 3HR

Lund Humphries is part of Ashgate Publishing

British Library Cataloguing-in-Publication Data
A catalogue record for this book is available from the
British Library

ISBN 0 85331 789 5

Designed by Peter Brawne/Matter
Printed in Singapore under the supervision of MRM Graphics

Ashgate US office:
Ashgate Publishing Company
131 Main Street
Burlington
VT 05401
USA

Distributed to the book trade in North America by
Antique Collectors' Club
Market Street Industrial Park
Wappingers Falls
NY 12590
USA

Acknowledgements
The author would like to acknowledge the generous support of Gimpel Fils, the Royal College of Art and the Arts and Humanities Research Board

Contents

Foreword

I first met Peter Kennard and his work during the GLC years in the early 1980s. His photomontages made a powerful impression, enhancing our campaign against nuclear weapons, as well as conventional and economic aggression against the peoples of the world. His work shows that aggression always has an economic basis.

I next encountered him when asked to be the speaking element in his recent works, *Welcome to Britain* and *Our Financial Times*. These installations were mind-openers, making you think and feel politically. It was interesting to be art and fun to move around such eloquent images. But although eloquent (and accessible for a politician too busy for the luxury of systematic art consumption), the images were not wonderful. They spoke the truth about the world at the fag end of the cold war and the aggressive resurgence of capitalism; about the conditions of too many people. Kennard is a revolutionary artist because he shows us what is really there, using with ease and force any medium necessary for his message.

At Gimpel Fils gallery in 1995, for *Our Financial Times*, I spoke of the terrible toll third world debt took on billions of people. How ultimately that debt affected workers in the west who lost their jobs when those debts forced third world countries into savage depression. How an escalating arms race against the Reagan- and Thatcher-defined 'evil empire' caused a world recession. How the 'evil empire' fell to a dreadful system where the average life span of a Russian man is now 58. How arms spending by corrupt third world puppet leaders, dependent on western arms manufacturers and banks, rendered millions more impoverished. How it is all so interdependent. Poverty and wasted life is not only over there; this corrupt system affects us too. There are homeless people sleeping rough in London with the same hopelessness at heart as a pauper in Managua or a starving child in Sudan.

In hitting at the heart of the matter, Kennard gives us hope. You can't begin to change something until you see what is really there. That is the message of Peter Kennard's work.

Ken Livingstone MP, Mayor of London

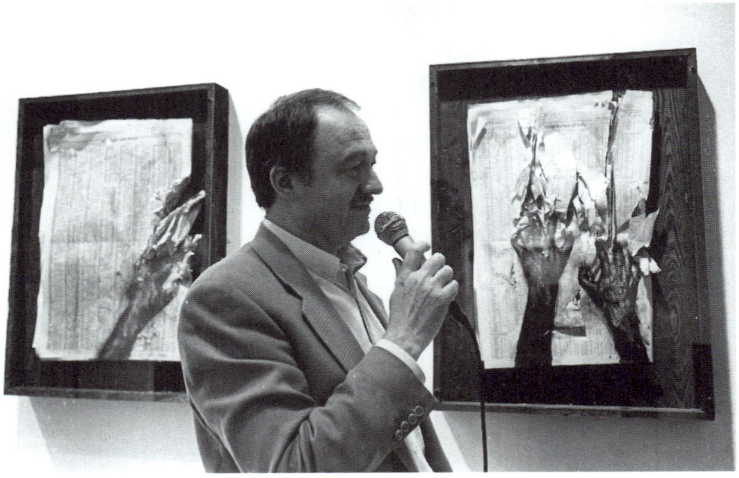

Introduction

Peter Kennard has all the credentials to render him an 'Unofficial War Artist'. He painted from the age of 13 in a coalshed; won a Leverhulme scholarship at Byam Shaw Art School five years later; worked hard to become the veteran of a raft of left-wing and radical campaigns, including CND and END (without ever signing up to pacifism), and along the way mastered an extraordinary range of techniques and materials which he integrated in spectacular fashion. Kennard's 'dispatches' effectively sabotage the role of the conventionally appointed variety, hand-picked by government to accompany their armed forces overseas to record the travails and trumpet the glories of military action. For Peter Kennard is more than a negative, more than merely unofficial. He is resolutely subversive.

Attempting to fit a multi-media, multi-faceted and – most of all – political and poetical artist into an existing tradition is bound to be at least partly a labour with the square peg and round hole. There is, however, one discipline into which Kennard slots comfortably. Called, by John Berger, 'a master of the medium of photomontage', Kennard has chosen this deeply unfashionable medium to convey categorical responses in an increasingly confusing world. It has given him freedom in using his training and talents as an artist, his skills as a self-taught photographer, a playful propensity with found images and carefully selected words, and his politicised rage in a range of symbols instantly recognisable to the visually literate. From posters of Margaret Thatcher as a truly Iron Lady to John Major twinned with the Mona Lisa; from CND banners with a broken missile impaled on its axis to the postcards of Cruise missiles rearing from Constable's bucolic idyll, *The Haywain*; broadening into more recent attacks upon the hypocrisies of City institutions and the political betrayal of United Nations human rights resolutions, Kennard has matched the medium and its highly-charged message.

The medium itself is largely a continental phenomenon that the British have never been entirely clear how to use or where to place. In that sense, as in many others, Kennard remains an unabashed maverick, forging his way in an art world become a market place that insistently values palliatives over challenges. How to establish the artistic or financial value of work that may be produced by a photographer, an artist, by both or by neither. Photomontage can consist entirely of found images, with or without found graphics; or it can be solely or partly composed of original photos or paintings, with or without authored calligraphy and illustration.

Or so photomontage's founding fathers determined. The pair who claimed its parentage, some eighty years after the invention of photography, were the German artists George Grosz and John Heartfield.[1] Even the French, keen to be the first in cultural discovery, recognised as much.[2] Michel Frizot's book on *Photomontage* is subtitled *Experimental Photography between the Wars*, marking what the author regards as the inception, heyday and decline of photomontage within a period hardly longer than a person's schooldays. Frizot traces its origins thus:

> 'Born in 1916, the progeny of Grosz and Heartfield, and again in Berlin in 1918 in the Dada group formed around Raoul Hausmann, Hannah Höch and Johannes Baader ... there is room for the suspicion that the invention of Dada photomontage as a means of disconcerting the viewer was designed to encourage a hope for the emergence of Truth from a lie.[3]'

Yet Frizot and Leiris are as wrong as Heartfield and Grosz, and for the same reason. Much store has been set by Grosz's comment, made to his friend and fellow Berliner in 1922, the theatre director Erwin Piscator: 'When John Heartfield and I invented photomontage in my South End studio at five o'clock on a May morning in 1916, neither of us had any inkling of its great possibilities, nor of the thorny yet successful road it was to take. As so often happens in life, we had stumbled across a vein of gold without knowing it.'[4] The concept of 'invention' was applied to a new art form that acknowledged Braque's *collages* and Picasso's *papiers collés* of the 1910s as its forebears. And it is indisputably true that many of their techniques were carried over into photomontage, just as it is true that many practitioners were (like Peter Kennard) artists well before they ever worked with photomontage.

But there is another, parallel, history – that of fine art's forever poor relation. For photomontage has been around almost as long as its prefix, photography. Ever since the single-imprint daguerreotype gave way to the infinitely reproducible printed image, photomontage has been with us. For the briefest period, the inside of a decade in the 1830s, the daguerreotype served as a modern-day replica of the miniature portrait so beloved of royalty in the business of forging dynastic and often distant marital alliances. The intention of these frequently hand-tinted originals in their oval silver cases was both to be true to life and to be life-enhancing. An extra touch of rouge to the cheeks, jet rather than greying hair, all could be fixed *after* the unique portrait was taken, regardless of whether the picture was painted or printed.

These one-offs may have assisted photography's claim to be a branch of High Art but did little towards establishing its credentials for realism. It was another French man, Niepce, who first succeeded in making a negative photographic image he then printed onto light-sensitive paper. He and Nadar on one side of the Channel, Fox Talbot, shortly followed by Octavius Hill and Robert Adamson (in Scotland) on the other, were soon experimenting in both adding and subtracting from new prints. Within fifty years, heavy box cameras and plate negatives were no longer essential to any but the most old-fashioned and stylised studio portraitists. Rolled film and 'instamatic' cameras – and Kodak's most famous slogan ever: 'You press the button, we do the rest' – were devised in the 1890s. The amount of control permitted to any amateur was in direct ratio to their skill. Any fool could 'press the button' and any laboratory process the results. (And did: more women were employed in processing and retouching film in Edwardian times than in any other industry outside the home.) But the variety of ways in which photographs were exhibited was also growing exponentially well beyond the confines of framed family snaphots on domestic

The familiar statement 'the camera doesn't lie' may be true but, like all clichés, is also banal. The camera lies all the photographer wishes it to, and can extend the lie ... by subsequent amendment

mantelshelves, out of the home and into the market and the media.

Photographs, by their unlimited capacity for reproduction, could have been the democratic medium *par excellence*. There is nothing uniquely irreplaceable or invaluable about a print. Yet, from the start, this essential difference to all previous fine arts was lost in a welter of misplaced debate. Was photography a science, a fine art or merely some kind of literal record of an external world? The familiar statement 'the camera doesn't lie' may be true but, like all clichés, is also banal. The camera lies all the photographer wishes it to, and can extend the lie to a greater degree by subsequent amendment. The horror recently expressed at the alteration of an assumed truthfulness by digital manipulation is similarly misplaced for there is nothing peculiarly authentic about photography *unless the photographer wants there to be*. Mao and Stalin famously had discredited and discarded colleagues removed from their company in official portraits:[5] as purges terminated their colleagues' lives, so air-brushing was meant to put paid to their public record and memory. There is little that digitising can do that cut-ups could not. It just does it better, more seamlessly. Photomontage was assisting at photography's birth.

Already in the nineteenth century, when photography was new, there arose an extravagant preference for adding rather than subtracting. It was a Swede, Oscar Rejlander, who made his deservedly forked reputation with a disproportionately famous representation of *The Two Ways of Life* (1857). Depicting the routes to heaven and hell, it naturally fell into what could have been called John Bunyan's *Pit of Platitudes*, the way of all flesh proving vastly more fascinating and susceptible to artistic interpretation than prayer, charity and devotion. Rejlander might protest that his large-scale parable required over thirty portraits taken individually, and in the interests of modesty, to spare the models from becoming voyeurs of one another's decadence and debauchery. It did not spare the monarchy from becoming adversaries in the battle between individual creativity and religious principle. Or, as the twentieth century would have it, art and politics. Queen Victoria, mother of the Nation, the Empire and nine offspring protested at its nudity, levity and lewdness. Prince Albert attended its inauguration and, according to tradition, insisted upon its purchase. (Perhaps the Queen considered private vice preferable to public display: Edinburgh Photographic Society loaned and exhibited only its 'righteous portion', the rest being discreetly screened behind a 'dark curtain'.)

As to Rejlander, what did he think he was doing, tampering with Nadar's so-called 'instrument of truthful record' within a mere decade of its invention? In the first instance, he claimed to be exploring 'the camera's usefulness to artists' and a no doubt elevated portrayal of 'various draped figures as well as the beautiful lines of the human form'.[6] More practically, he was doing something subtly different to applying the more obvious method of simply reshooting an arrangement of existing prints. Instead, he attempted to lay out the entire sequence of plates together but to print them one by one, already positioned. According to a witness: 'Each [image] in turn was laid upon the sensitive paper and all except the part that was to be printed was covered with black velvet'.[7] Although, to contemporary eyes, the individual components look oddly out of scale, immense care was expended in rendering these disparate portraits integral to a final work measuring 31 by 16 inches. Modestly, Rejlander concluded that if his work was not to be taken as equivalent to a painted epic, then at least he might 'show the artist how useful photography might be as an aid to their art, not only in details but in preparing what might be regarded as a most perfect sketch of their composition'.

Photography was thus bifurcated from the start. The subtext to the debate over its definition as New Science or High Art was the indecision over its interpretation. It is hard, now, to consider seriously Delaroche's cry of despair uttered in 1839: 'From today painting is dead'. Photography could be integrated into a fine art movement, as witness examples from the Pre-Raphaelites to the Surrealists to present-day Brit Packers, but it also has a role of its own. That photography has an intimate and inviolate connection to the outside world is undeniable: without a photographable object, there is no photograph. But what happens when the object is also the subject, an active agent of its own portrayal? An early example was when possibly gullible children agreed to be dressed up and photographed: Rejlander claimed that the portrait of a weeping urchin sold over a quarter of a million postcards and raised hundreds of pounds for Dr Barnardo's Homes for Children. Additionally there is, of course, the photographer's own subjectivity. Rejlander used his sensitivity both to his subject and to his market to 'create an image'. And of course he chose one that, *pace* Dickens, could be found in any city slum. A visible reality was only enhanced by artistic invention, whether painted or photographed.

Such early episodes in the history of photography had a significant impact on how photographers understood their work, and on how the public read it. For there is little intellectual and no moral distinction to be made between a manipulated image in the sense of a studio pose, accompanied by the appropriate costumes and props, and a photomontage. The only real difference is that a studio pose involves a collaboration between photographer and subject; a photomontage requires no such collusion, the artist(s) alone decide on the content. Arguably, the Pictorialist Movement that paralleled and in many ways emulated the Pre-Raphaelites was founded on the felicitously named 'combination prints'. Many literally combined cut-outs matching characters and backgrounds and often followed artists' sketches. Others simply combined the two, sketches and photos alike, using realism in the services of art to sharpen its impact. This was photomontage at its most primitive.

While the seed of propaganda photography was sown by the fictitious Barnardo's children, its most famous nineteenth-century use was undoubtedly that surrounding the Paris Commune of 1870. This mass uprising, which seized and held power for only sixty-two days as Prussian forces advanced upon Paris, generated a frenzied appetite for 'news'. The confusion resulting from civil insurrection and invading armies generated a propaganda war, in which partisans on all sides claimed to be the guardians of patriotism, and of

Like a magician's sleight of hand: now you see it, now you don't – and when you 'see' something, it is least likely to be 'really' present

the one accurate version of events. Photography appeared as the perfect medium for substantiating claims of own-side heroism against enemy atrocities and soon the industry fabricating 'true' or 'living' images approached that manufacturing splinters of a 'One True' Cross. Suddenly eye-witness portraits of generals on the guillotine, aristocrats dying in their four-posters and wild-eyed murderers repenting on their knees entered mass circulation.

According to Stéphanie Sotteau and Quentin Bajac,[8] photographs by one Eugène Appert (about whom we know little, but who happened to share his name with an anti-Commune General) served just such a jointly judicial and commercial purpose. Entering the prisons and linking his portraits of inmates to lurid 'scenes of crime', at times stage-directing their reconstruction, Appert claimed to be serving Paris's City Fathers. But he also sold thousands of cheap prints – curiously enough not least to the condemned and their families, who savoured the record, however contrived. As the authors conclude: 'Perhaps, finally and in their time, the troubling force of these images resides in the constant alternation between true and faked ... What they may lose in verisimilitude through copying traditional historic techniques of epic painting too fervently, Appert's photomontages regain in visual intensity. By allying the naturalism of photography to the dramatic strength of historical painting, both contribute to construct a myth and falsify history in the eyes of his spectators.' It was a legend that viewers were co-opted into and to which they eagerly adhered.

What matters is that they all knew it to be untrue, not only in image but often also in fact: the bodies of dead Communards were clothed in aristocratic outfits to make up the numbers displayed and photographed on trestles, as supposed evidence of the revolutionaries' ferocity. The significance of the montages by Appert among others[9] was that the real myth lay in taking seriously seeing as believing. Like a magician's sleight of hand: now you see it, now you don't – and when you 'see' something, it is least likely to be 'really' present. While some people presumably bought prints and newspapers to prove the rightness of their political position, others merely wanted to be able to give a concrete illustration of its righteousness.

Jules Raudnitz took the technique to its extreme. To our eyes his series on the 'Red Sabbath', which included *Saturnalia on the Place Vendôme*, *The Devils of the Bastille*, and *The 'Pétroleuses' at the Ministry of Finance*, may merely look ludicrous. They were, however, immensely popular in their own day, presumably with a clientele who preferred to believe that the orgiastic Saturnalia included Roman attributes. Devils came equipped with horns and masks; and the *pétroleuses*, like their forebears at the guillotine, the (similarly fictitious) *tricoteuses*, sported hideous animal heads, suitably resembling ancient monsters of war and pestilence. The importance lies in the use of photography rather than, say, the familiar skills of a cartoonist or satirist. The result harks back to the previous century and the work of Hogarth or Gillray, as it also looks forward, anticipating the grotesque caricatures of Daumier, even Goya.

Interestingly, photomontage was little vaunted as a propaganda technique during our Edwardian period. So little so, in fact, that it was perfectly feasible for Grosz to boast of his new 'discovery'.[10] In effect, Appert was merely an early instance of what soon became so widespread as to be commonplace: the manipulation of print images and the harnessing of photomontage in the promotion of the status quo or, as in his case, the outrightly reactionary and deliberately misleading. During the First World War the hijacking of photomontage to propagandise an armed conflict or government-of-the-day cause reached its apogee. The ban on permitting photographers to document military action gave carte blanche to the authorities for a rich variety of interpretation and reconstruction. What is denied has a necessary impact on what is created: just as Prince Albert had ordered photographers going to Crimea 'no dead bodies', Henry Morris noted that 'All the public got to see of the First World War in photography was emasculated by the censor and sprayed with disinfectant'.[11] If photography was not telling the truth during this period, what was?

It was during this unbelievably bloodless war-to-end-all-wars that photomontage was born as a radical art tradition. And it was cast not only in a new politics but as a fresh art form, image and text, in magazine format. Formerly, even if you doctored your printed portraits, you remained a photographer. All of a sudden you could be photographer, artist, or neither. Simply by cutting and pasting – techniques at the command of every nursery school infant – you could assemble a photomontage that would achieve the heart's desire of all radical artists worth their name: to shock the viewers into consciousness of a significant political truth.

For photomontage is æsthetically inseparable from the radical movements with which it is inextricably associated. They cover the spectrum from Communist and Socialist monoliths to every splintered faction including German Spartacists and Russian Trotskyists. It surfaced at moments of crisis, as a rash of posters generated for the anti-Fascist Republican government during the 1936–9 Spanish Civil War, mostly by 'artists unknown'. At others, it was co-opted by anti-Party political forces, including Syndicalists and Anarchists. It was even adopted by the Italian Futurists and then the Vorticists, with their links to Suprematism and so to Fascism. Despite photomontage's revolutionary credentials, its trademarks of instantly recognisable messages and cartoons of immediately recognisable individuals projected a fresh era and identity which could serve the cause of populism and the cult of leadership on whatever side.

The cradle of this hybrid activity was Europe at a time of immense social unrest and instability, with considerable movement between countries, even continents. From the Mediterranean to the Baltic, from Russia to Holland, and most of all in Germany, France and among Central European émigrés, photomontage flourished. Man Ray, the endlessly versatile North American who settled in Paris, becoming inventor of the 'Rayogram' and experimenter with everything photographic, declared himself to be not a photographer but a *fautographe* for the embellishments and so falsifications of his images. The Chicago School was founded and composed largely of central and east European exiles, many of whom (like László and

Photomontage ... became the ideal link between incipient desire and its object. It was therefore ideal for advertising

Lucia Moholy-Nagy and Naum Gabo) introduced their proficiency in photomontage to the United States. The Russians carried photomontage through a rich variety of artistic outlets (including book jackets and magazine covers, allied to literacy campaigns). They excelled in the integration of graphics with 'taken' rather than 'found' photographs.

Propaganda works best with achievements to boast about and the political and economic transformation of the USSR was promoted by Alexander Rodchenko and Gustav Glucis, established as photographers rather than as fine artists. The fine line between political propaganda and commercial advertising was drawn only according to the 'product'. This, in turn, was determined by the adopted politics and even the native country of the propagandist/advertiser. West European 'competition' was East European 'emulation': the jargon altered along with the images, but the style owed much to the classicism of a black-and-white photograph with a strong geometric balance of primary shapes that would prove eye-catching even from a distance, a play on scale and shadow, often incorporating the human form (most often an eye, returning the viewer's look) and some striking lettering, typically red.

It was Tretyakov who defined photomontage by content rather than merely by style: 'If the photography, under the influence of the text, expresses not simply the fact which it shows, but also the social tendency expressed by the fact, then it is already a photomontage'. Brecht went further, contrasting the limitations of a photograph with the power of a photomontage: '... a simple reproduction of reality rarely reveals anything about reality ... the human relations and functions inside the [Krupp works or a GEC] factory are not explicit in a photograph ... so something must be built up, something constructed, something artificially posed'. (Both the above were quoted with approval in *Photomontage Today: Peter Kennard*, a video of Kennard at work in 1983.)

This notion of getting inside 'human relations', using created art over documentary reality, is oddly akin to a further aspect of photomontage. Dadaists and Surrealists intended to disrupt and confront rather than engage in the political arena. Drawing heavily on Freudian theory, they rendered confrontation with the self as relevant as that with society. The notion that the human psyche responded to the workings of inner forces that might only be understood through analysis ran parallel with neo-Marxist interpretations of a proletariat manipulated by the power of business and capitalism. Despite the penchant for Modernist manifestos their practitioners balked at replicating old-style programmes for reform or revolution. Dada and Surrealism permitted the liberation of the unconscious in the name of art. Their techniques included the attempt to channel 'irrational' or 'uncontrolled' elements of the human psyche in artistic creativity via such activities as 'dream painting' and 'automatic writing'. These were, of course, entirely at variance with the intellectual control and direct communication essential to photomontage.

Aside from the difference of aims and techniques, psychoanalysis played a part in the manipulation of photomontage imagery. The felicitous juxtaposition of text and photograph, of the extraordinary in the everyday and the association of the banal and the surprising was intrinsic to both. One has only to view a montage like Janusz Maria Brzeski's *Even Faster*[12] which shows elements of a rapid Soviet industrialisation (workers beside a train piston, a car, a factory chimney), overseen by a ring-mistress sporting only boots, bikini and whip, to have a hint of possible psychoanalytic content. Conversely, if perversely, Moholy-Nagy's satirical *Eternal Feminine* gives the viewer another woman in bikini top and shorts. Here she is an athlete running through the walls of an enveloping sphere, and the voyeurs are a circus clown and a cowboy dwarf.[13] Transformation on both the political and personal level led to photomontages on the theme of metamorphosis, typified by Wanda Wulz's superimposition prints of *Me + Cat* (1932). It was, of course, left to Max Ernst to make the art/photography movement link specific through his montage of *Loplop Introduces the Members of the Surrealist Group* (1931).

Photomontage thus became the ideal link between incipient desire and its object. It was therefore ideal for advertising, particularly with the advent of the new picture magazines of the 1920s, and with the Bauhaus preferences for sharp lines and stark black-and-white, so particular in Germany in the 1920s and 1930s. Grete Stern, who took over Walter Peterhans' studio after he fled, made her living with her friend and colleague Ellen Auerbach employing photomontage to advertise hair oils, corsetry, gloves and other accessories. When she too finally had to escape Nazism, she went to Argentina, where – in a capital city obsessed with psychoanalysis – she doctored her own photographs to illustrate the impromptu analyses of a newspaper doctor, heading up a column that purported to reveal the inner meanings of dreams sent in by a tireless supply of readers.

Non-photographer but political activist John Heartfield, out of the same stable and period as Stern, maintained his mission and followed it to his end. At the time of his death, it looked very much a dead end: his work was suspect in the Soviet Union and rejected overseas. Brecht had been obliged to provide him with a 'reference' for the Soviet authorities, and he had redefined photomontage to leave out the politics: 'A photograph can, by the addition of an unimportant spot of colour, become a photomontage, a work of art of a special kind'. When he left England for East Germany in 1950, it had been in hope. As hope faltered his work stagnated.

Yet Heartfield was already cynical and economical in the wake of the First – 'Last' – World War. Disillusioned still further, he recycled more and more of his early work, often altering only the slogan. The more the world turned the more it remained the same and the more history he witnessed repeating itself. Communist Party jargon like *Where capital lives, peace cannot live* (1932) over a bayoneted dove of peace is replaced by a globalised *Never again!* (in 1960). *Like brothers, like murderers* (1933) is applied less strictly to German Brownshirts and Italian Blackshirts than to the threat of Fascist revivalism in a postwar Federal German Republic (where Heartfield made his home after 1950). One of the last montages he completed,

The extent to which energy and polemic has been devoted to the futile propaganda exercise of ‘keeping politics out of art’ belongs to another story, but is worth noting for its Englishness

collaborating again with his brother Wieland Herzfelde, shows a cinema audience watching a newsreel of Japanese atrocities in China (1937). It was captioned: ‘Today you watch a war on film, happening far away and overseas. But beware: if you don't unite in self-defence, tomorrow it will kill you too!’ Thirty years on, the caption stayed the same but the film shows US atrocities in Vietnam. The style and tone of his work, though, popularised here primarily in the pages of *Picture Post* was attenuated to vanishing point in the 1950s, a fate shared with the magazine.

Peter Kennard's own work in photomontage came of age with the Vietnam War. The over-riding need was to find a popular and adaptable artform through which to alert and communicate. The anti-war movement of the 1960s and 1970s was born of disgust at British complicity in perhaps the bloodiest century in world history. Globalisation brought the war home. Not only were we in the century of ‘World’ Wars, but media technology and new speed of communications could heighten our consciousness of what was being done in our name as never before. And Vietnam was the last war of the last century in which the United States was involved and where there was little restriction on the images sent back. So often, in fact, have photographers been blamed for ‘losing us the battle against the Vietcong’ that government and military authorities have imposed draconian conditions on war photographers, film-makers and even *official* war artists ever since.

It is interesting, therefore, that Peter Kennard chose to make Vietnam the subject of photomontage rather than photography. According to art historian Dawn Ades, who detects a homage to Heartfield both on the covers of *Private Eye* and the posters of R(adical) A(lternatives) to P(rison) in the 1960s: ‘Heartfield's influence ... is strongest ... in Kennard's anti-nuclear posters such as the photomontage using Constable's *Haywain*’.[14] Where the *Eye* and RAP confined themselves primarily to domestic political issues, Kennard always starts from an international – and internationalist – standpoint, rooted in a British tradition. And, as the Metaphysical poets insisted four hundred years ago, every artist's search is for the particular in the universal. The modified *Haywain*, mingling two centuries' accrued nostalgia for a countryside in decline bristling with the weapons that marked us (in the language of the time) as an offshore missile base for the United States, struck such a profoundly emotive chord that postcards of the montage sold in hundreds of thousands. A perfect blend of the familiar with the horrific now in mass circulation as in popular consciousness.

Britain has never, however, been that good at a sense of internationalism beyond one of empire. The extent to which energy and polemic has been devoted to the futile propaganda exercise of keeping politics out of art' belongs to another story, but is worth noting for its Englishness, appropriate to the maritime endeavours of a Canute. Kennard's images, which may make unexpected connections between, say, the Suffolk countryside, US missile enclaves and global destruction, belong in a continental tradition. The brief but powerful flowering of montages produced on hoardings during the development of London's Docklands in the 1980s by Loraine Leeson and Peter Dunn (who called themselves workshop artists) was a specific response to a particular situation: neither artist is still active in using photomontage.

The only book/journal to explore or theorise this incarnation of photomontage was *Photography/Politics*. It read as if midway between an academic analysis and a radical manifesto.[15] Edited by Jo Spence, Simon Watney and Patricia Holland, the boldness of the politics in the title became a little obfuscated by the language of co-authorship. The introduction to *Photography/Politics 2* opens: Photography is a central ideological marketplace of capitalist society' and closes: ‘We acknowledge the continuity of certain areas of photo-practice which will continue to be relevant in their opposition in relation to the much larger continuity of oppression and subordination inherent in patriarchal capitalism and its systems of self-representation’. Meanwhile the internet cannot find anything current to list or link under ‘photomontage’ at all.

Kennard sits equally ill with such pronouncements, but where does a political artist find his place? He may be widely reviewed, but his politics are widely disregarded. The Saatchi gallery risked buying one pallet, perhaps less to show good taste than to prove their open-mindedness towards a successful *enfant terrible*. He remains an anomaly on the books of Gimpel Fils, his Davies Street gallery. Nonetheless René Gimpel supports him loyally. More, he boldly welcomed Kennard's art auction on behalf of the independent candidate for Mayor of London, knowing that Ken Livingstone's cause would attract attention but that picture sales of Peter Kennard's attacks on capitalism and militarism are unlikely to be enhanced.

The internal contradictions of the art market are such that Kennard's work seems to find its natural outlet in the most unlikely places. Yet he takes a certain pleasure in introducing his work into the acme of state and private enterprise, so that they and not the work look oddly out of place. He talks in his text[16] of the packers' incredulity at being asked to ship a load of mutilated wooden pallets. The invasion of one of the capital's more hallowed spaces (the classical concert centre at the Royal Festival Hall) with what Kennard called looking, from a distance, like ‘a pile of debris’ was another such an instance, a part of the ‘pile’ in question having been hacked from the floorboards of the house where he worked. Screened with photographic images, the non-arbitrary assortments of wood, manifesting as the pallets on which the homeless regularly sleep, or as the lecterns from which the great and the ghastly pontificate on such matters as share prices, are regularly rearranged to suit the case he has to present. Polemics, here, comes harnessed to both the practical and the outrageous, very much in line with the post-1980s ecological propensity for recycling and with the persistently outmoded Heartfield.

Social fashion is as embedded in the language of what he does as in the medium he chooses to do it in. Globalisation became the buzzword of the 1990s, applied as much to moving money as labour around the planet. Internationalism is the word that Kennard has

John Berger has rightly described what he does as 'pure and dirty' and Peter Kennard feels rightly complimented

hammered home and refused to amend since the late 1960s. He is far more interested in by-products of the *Financial Times*'s global markets than in the markets themselves: in the mass migrations of those in search of jobs and homes; in those who end up virtually indistinguishable from the rest of the detritus in our 'cardboard cities' under motorways and around train stations. A basic precept of found images/photomontage is less that the world is your oyster than that the world's cast-offs are today's wearables: last year's newspapers and, in Kennard's case, any old piece of material (wood, cloth, even dust) that seems descriptive of an obsolescent society will serve a fresh purpose in awakening the viewer to shocking messages.

For Kennard it is always the human element that counts, even when his montages are bristling with weapons; scarred with presumably toxic waste; or come bearing banners of UN Declarations or lists of share prices from the *Financial Times*. John Berger has rightly described what he does as 'pure and dirty' and Peter Kennard feels rightly complimented. 'War is dirty work' is his only comment. It is more often authors than critics who comprehend Kennard's take on the world, politics and art. The indivisibility of all three lead him to segue from the killing fields of the former Yugoslavia to the dying streets of inner cities; from using his own photographs to appropriating 'found' images or collaborating with other photographers (principally with documentary photographer Jenny Matthews); from working out of a mixture of rage and passion that has him physically dramatising his own montages using everything from agitprop theatre to campaigning outside the Stock Exchange.[17]

Unexpectedly, perhaps, it was Matthew Arnold who declared that 'Men of culture should have a passion for equality'. The implication is that one is tantamount to the other. Culture, of course, is indivisible: Kennard is as widely read in literature as in fine art, his reference points are ubiquitous. Yet the fusion of politics and culture can be an explosive one, not least when a political system intervenes into a medium that would itself make political inter- ventions. Louis Aragon's comment (*apropos* of Mayakovsky) contains a warning: 'All too soon, poetic suppression was superseded by social suppression or, to be more precise, under the pressure of events, in the struggle in which the artist was embroiled, the two prohibitions were merged: the only poetry was 'in the revolution'.[18] All this is highly reminiscent of Fidel Castro's: Within the Revolution everything; outside the Revolution nothing'.

Kennard leaves neither poetry nor politics behind him in his imaginary travels to real places. Having worked with a number of contemporary poets and writers, including Peter Reading, Ric Sissons, Hilary Wainwright and E P Thompson, his last *Domesday Book*[19] alternates his own verse and image on the page. It's what Kennard himself describes as 'a sort of sustained rant' and Harold Pinter, in his foreword, as 'a brilliant and ghastly tapestry about power, desolation, destruction, death and "the market" [in which] word and image are locked together in a deadly and convulsive marriage'. Found pictures of starving African infants and marching Chilean soldiers alternate with constructed close-ups of skin over-printed with shares indices, or of stock reports streaked indecipherably with carbon. An iconography familiar from his earliest work with photomontage uses unrecognisable faces perilously insulated with gas masks or helmets; barbed-wire fences that interdict but do not insulate; weapons that are brandished against which bare hands can only claw. The human body is inherently vulnerable. The body politic, or the 'military-economic complex', remain faceless. Exposed faces, beside which Kennard merely conjures with the one word 'speak', belong to the powerless. A further project (which also became a book), is called *Unwords*.[20] Its starting point was the quantity of clauses in the amended UN Conventions and Charters, dissipated and torn by hands that can never either get to grips with them or receive their handouts. His work makes visible what heads bushy with missiles, eye-sockets stuffed with US (and, for good measure, USSR) flags, cannot sense.

Kennard's fury is palpable and has failed to dissipate with the years. Yes, it is a sick society indeed that overlooks poor people sleeping rough but pays critical attention to an art exhibition that illustrates their situation.[21] Kennard makes the invisible the visible by literally bringing the homeless and unemployed into the galleries where he shows his work. Photomontage owns a critical shock factor. By working on two levels, seducing the viewer with a familiar image that, on closer inspection, turns out to have been subtly – at times blatantly – subverted, it is as though he seeks to focus both the conscious and unconscious mind. Lulled by the subliminal familiarity of, say, a CND symbol, our attention is suddenly drawn to the missile broken on its axis. The same device was employed by Heartfield in adapting a crucifix into a swastika:[22] the juxtaposition of religion and politics is always a disquietening one. Curiously Kennard also started out obsessed with the body's cruciform possibilities.[23]

Art in the service of politics has a chequered history. It was the great Chilean poet and Communist Party spokesman Pablo Neruda who marked the hiatus between his poetry and his 'pamphleteering in verse'. Kennard's work disagrees: from his earliest impromptu exhibitions, he is consistent in both his fire and his targets. Since then, he has been the object of interest and misunderstanding in roughly equal measures. Leaf through his first scrapbook and there are the reviews of an initial London exhibition at the Zeez Arts Gallery in October 1970. They span the political spectrum in publications as diverse as *Tribune* and *Queen*, *What's On In London* and the *Daily Telegraph*'s 'Way of the World', the *Observer* and *Art and Antiques Weekly*. It takes little conjecture to figure out which announces: 'At last! A socially conscious artist who puts subject matter and content before formal æsthetic preoccupations'[24]; which rephrases praise as critique in: 'Aggressively revolutionary in content, his beliefs are extended to the technique'[25]; and which settles for a nod at the 'experienced etcher and print maker... [whose] technique, as well as scale, gives these close-ups of violent existence new pictorial flavour'[26]. Only Caroline Tisdall, writing a few years on, manages to be politically direct: '[Kennard]

It is a sick society indeed that overlooks poor people sleeping rough but pays critical attention to an art exhibition that illustrates their situation

was possibly the first English artist working with news-photo based material to regularly produce high quality images for the *Workers Press* and then *Socialist Worker* ...'[27]. Kennard was soon also to be working regularly for the *Guardian* and CND, END and the *New Statesman*, even the Labour Party – of which, however, he has never become a member.

To adjust McLuhan only a little, the medium may change but the message remains the same. Kennard is prolific across the artistic media. His targets stay remarkably consistent. The enemy remains faceless; humanity is with the victims. War is rarely in the interests of any but warmongers; the planet is as fragile as its population. His obsessions are trite when spelt out, overwhelming when displayed without stating the obvious, without rational discourse. An image that functions on a symbolic as well as an æsthetic level is one you remember. One which arrives unpredictably like a collage on a postcard, like a face screened onto a wooden palette or placard, like a photomontage on the financial pages of a daily newspaper, burns itself into your mind. Peter Kennard's use of montage rather surprisingly fits within a tradition as old as photography and with the political force of a world at war with itself.

Amanda Hopkinson

Notes

1 They anglicised their names (from Georg Gross and Helmut Herzfelde) in protest at the Kaiser's injunction, during the First World War, to salute fellow-Germans with the patriotic greeting: 'God Punish England'. Naturally, permission for the name change was denied but then, as both men were forced to flee by the rise of Nazism, the changes suited their move to an anglophone environment.
2 See Michel Leiris' introduction to *L'age d'homme*, Gallimard, Paris, 1939 (English edition, *Manhood*, Jonathan Cape, London, 1968).
3 Michel Frizot, cited, from the introduction titled 'The Lying Camera'.
4 George Grosz, 'Randzeichnungenzum Thema', *Blätter der Piscatorbühne*, Berlin, 1928. Quoted by Peter Selz in *Photomontages of the Nazi Period*, Gordon Fraser/Universe Books, 1977 (German original Carl Hanser Verlag, 1972), p.7.
5 David King, *The Commisar Vanishes*, Canongate Books, 1997 (first published in 1997 by Henry Holt & Co Inc., an imprint of Metropolitain Books).
6 *Photographic Journal*, vol.1, 1858, p.193.
7 Walter Woodbury in *Photographic Amusement*. Cited by Beaumont Newall in *History of Photography: From 1839 to the Present*, Museum of Modern Art, 1964, p.32.
8 All quotations regarding the 8170 Commune are taken from *La Commune photographié*, Edition de la Réunion des Musées Nationaux, 2000, Chapter IV, entitled 'Eugène Appert, les premiers photo-montages politiques?' Text translations by Amanda Hopkinson.
9 Including Trémelat, Verdeil, Vauvray, Muriel, Liébert, Durand, many of whom launched their careers with the gift of opportunity provided by the Commune.
10 As Grosz worked increasingly in fine art media, rather than photography and graphics, his partner came to be far more closely associated with photomontage. Brecht's famous reference for his comrade Heartfield describes him thus: 'John Heartfield is one of the most important European artists. *He works in a field he created himself, the field of photomontage.*' [My italics.] Taken from John Heartfield's biography by Marz, p.437.
11 Quoted by Rainer Fabian and Hans Christian Adams in *Images of War*, Imperial War Museum, 1983.
12 From his cycle *Birth of the Robot*, 1933.
13 Moholy-Nagy, undated. Moholy-Nagy was also the first to introduce psychoanalytic terms into his captions, *viz* in his *Mass Psychosis* of 1927, making the link to a Marxist construct of 'the masses'.
14 Dawn Ades, *Photomontage*, Thames and Hudson, 1976, revised 1986, 1996, p.58.
15 Only two volumes of this 'permanent, ongoing' project appeared (Comedia Publishing, 1985 and 1986).
16 See p.38.
17 See pp.20–1 and 60–1.
18 Louis Aragon, 'John Heartfield et la Beauté Révolutionnaire', pp.29–32 in *Photomontages Antinazis*, edited and introduced by Denis Roche, Editions du Chene, 1978. Translation from the French, Amanda Hopkinson.
19 Foreword by Harold Pinter, *Domesday Book*, Manchester University Press, 1999.
20 *Unwords*, Bluecoat, 1996.
21 The 1992 exhibition shown at the Towner Art Gallery, Eastbourne, as part of the Cross-Channel Photographic Mission, then at London's Royal Festival Hall, in 1994, adjacent to Waterloo's 'cardboard city'.
22 Made for *AIZ* magazine in 1933. It shows Christ bearing his crucifix, to which a Nazi is nailing the additional swastika pieces. The caption reads 'Without this, the Cross was still not heavy enough'.
23 See p.34.
24 Margaret Richards, *Tribune*, 2 October 1970.
25 Peter Fuller, *Arts Review*, 26 September, 1970.
26 *Art and Antiques Weekly*, 10 October 1970.
27 Caroline Tisdall, The *Guardian*, 18 October 1977.

Bibliography

Ades, D., *Photomontage*, Thames and Hudson, 1976, revised 1986, 1996, p.58

Buchler, P., *Ghost Stories*, Proboscis, 1999

Evans, D. and Gohl, S., *Photomontage: A Political Weapon*, Gordon Fraser, 1986

Evans, D. and Londger, A. (eds.), *John Heartfield/AIZ/VI 1919–1936*, Kent Gallery, New York, 1991

Frizot, M., in introduction to *Photomontage: Experimental Photography between the Wars*, Thames and Hudson, 1987, translation 1991

Herzfelde, W. *et al.*, *John Heartfield: Photomontages of the Nazi Period*, Gordon Fraser/ Universe Books, 1977

Holland, P., Spence, J and Watney, S. (eds.), *Photography/Politics*, vols I & II, Comedia, 1985/86

Kennard, P., *Domesday Book*, Manchester University Press, 1999

Rees, A. L. and Borzello, F. (eds.), *The New Art History*, Camden Press, 1986

'"Critical Decade" (black British photography in the 80s)', *Ten 8*, vol.2, no.3

Photomontages Antinazis, Carl Harper Verlag, Munich, 1972 (French edition, edited and introduced by Denis Roche, Editions du Chene, 1978)

Author's note

As I write this, the United Nations is pulling out of East Timor days after the elections in which the majority voted for independence. There is terrible bloodshed. The Indonesian military is on a killing spree. Some individual members of the UN who were there to protect the East Timorese are bravely refusing orders from the UN in New York to leave their compound in Dili. The world watches an awful betrayal. My country has been arming the Indonesians for years: guns, armoured cars and Hawk jets. We are steeped in the blood that is flowing.

How do I write about my work while this is happening? I don't go into a studio every day and lock the door against the world. I don't subscribe to the idea that artists should just emerge from their studio every couple of years with enough objects for a show. That the world outside can go hang. That the artist is independent, a free spirit. That the work is autonomous, having its own internal development. My own practice has been opposed to this notion. There is a formal development in my work but it doubles back on itself. It is charged with the outside world, at this particular time, in this particular place. Today, if I had to put together a show for a gallery in England, I would choose all the work I have done related to the United Nations, going back twenty years. It would be put together to make the horror of East Timor now, at this moment, the important issue. There is a vast gap between the rhetoric of the UN, its language, its declarations, its articles on human rights, and the reality. In my work I have tried to bring the rhetoric and the reality together to impact on the page. I try to show the language of the UN being smashed and broken by the suffering of the victims in an international game of world diplomacy.

The same image that I made to protest at the Gulf War has been used against the war in Kosovo, and could be used against the massacre in East Timor. The same montages of arms dealers that I made 25 years ago could be printed in a newspaper tomorrow as a condemnation of the annual international arms fair which opens in Chertsey tomorrow. The same dealers feed the same barbaric regimes with military hardware for the same repression of their own people now as 25 years ago.

Independent æsthetic development is a deeply flawed concept the minute I look out the window. A completely linear chronology is an impossibility when discussing my own work. It's the resonances over the years that might enable me to unlock my own history. Images that are already montages made up of fragments sidle up to each other, jostle, fold into

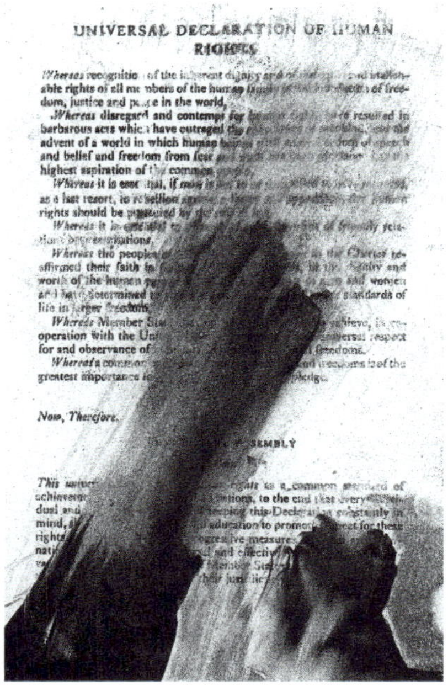

Left
Unwords 1/1996/Carbon toner, charcoal and pastel on paper
First published as a frontispiece to *Unwords* (Bluecoat, 1996). An exploration of the Charters and Declarations of the United Nations. The work in *Unwords* was begun in June 1995, when the UN was celebrating 50 years since the signing of the UN Charter

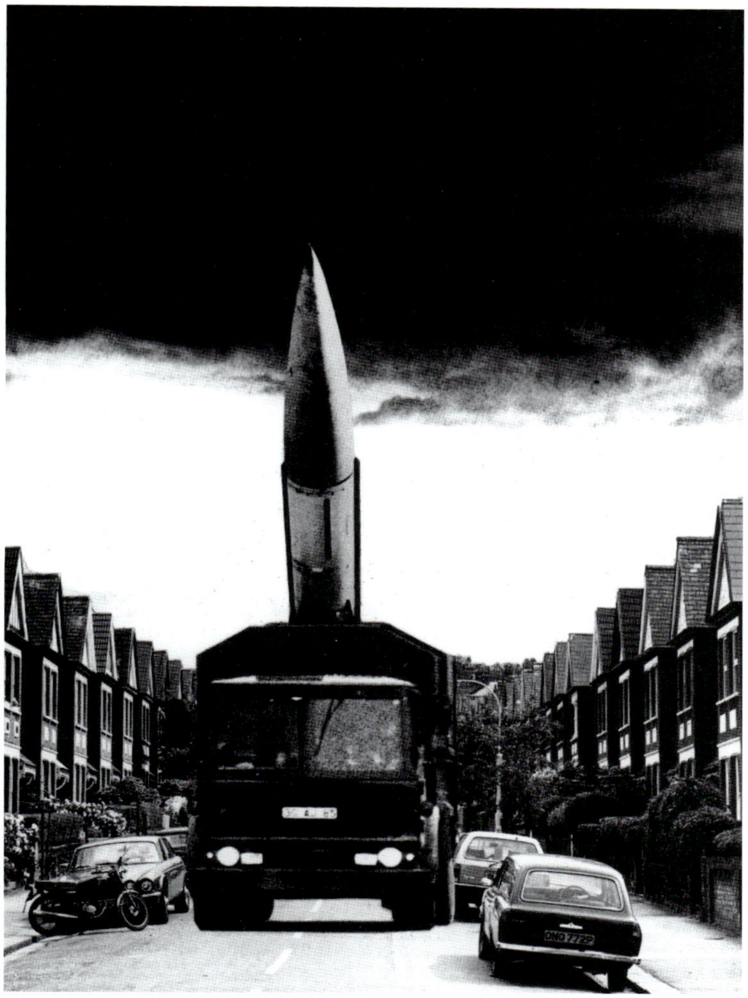

Left
Street Scene/1984/photomontage
First published as a poster for the Campaign for Nuclear Disarmament (CND) to protest against the movement of nuclear materials through densely populated areas

Below
The Gamble/1986/photomontage

one another, and in so doing make up another set of correspondences.

Over the last 30 years, as I've written statements, as my work has been reviewed, as images have been published in papers, made into posters and magazine covers, I have dumped the evidence into piles of papers, unsorted, disorganised. These piles are the evidence I must sort through in some way. They are in a room in Newington Green, north London. In the writings that follow I call these piles Archive A, although it would make an actual archivist shudder with horror. In the spill of material, there is, just discernible in places, a separation of elements – newspapers, negatives, montage originals, slides, etc. I'm using the piles of Archive A as the material trigger for my memory, as snapshots of my history. Bits from interviews I have given and manifestoes and statements that I have written will be quoted directly alongside the main body of the text, to give a sense of the actual historical time in which the work was made and act as a scaffolding on which to build the fragments of autobiography.

The piles have built up until now, when they overflow in chaos. They are the traces of the work in action, how it went into the world. Every time I've tried to put order into the piles I've been defeated and just added to them. Looking back

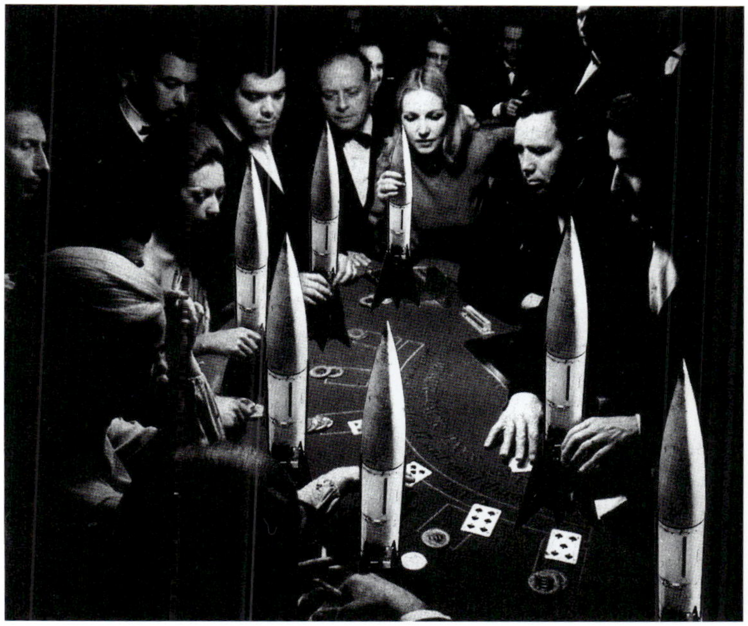

Right
News Bills/1998/carbon toner, charcoal on paper with metal
Installation of 'roof-rack' show in *Rencontres Internationales de la Photographie*, Arles, France, 1998

Below left
Values 1/1974/photomontage

Below right
Values 2/1999/photomontage
The photomontage from 1974, first made for *Workers Press* has another element added 25 years later for *Domesday Book* (Manchester University Press, 1999)

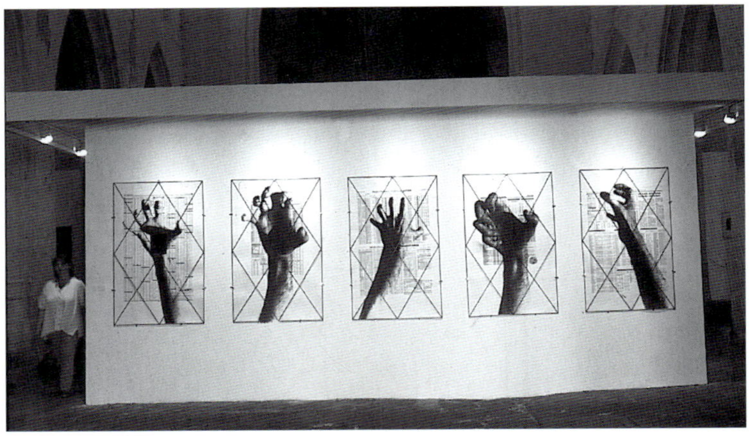

always seemed a denial of looking forward, of making the next thing. But now, to reconstruct my memory, I dip into the piles, so that any image can appear from any time, any place, any context. My story is locked into these towers of old papers, magazines, artist's statements, manifestoes, and jottings. If I can dam up the flow into related streams of imagery, a structure could emerge that would be adjacent to me living now, and through looking back, avoid looking back for the sake of it. So as not to turn into a pillar of salt, looking back must be for the sole purpose of looking forward, finding out ways to speak and to speak out now, in this period we're living through, where there is an inexorable pull to become distanced, cut off, ironic, detached from a reality processed through the agendas of CNN (for CNN see a million other logos flash by). It's as if I'm being interviewed by my own archives. Being led by the work into the methods and moments of its production.

In another building a mile away is my studio in an old factory in London Fields. There the bulkier work, large prints and parts of installations are piled up in two adjacent spaces. I call this Archive B. I see all of it as raw material to be reconstituted according to place, context and time (at this time East Timor). Year after year the work piles up. Since 1989 my work has become bulkier and is used as movable elements in a continuous installation. When I get asked to put some work up in a public space it is often from an organisation that is not on the official art circuit. They are probably skint; local funds have been diverted to an official venue. In these situations my shows are often determined by the size of the van they can afford to hire to move the work. It can be a 8.5cwt show, a Luton van show, or, as last year, when I showed at the Arles Photo Festival and they wouldn't pay for transport, a roof-rack show. The different pieces of work are juxtaposed in relation to economic necessity.

I flit between Archive A and Archive B like an accident investigator at a crash, sifting the remains for evidence. I know where to start, with paintings made in a coal-hole in Maida Vale 35 years ago. From there, sparks light up fragments of soot in a flash of illumination that I try to pin down.

Peter Kennard
12 October 1999

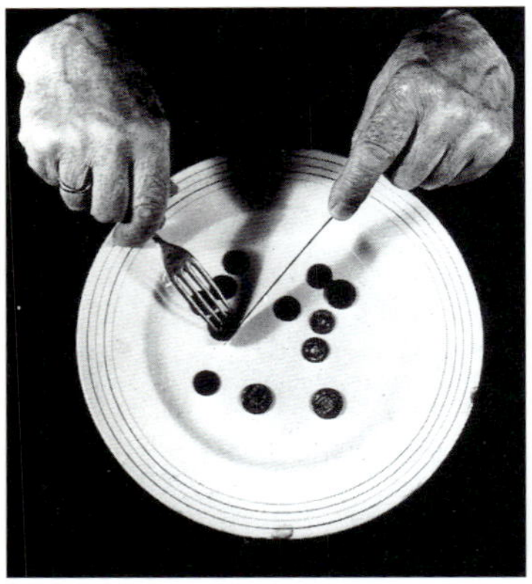

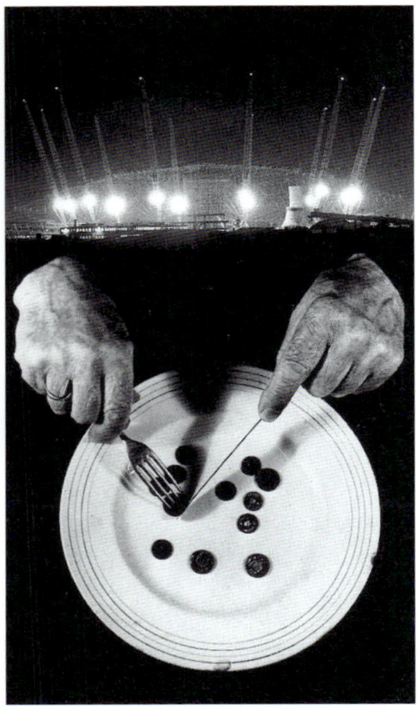

Dispatches from an Unofficial War Artist

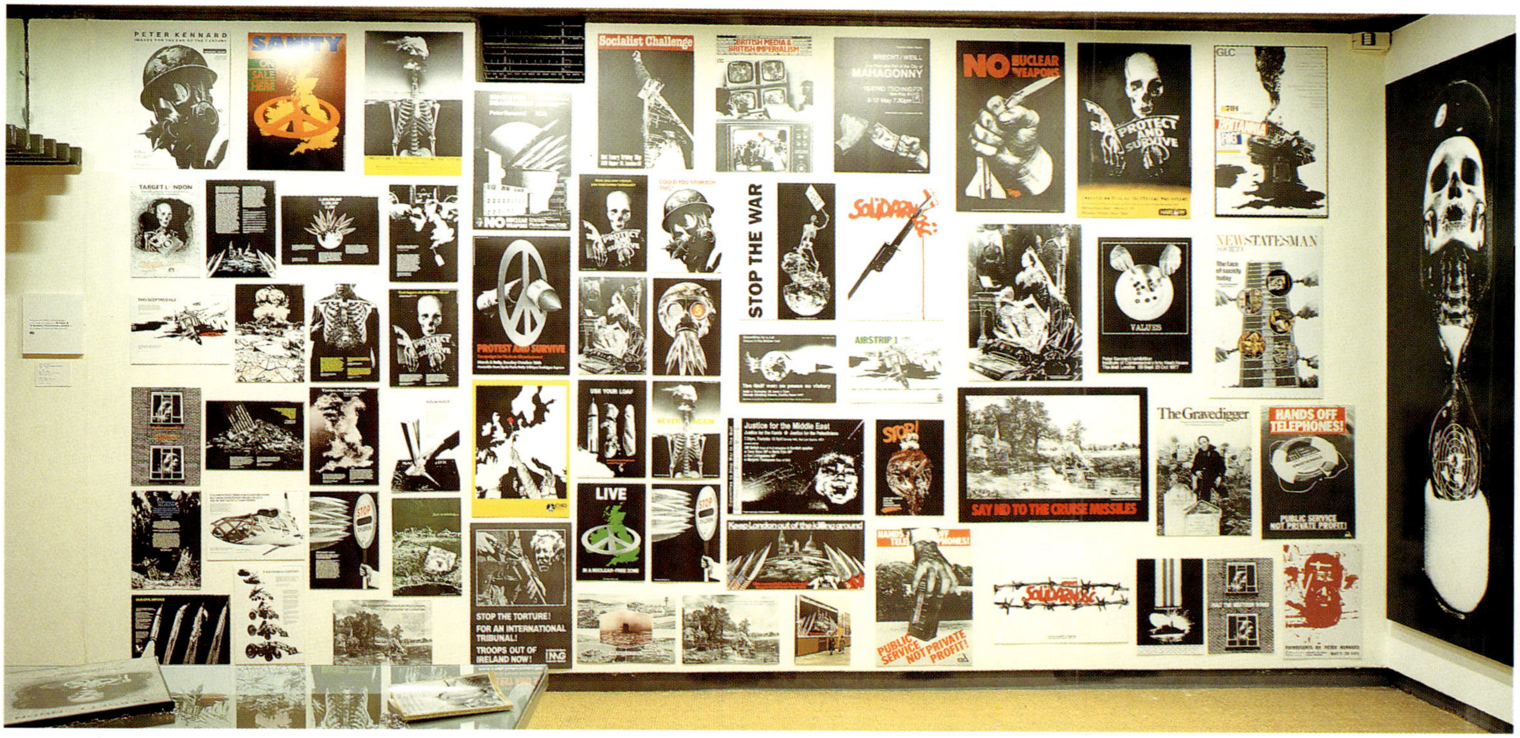

Photomontages in Print 1972–92
An installation containing 20 years' worth of photomontages printed in newspapers, magazines and on posters and book covers in *The Cutting Edge*, Barbican Art Gallery, London, 1992. The space included a table at which people could study many of the publications within which the images were included

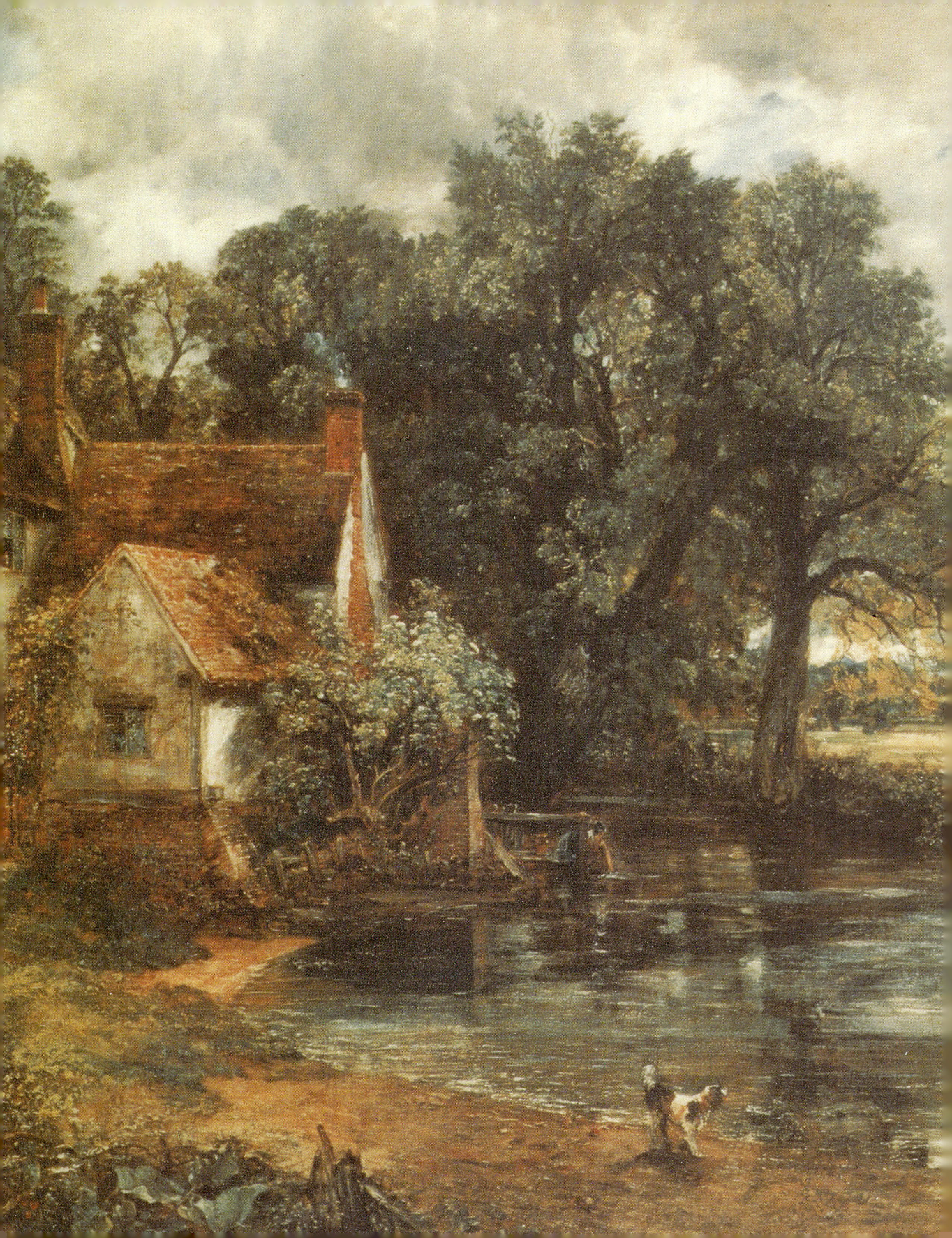

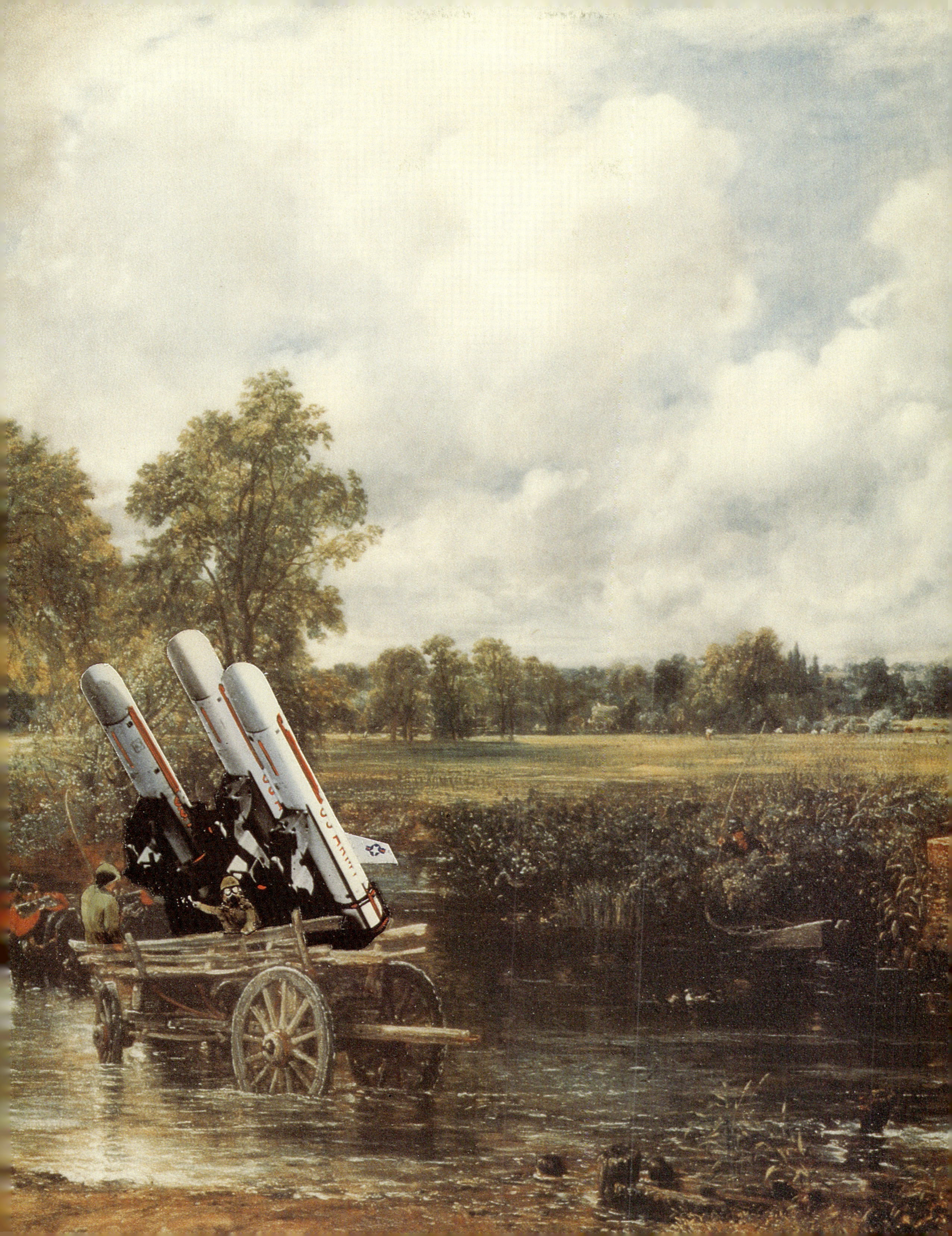

Previous pages
Haywain with Cruise Missiles/1980/ photomontage
The full title, which changed over the years in relation to the movements of the Cruise missiles, is *The Haywain, Constable (1821), Cruise missiles, USA (1983–1988)*. The painting *The Haywain* by John Constable is a well known part of British heritage. It shows a stretch of water below Flatford Mill in East Anglia, near where US bases were stationed

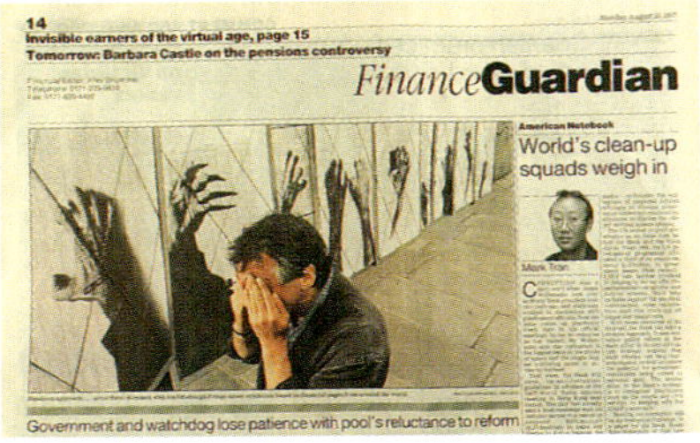
14
Invisible earners of the virtual age, page 15
Tomorrow: Barbara Castle on the pensions controversy

FinanceGuardian

World's clean-up squads weigh in

Government and watchdog lose patience with pool's reluctance to reform

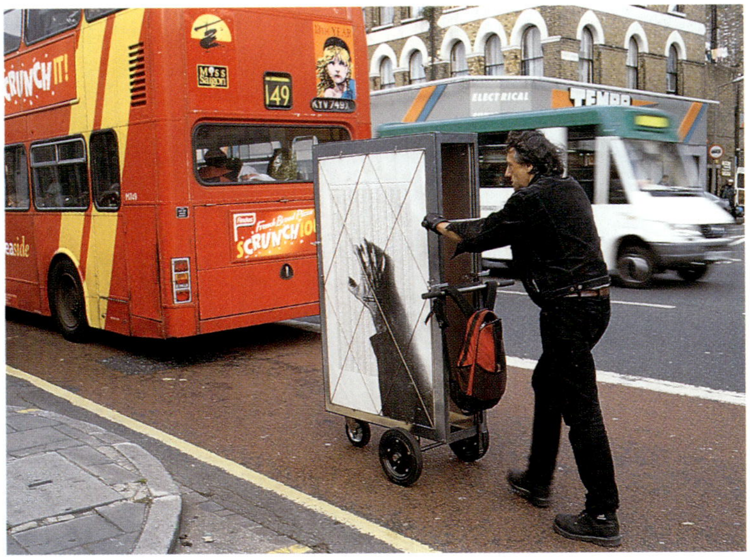

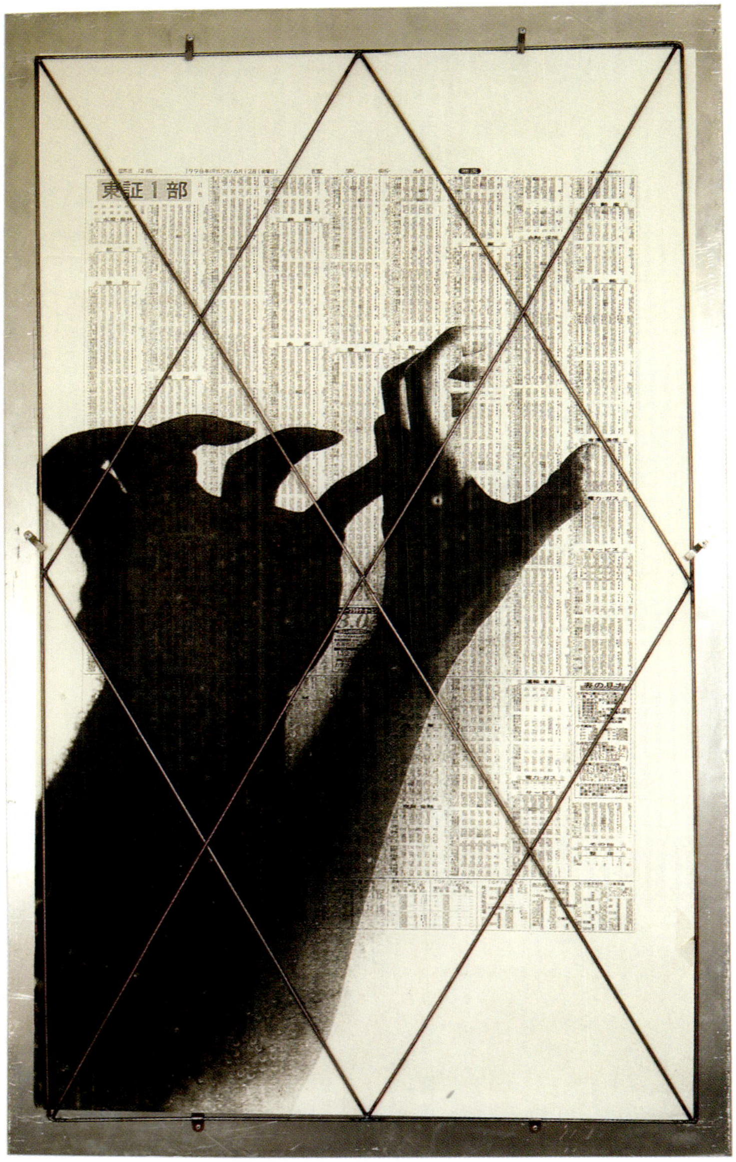

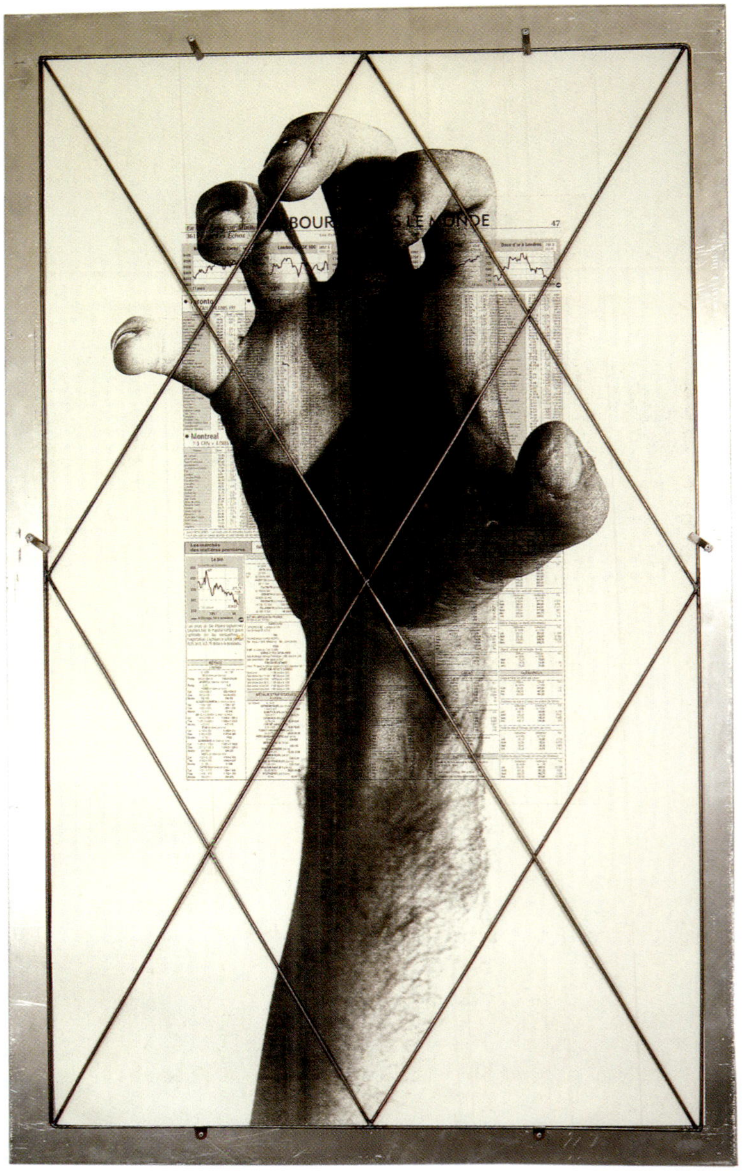

Top
A photograph on the finance page of the *Guardian*, of *News Truck* taken when it was on the streets of Edinburgh as part of the Edinburgh Festival, 1997

Above and opposite
News Truck/1997/carbon toner and charcoal on paper with metal and rubber
Between 1997 and 1999 ten large news-screens were regularly transported in the truck to the City of London, where they were unpacked and lent against the wall of the Stock Exchange. In each screen is the image of a hand overlaid on a stock market report from an international newspaper

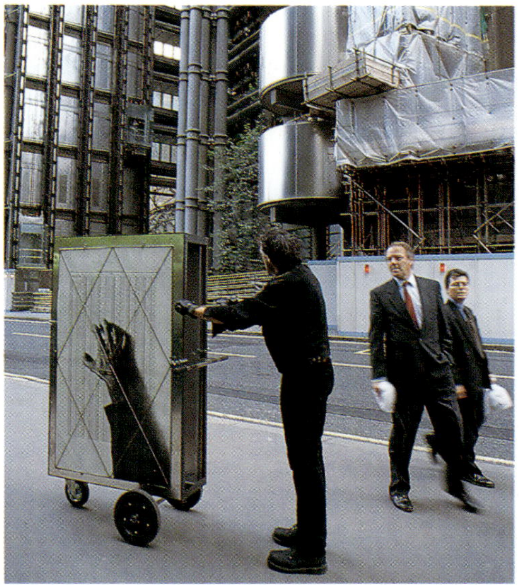

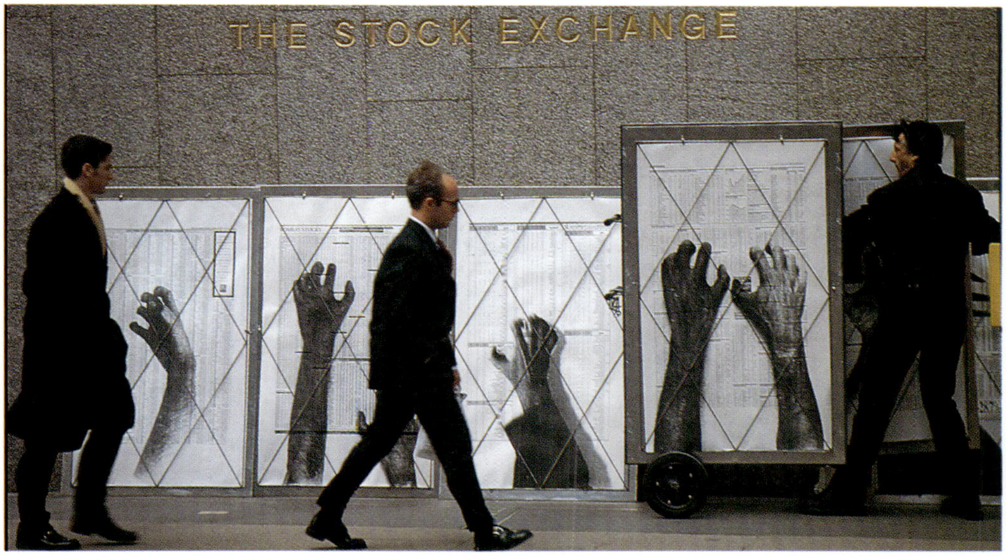
THE STOCK EXCHANGE

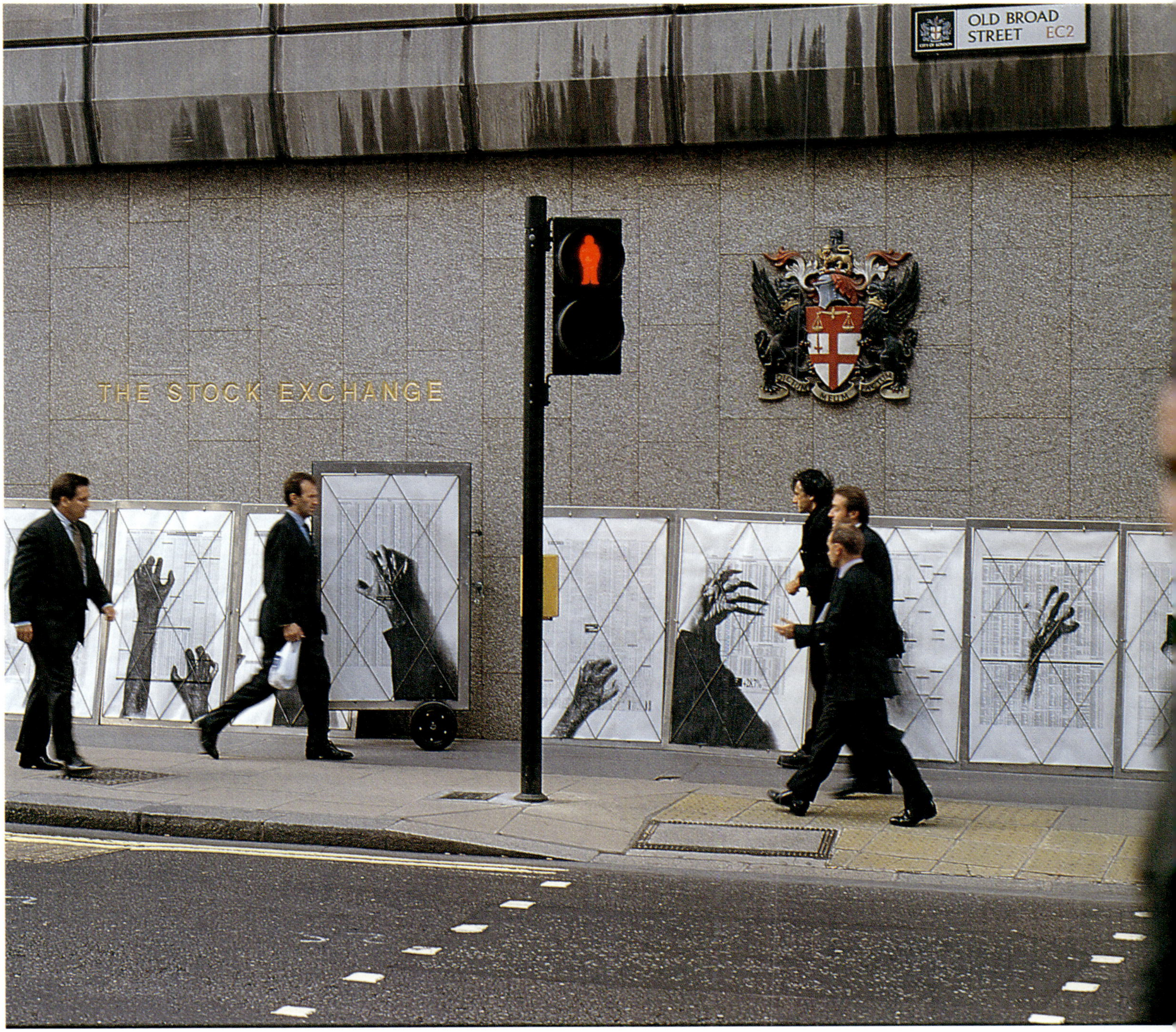
OLD BROAD
STREET EC2
THE STOCK EXCHANGE

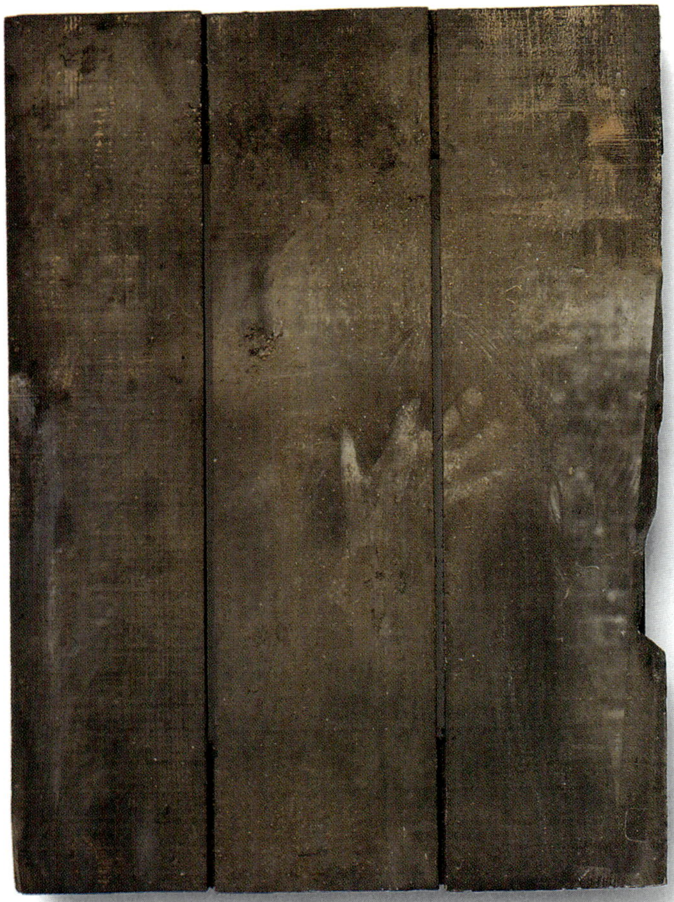
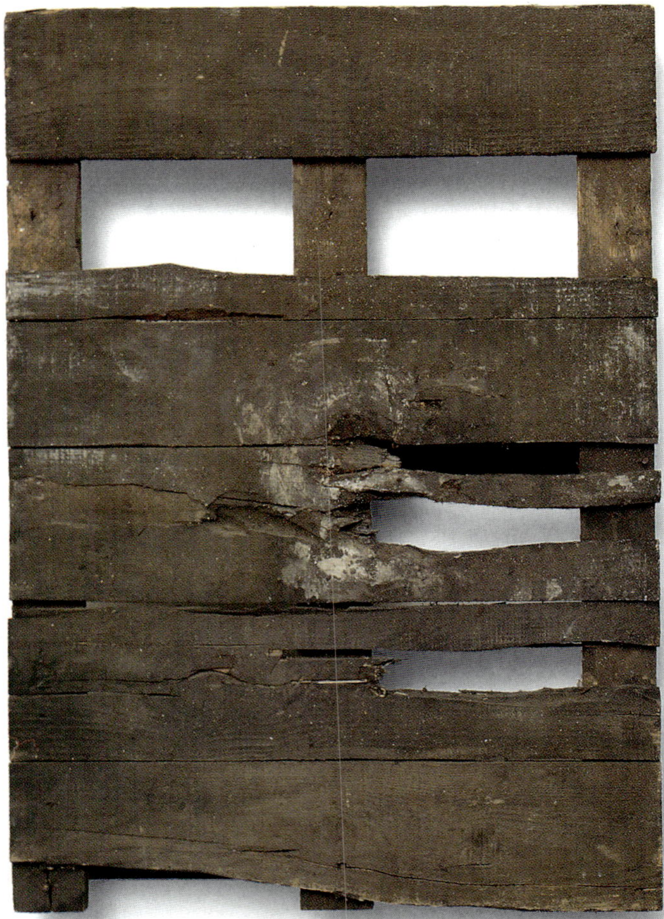
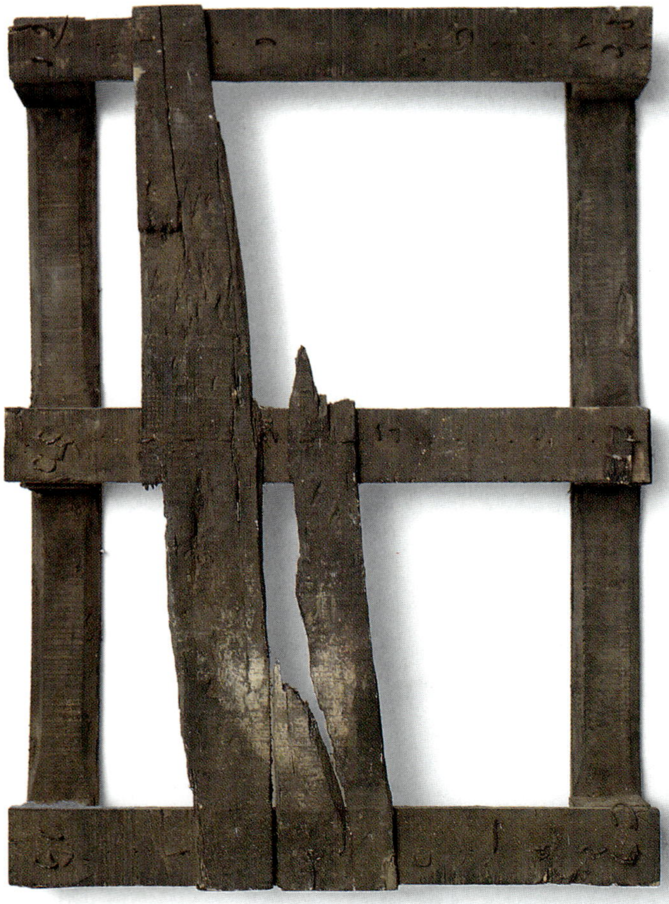
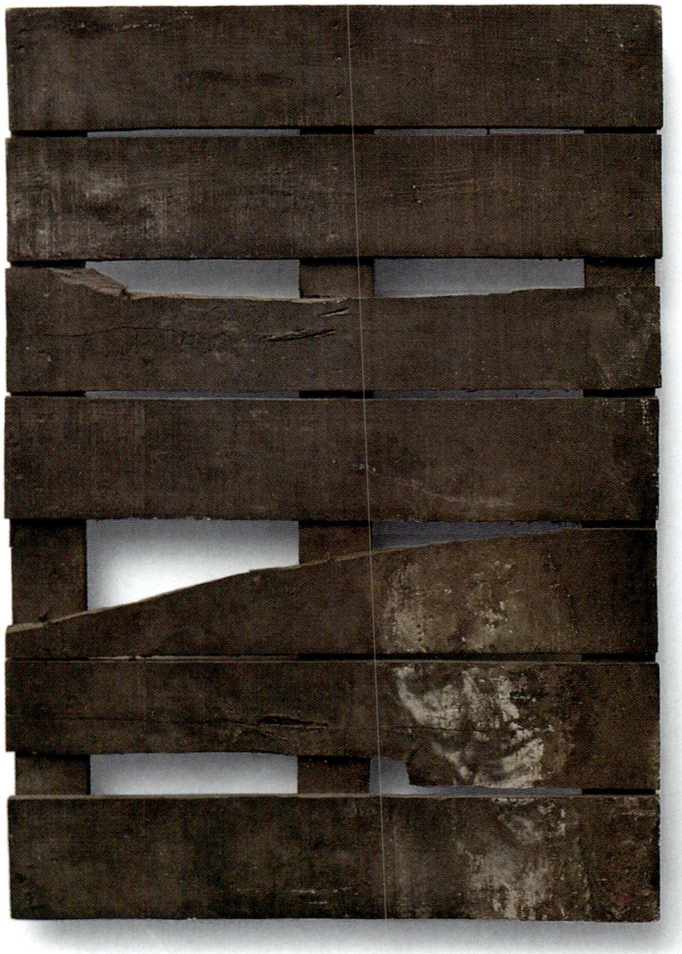

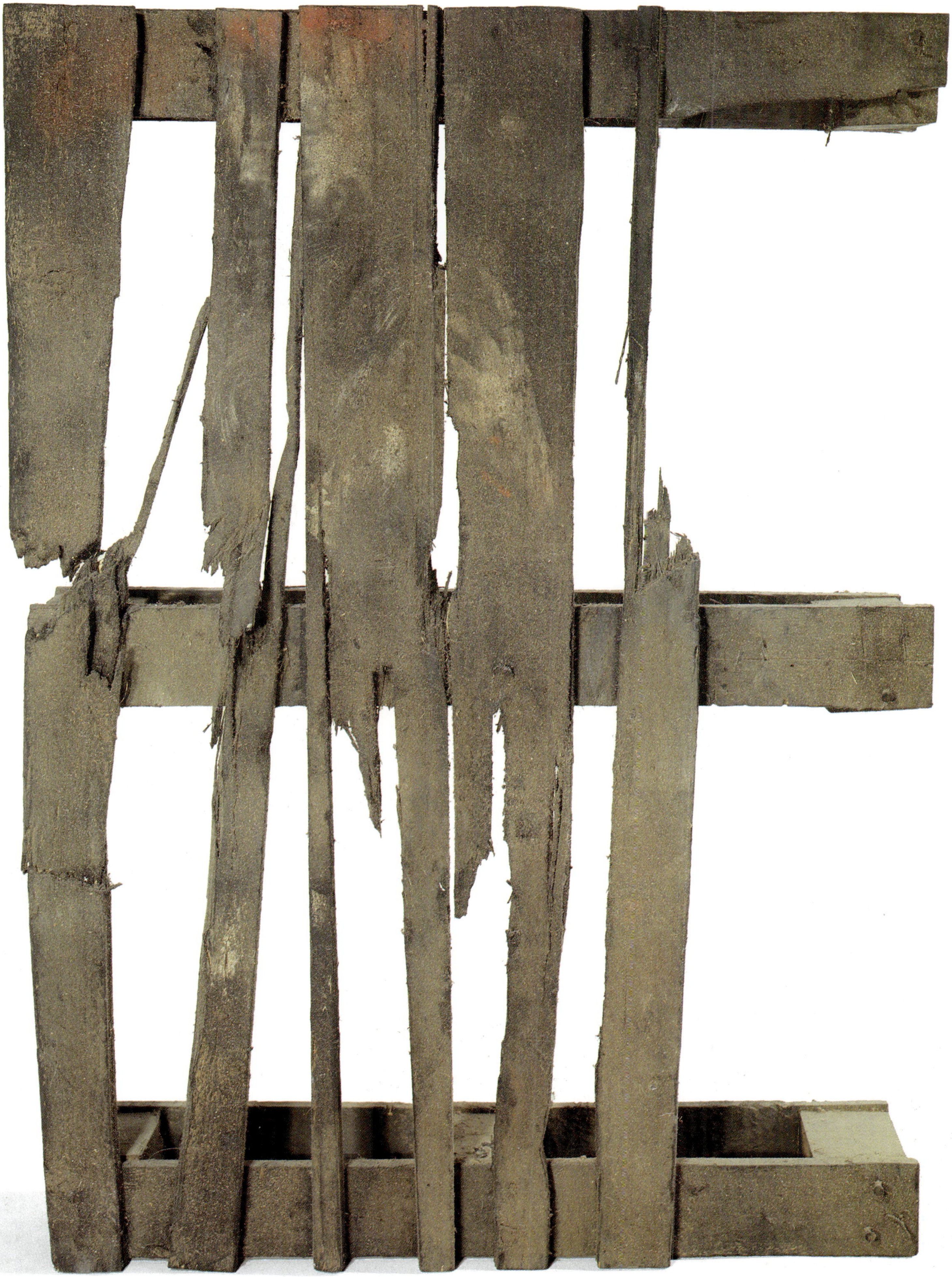

Previous pages
Page 22, clockwise from top left
Pallet 5/1988/dust, oil, acrylic and photograph on wood

Pallet 10/1989/dust, oil, acrylic and photograph on wood

Pallet 2/1988/dust, oil, acrylic and photograph on wood

Pallet 7/1989/dust, oil, acrylic and photograph on wood

Page 23
Pallet 15/1990/dust, oil, acrylic and photograph on wood

This page, clockwise from top left
People's Dome/1999/mixed media
Installation, Gimpel Fils, London, 1999, as part of solo show *Domesday*.
A pile of pallets and placards are placed under the protection of a torn umbrella, its struts extended to create a dome. A quiet voice is heard coming out of the pile, repeating the word 'speak'

Welcome to Britain/1994/mixed media
Installation, the Royal Festival Hall, London. The poet Peter Reading collaborated on this work with 16 pages from his poem *Perduta Gente* being printed onto placards. The traffic light was set permanently on red

Placards/1996/mixed media
Installation, Old St Chad's Church, Shrewsbury. One of three exhibitions in Shrewsbury shown simultaneously as part of *Unwords*

Home News/1992/mixed media (detail)
Installation, Towner Art Gallery, Eastbourne, as part of solo show *Welcome to Britain*

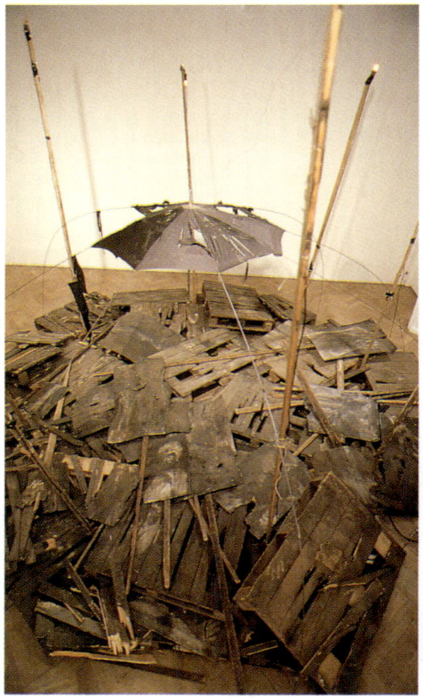

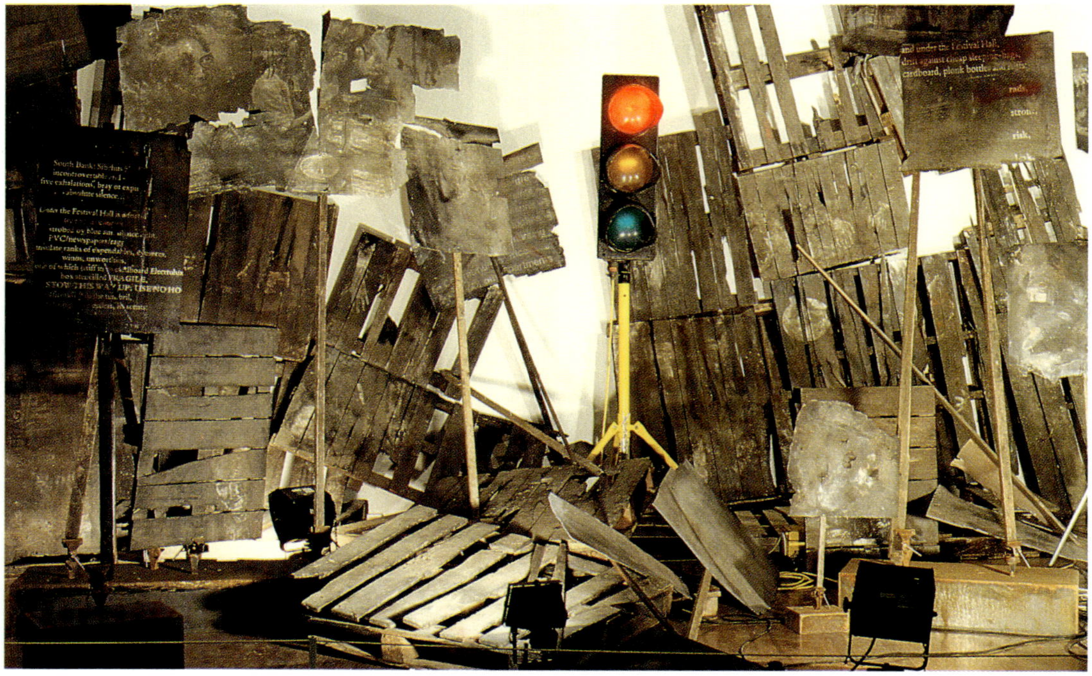

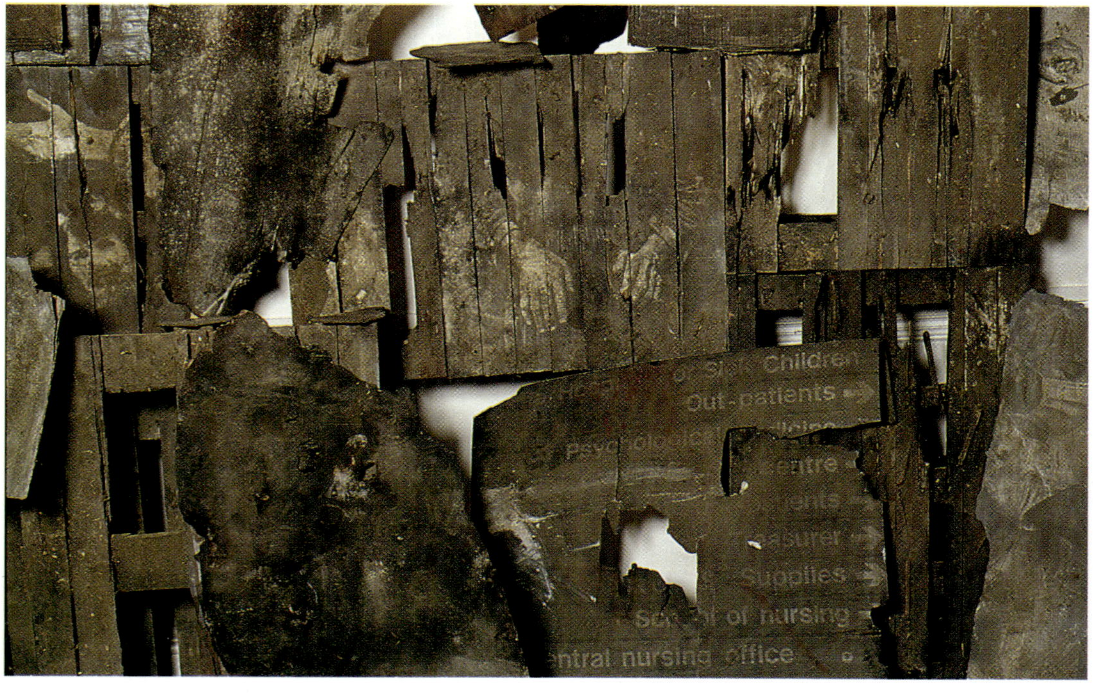

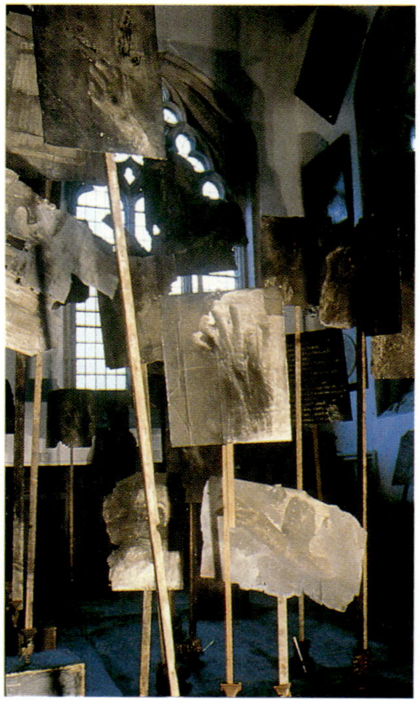

Below
Welcome to Britain/1994/mixed media
Ken Livingstone speaking from the midst of *Welcome to Britain* at the Royal Festival Hall on the last day of the exhibition

Overleaf left
Newspaper 4/1994/carbon toner, charcoal and pastel on newspaper

Overleaf right
Newspaper 8/1994/carbon toner, charcoal and pastel on newspaper

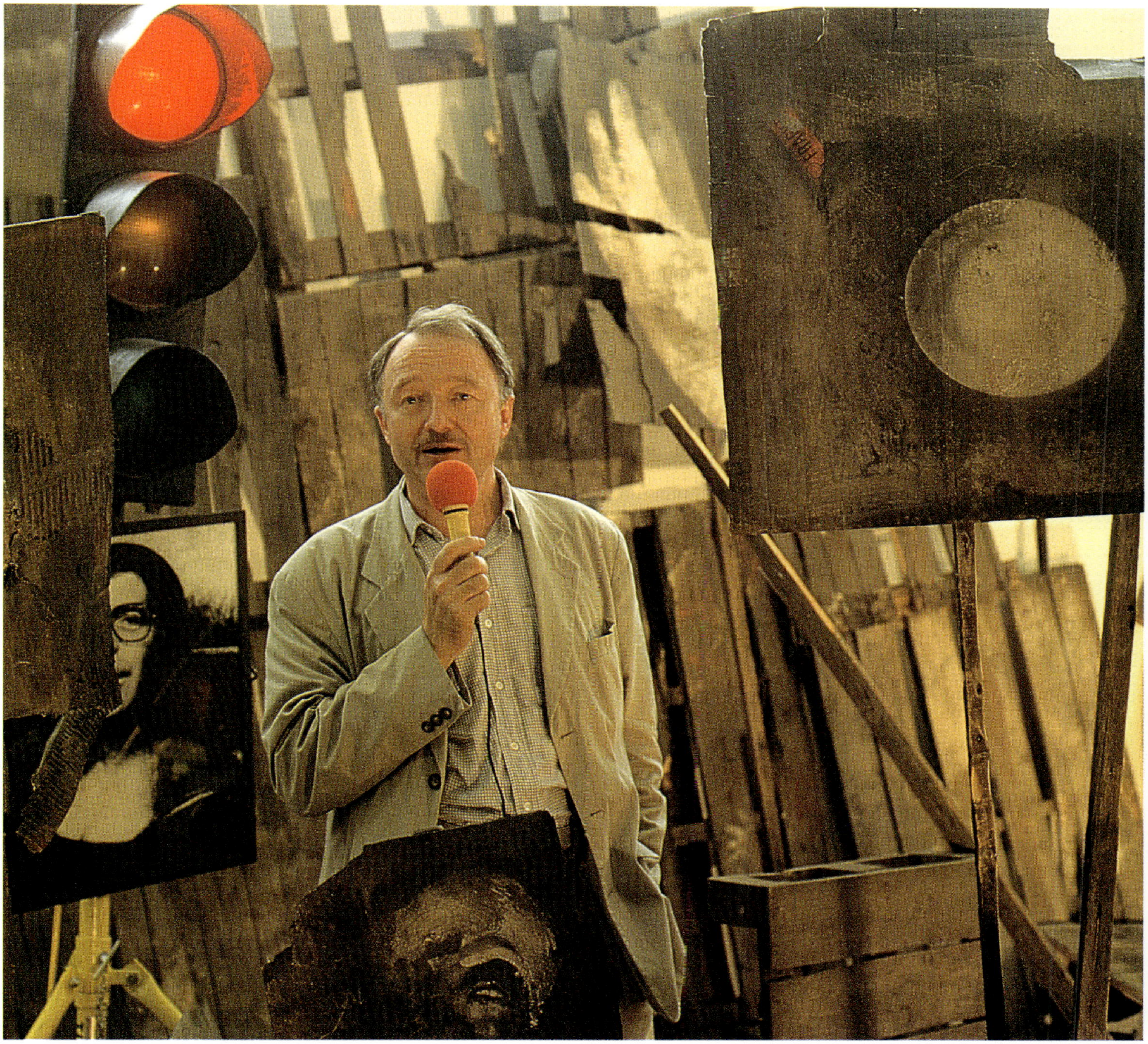

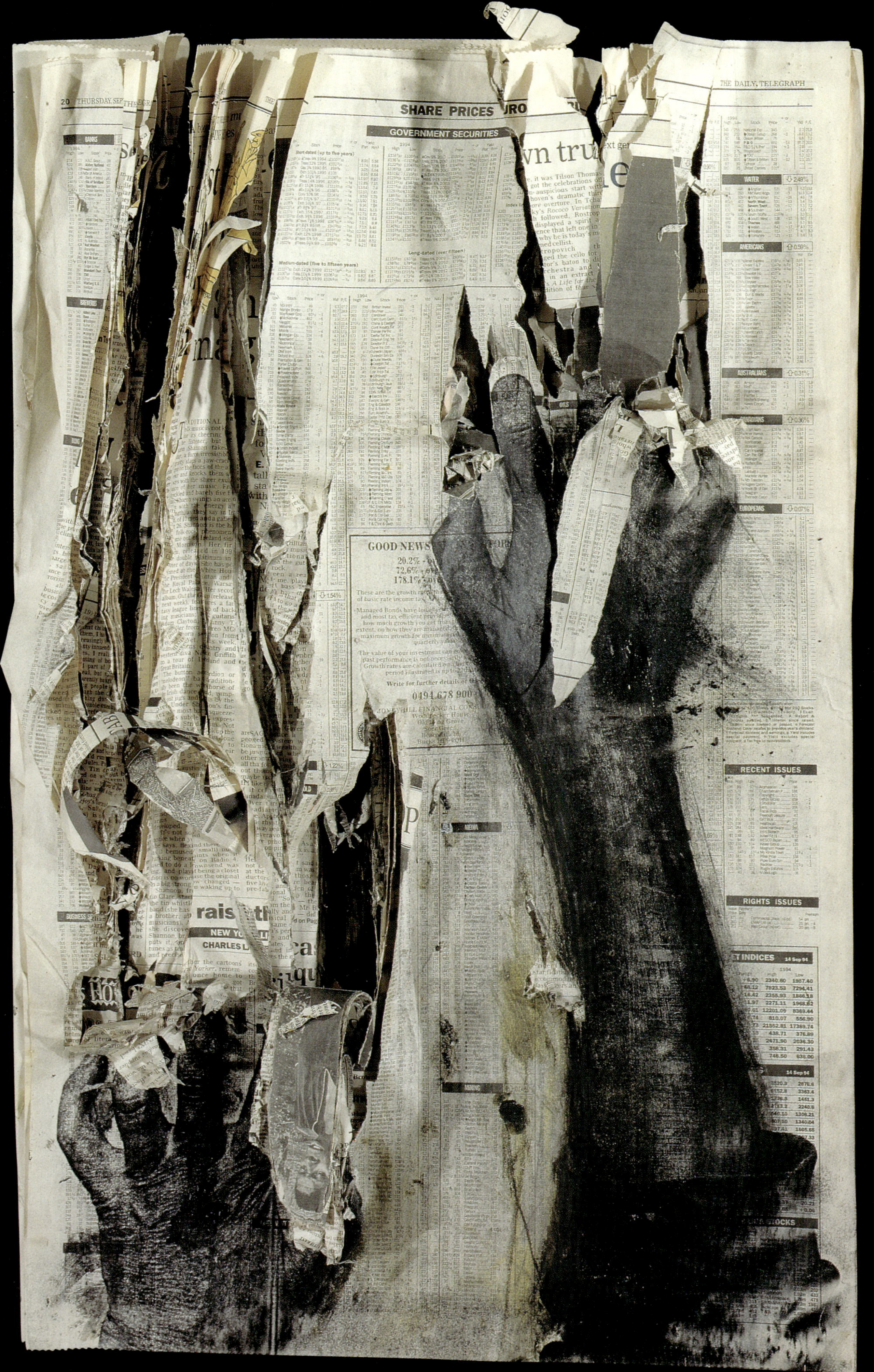
THE DAILY TELEGRAPH
SHARE PRICES
GOVERNMENT SECURITIES
WATER
AMERICANS
AUSTRALIANS
EUROPEANS
GOOD NEWS
RECENT ISSUES
RIGHTS ISSUES

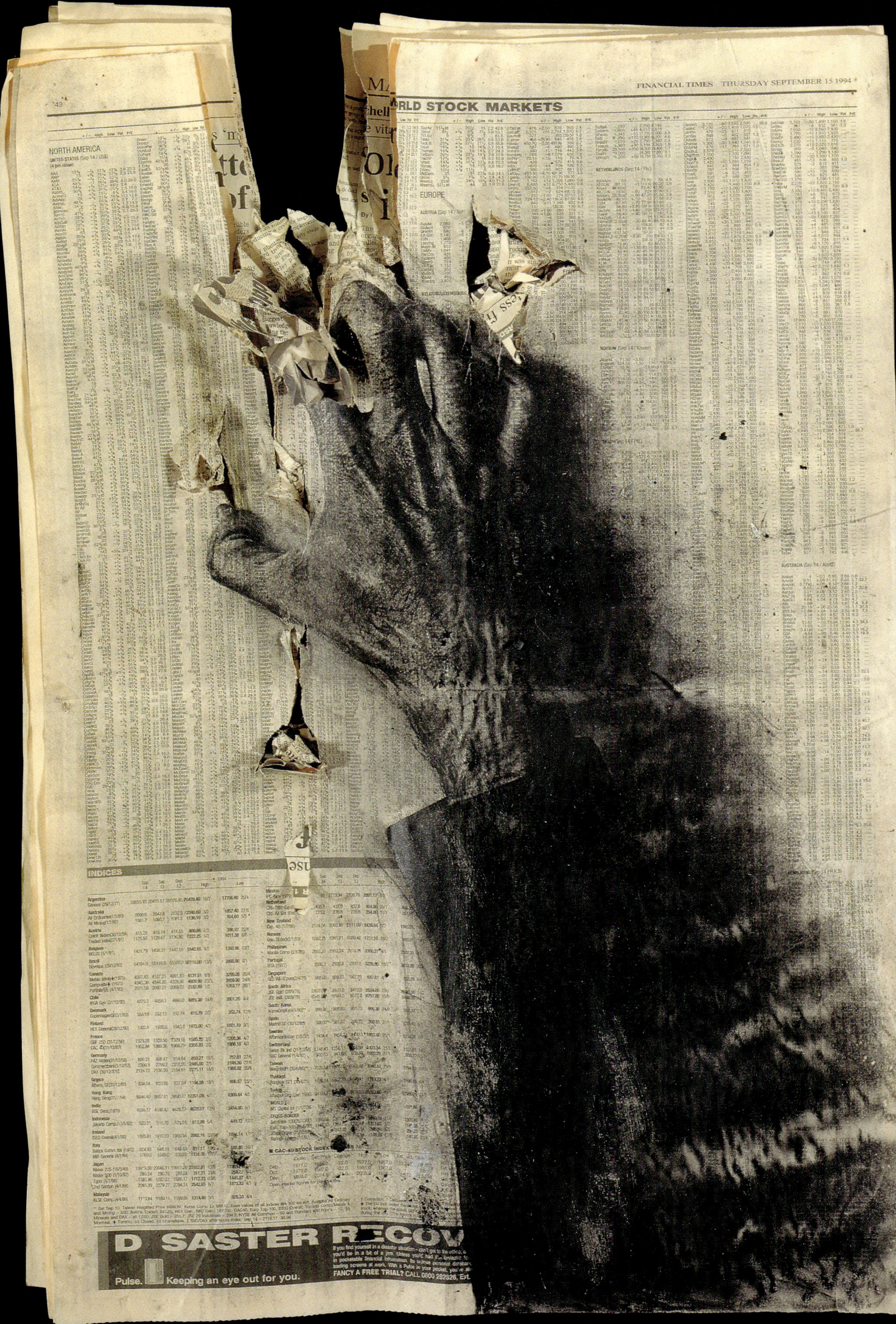

FINANCIAL TIMES THURSDAY SEPTEMBER 15 1994
RLD STOCK MARKETS
NORTH AMERICA
EUROPE
INDICES
D SASTER RECOV
Pulse. Keeping an eye out for you.

Clockwise from right
Sanity Poster/1982/photolithograph
A poster, designed by Peter Brawne, using the photomontage *Disarming Britain* advertising *Sanity*, the monthly magazine of CND

Firth of Clyde/1981/photomontage
An image of a nuclear submarine was inserted into an actual postcard and reprinted by Leeds Postcards for CND

A selection of badges made between 1982–85 showing photomontages being used by the disarmament movement

Broken Missile/1980/photomontage
Reprinted on a tee-shirt, 1982

Opposite
Defended to Death/1983/photomontage
First commissioned as a cover for *Defended to Death: a Study of the Nuclear Arms Race* from the Cambridge University Disarmament Seminar (Penguin Books, 1983)

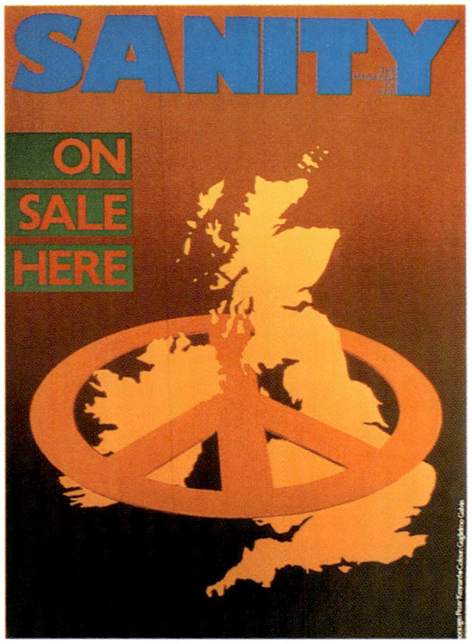

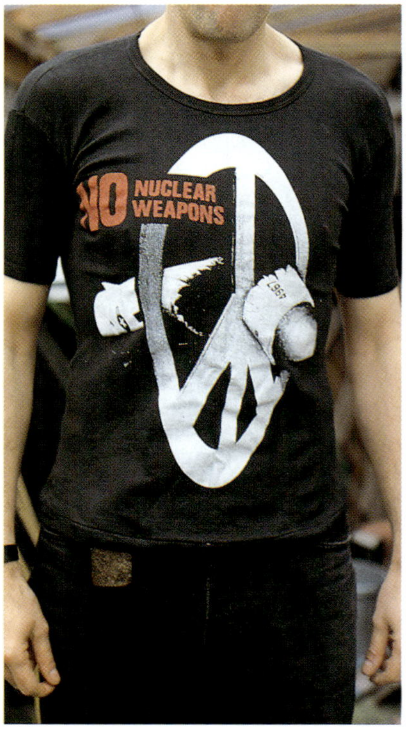

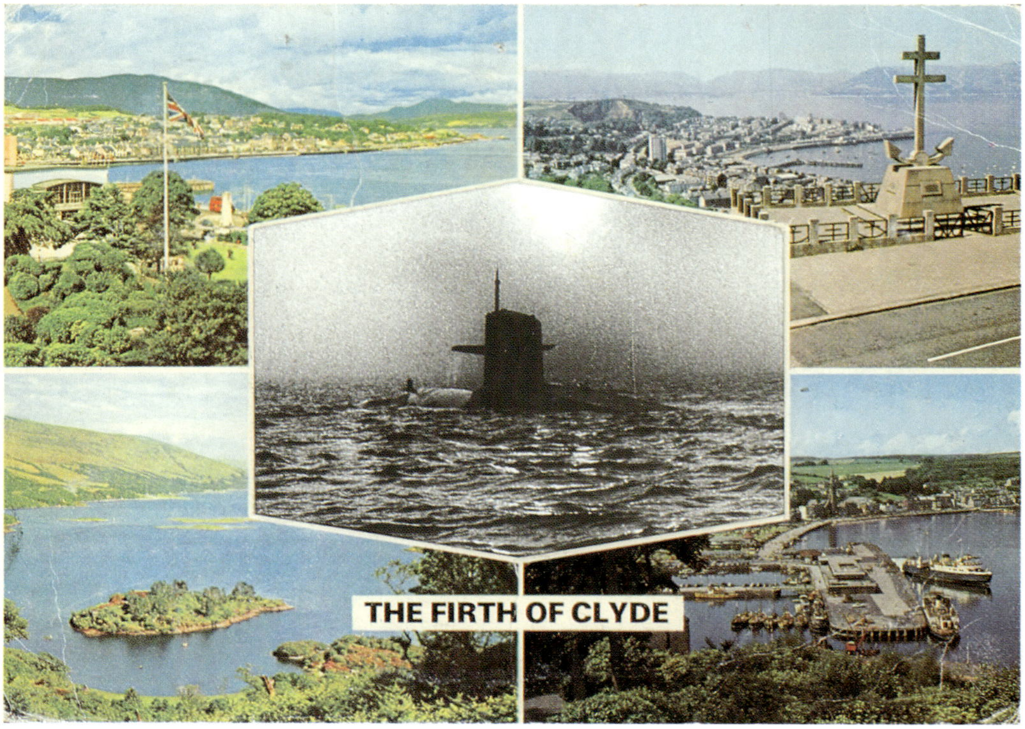

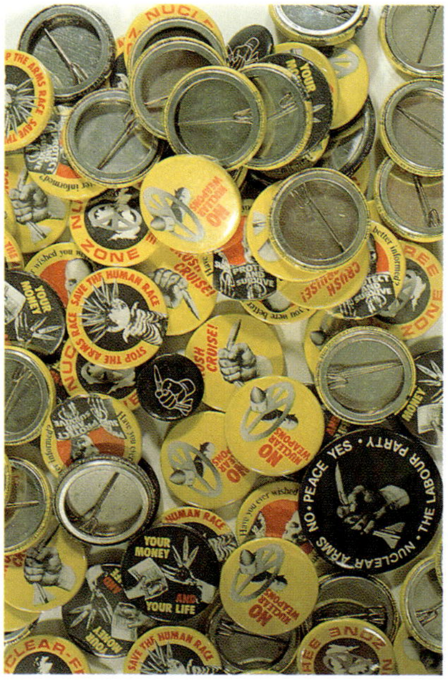

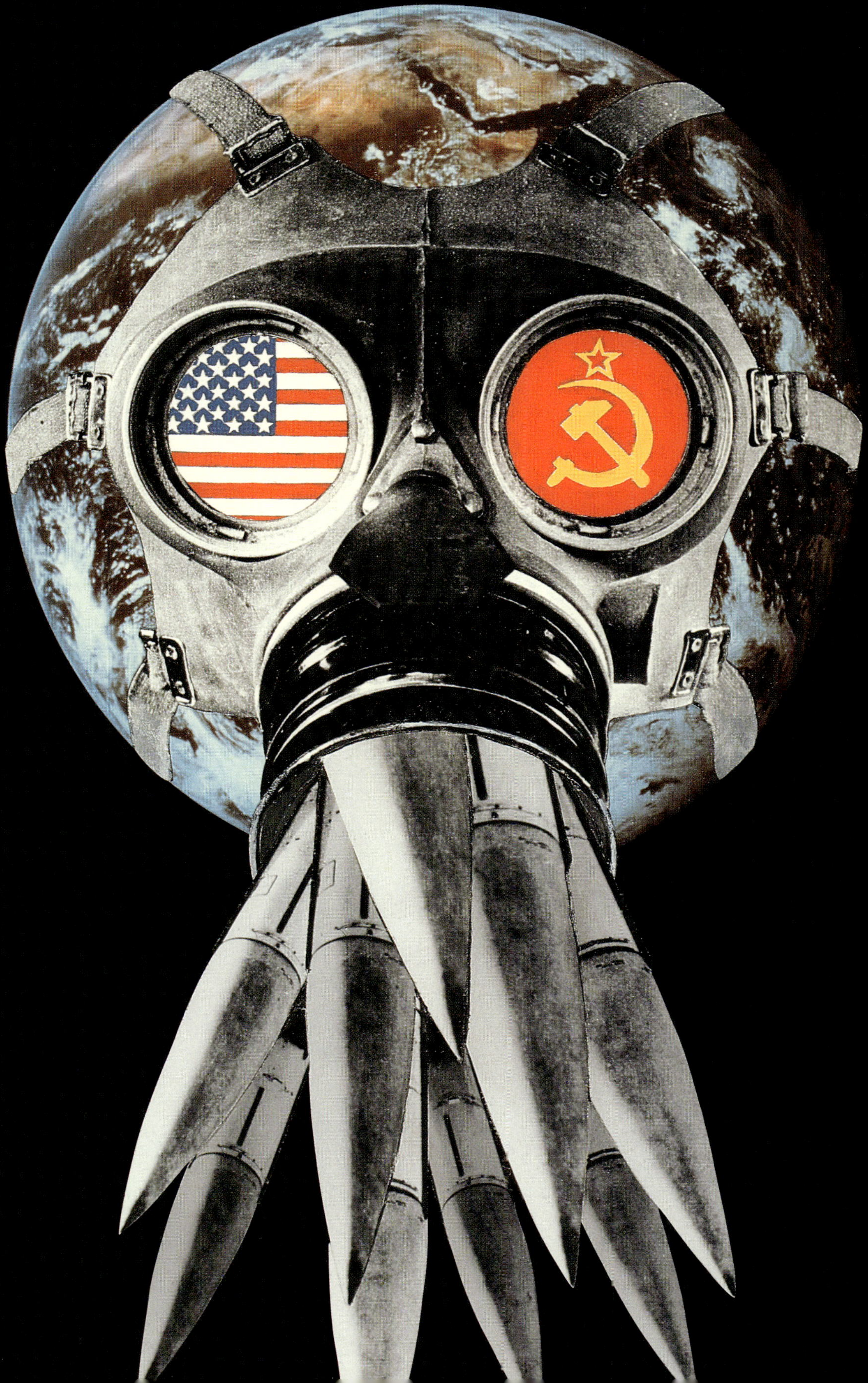

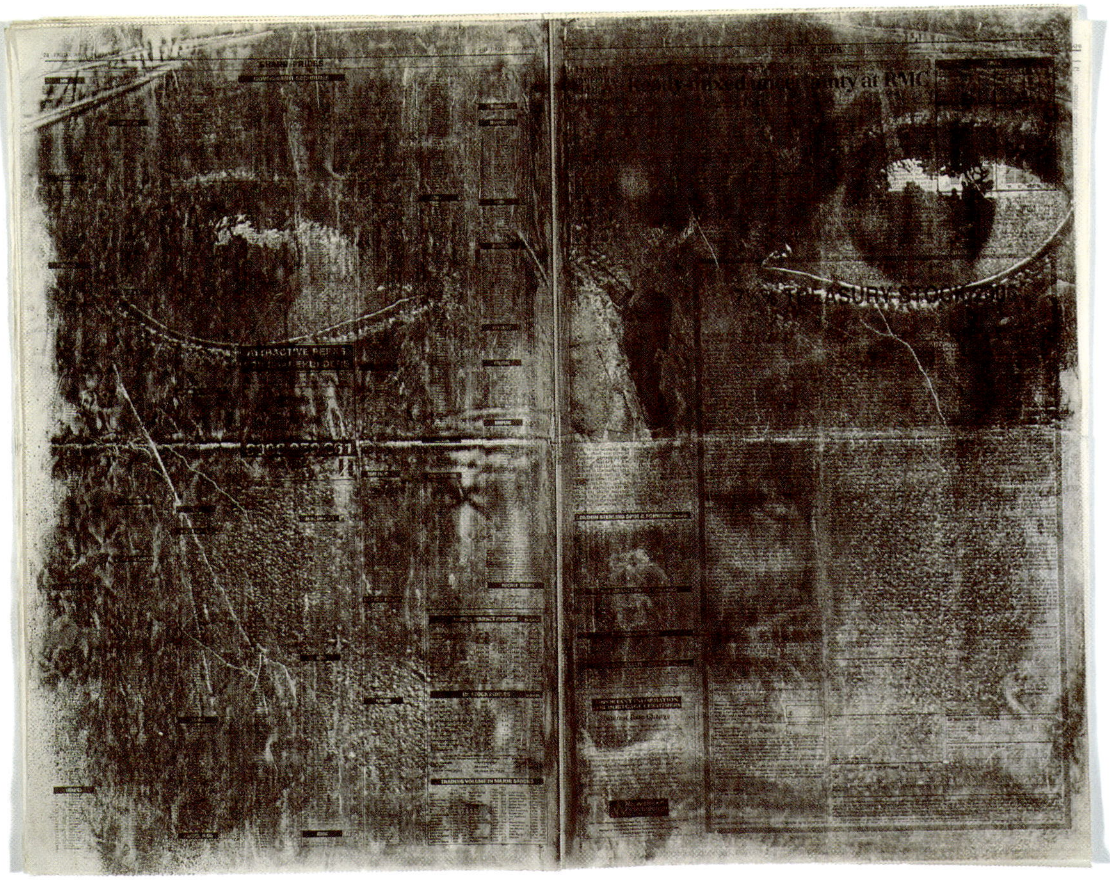

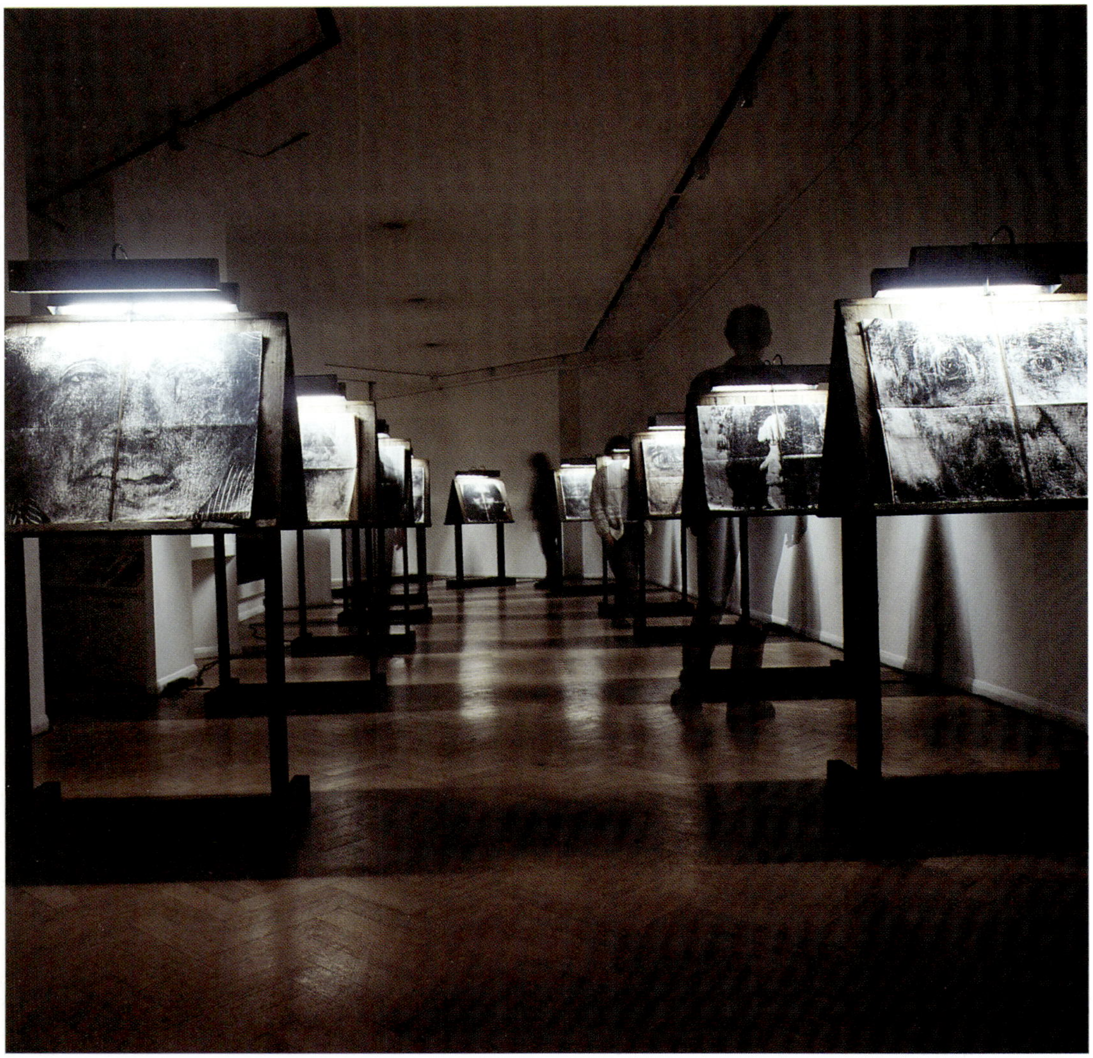

Above left, below left and right
Reading Room/1996–97/carbon toner, charcoal and pastel on newspaper with wood and metal
The installation consists of 42 international newspapers turned to the stock market pages, placed on 21 lecterns, each individually lit. On every paper is the image of a human face. First shown at the Bluecoat Gallery, Liverpool, and exhibited widely since

Above left
Single newspaper from *Reading Room*

Below left
Installation, *Reading Room*, Gimpel Fils, London,1997

Opposite
Single lectern from *Reading Room*

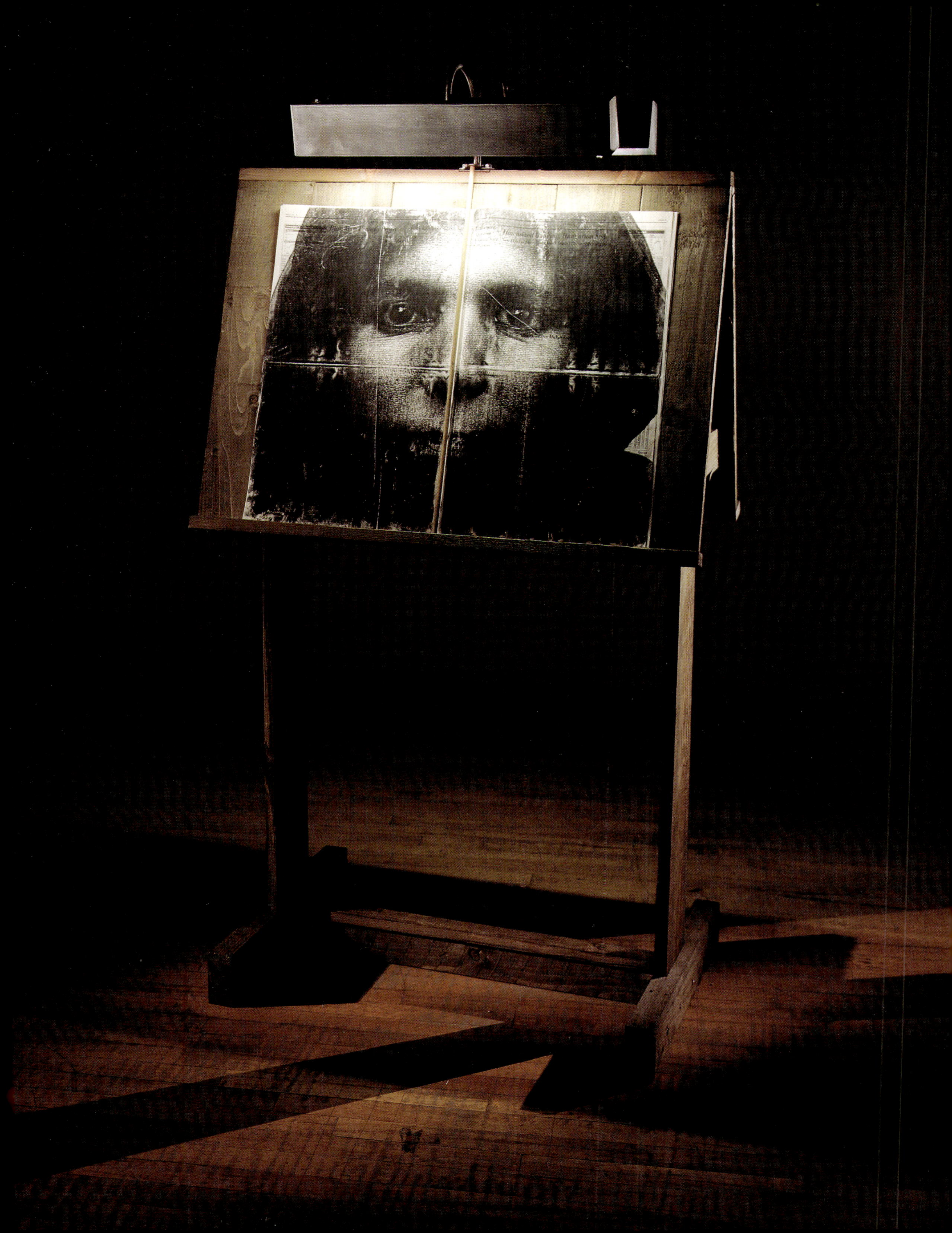

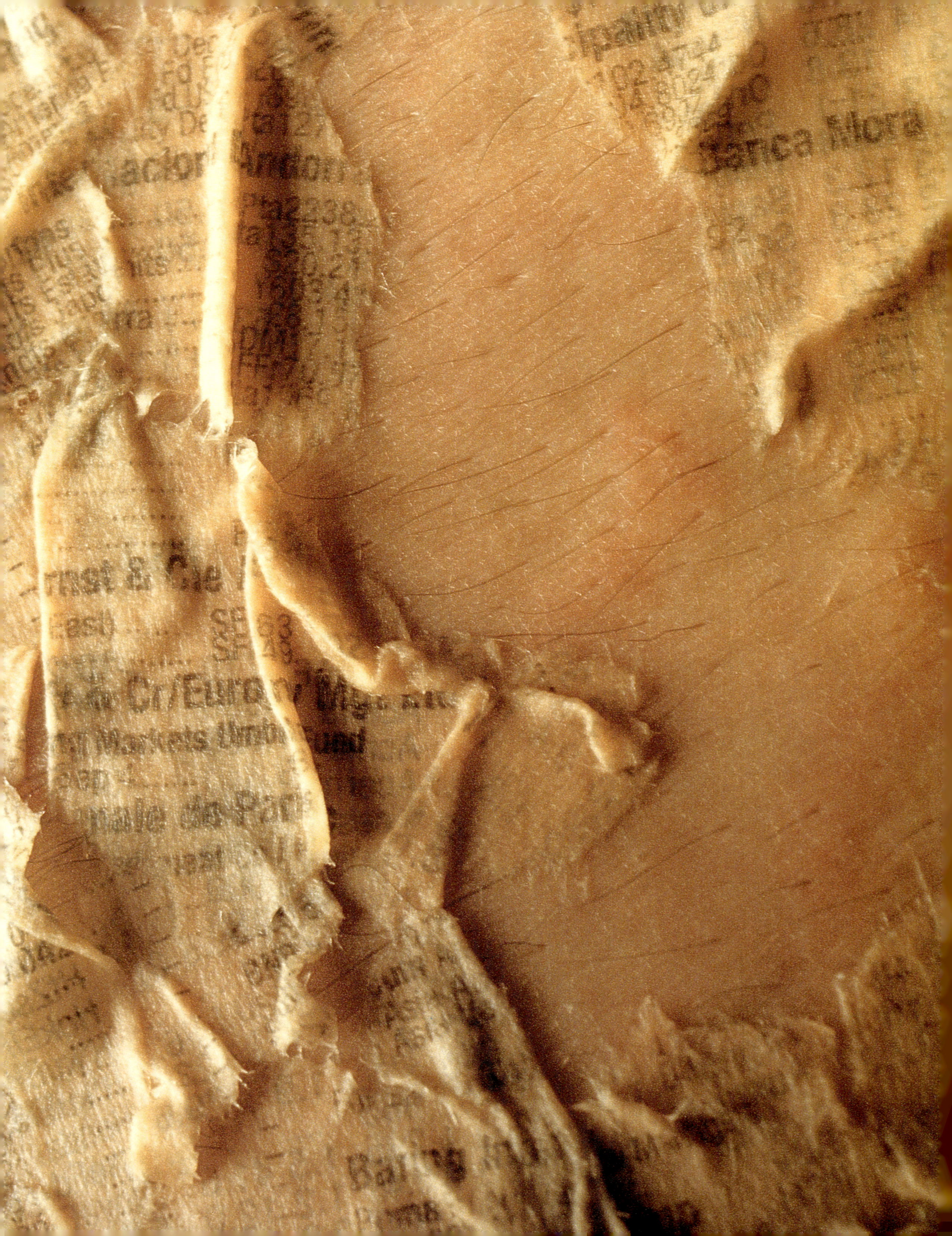

Today, artists all over the world are looking for methods to rip apart the smooth veil covering official lies, to make work that can equate the price of weapons and affluence with the fact of poverty, starvation and the planet's destruction. We are bombarded by more images that reveal less than ever before.

The *Guardian*/26 March 1990

Left
Skin 18/2000/C-type colour photograph

Right
Resolutions 5/1995/carbon toner, charcoal and pastel on paper
From a set of ten large photo-drawings based on images from the former Yugoslavia. These are overlaid with text from some of the hundreds of resolutions which the UN Security Council made on the former Yugoslavia between 1991 and 1995

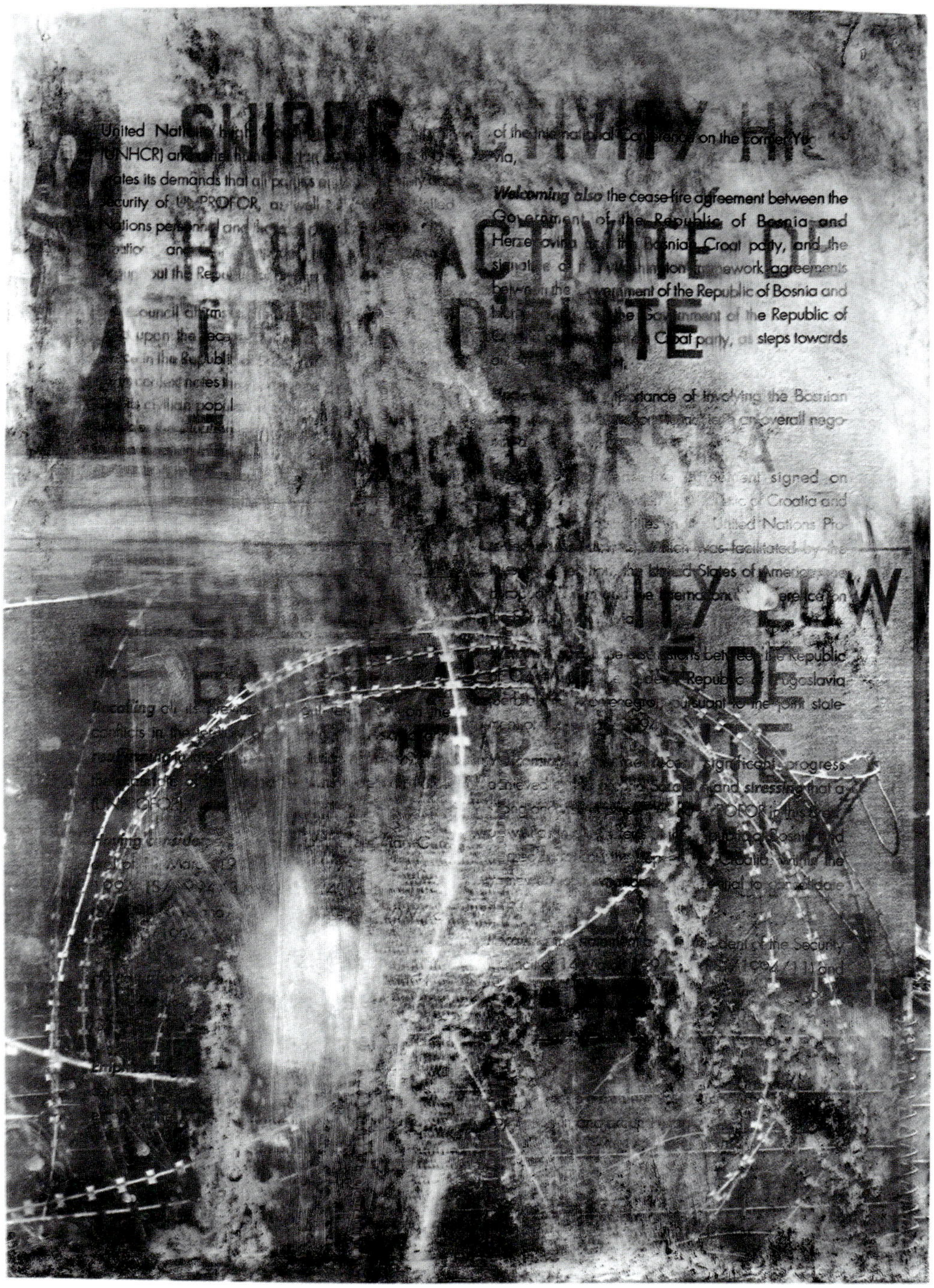

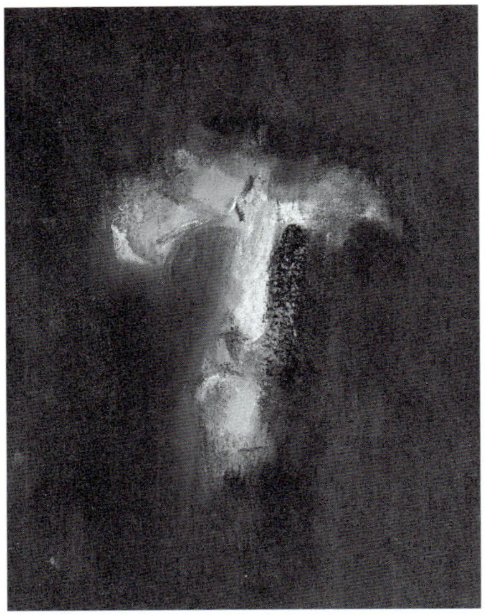

Left
Head/1966/oil on canvas

Below left
Vietnam Cross/1965/pencil on paper

Below right
War/1966/oil on canvas

Opposite above
Self Portrait/1967/etching and drypoint on paper

Opposite below
Raft of Pallets/1988–99/dust, oil, acrylic and photograph on wood
The pallets are reconfigured into a raft for *Domesday Book* (Manchester University Press, 1999)

Archive A: Coal-hole

I first pick up a pile of paintings from my teens. I was born in London in 1949 and began painting and drawing intensely when I was about 13, and it took me over. My brother Christopher and I were brought up in a top-floor flat in Maida Vale. I had a tiny bedroom, and as my need to paint increased I looked for somewhere to make work. I found a shed in the yard at the back of the flats that had been a coal-hole in the 1950s and was now empty except for coal dust. It must have been about four by seven feet. I cleared it out and worked in it, making collages, constructions and paintings. There was no light, so the door had to be kept open. Later, my parents emptied the larder opposite my bedroom, which was even narrower, but allowed me to work at any time, day or night. I spent a couple of very intense years, in the hours when I wasn't at school, making small work in any material I could get my hands on. I scoured building sites for wooden boards, hardboard, bits of metal or anything else I could find to paint on and worked incessantly. Looking back, I can see now that it was a way of building a world I could control. I was intensely shy and making art was a way to show the emotions I wasn't able to communicate in other ways. I worked through influences – Picasso, Bacon, Sutherland, and Giacometti – the work always coming back to the human form, especially the human face. This obsession with the human face has re-emerged in my work recently. The means to the end are different, the reasons for making the work are different, but the need to make the human image speak was established for me in those adolescent years.

I left Marylebone Grammar School at 16, and got a Leverhulme scholarship in 1965 which enabled me to go to the Byam Shaw School of Art, Notting Hill Gate, London. I was one of those art students (I see them now as a tutor in art schools) whose life is totally transformed by art school. The private intensity of making work, a strange internal compulsion, is suddenly acceptable, normal, socialised. Making art becomes as everyday as brushing your teeth. It's a closed environment that allows and encourages what is in all of us, but is offered to only a few. The baked-bean production line managerial structures that have been attacking art schools for years now are completely wrong-headed. As they emanate from the wrong heads, this is a given.

At the Byam Shaw my work concentrated on the human form. Every face I painted seemed to transform itself into a cruciform shape, the eyes being the horizontal, the nose and mouth the vertical. Looking at my sketch books from this period, I see a drawing of a cross that I called *Vietnam Cross*, and another one of tiny images of dead figures piled up that – looking back – is clearly influenced by Goya's etchings. The intensity of first seeing Goya's *Disasters of War* remains with me. I still have a small paperback of

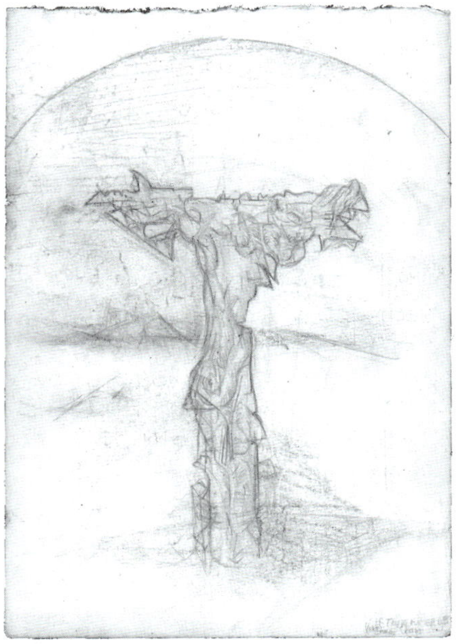

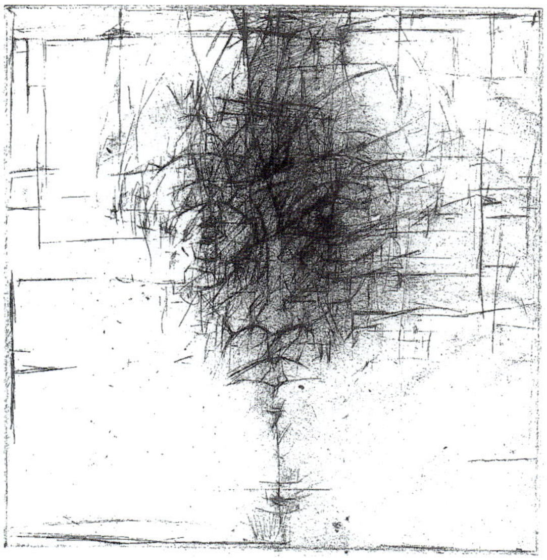

reproductions of the etchings that I bought at that time. The book is now collapsing; every page now separated from the spine. Goya's etchings shine an intense and merciless light on inhumanity and cruelty. He showed how the horrors appear as a flash out of darkness. I can remember the beginnings of my own attempt to look at what was happening outside, not just at the essence of what it is to be human, but at the social forces creating that essence. It wasn't a conscious move, I was still politically illiterate. My head was full of painting and poetry, but something else was happening. I became frustrated with the fluidity of painting, the fact that whatever form the image started from, it was transformed by the act of painting into something else. Paintings that moved me, and still move me, were those that were formed by paint, not drawn and filled in. Late Rembrandt, Bacon, Sickert, late Bomberg – that sense of using paint as coloured shit. But I felt the need to have more control over the image, so I spent the second year at college making etchings and drypoints of images of the human head. Through the etched line I could gain control of the image, and looking back now I think that printmaking equated with my growing desire to look at subjects beyond personal experience. I combined the precise line of etching with the line of drypoint which is more a line of attack. The burr of the drypoint line, in registering the violence of its own making, was a symbol of my desire to express through the human subject the brutal physical attacks on people that I knew were happening, especially in Vietnam. That sense of ripping into an image, unveiling a surface, going through that surface into an unrevealed truth, is at the core of photomontage, which I started doing two years later.

Archive B: Pallets 1

A pile of pallets, ten feet high. In 1987, my work went back twenty years, to those images of heads from my youth. A mixture of personal experience, disillusion with organised politics and the use by the media of innumerable digital photomontages caused me to question the effectiveness of photomontage as a critical, social probe. My practice split into two. I decided I would make photomontages for specific campaigns (against the Gulf war in 1991 for instance when I produced photomontages for newspapers and posters and worked with Jan Woolf in the first of many fruitful collaborations on a show against the war at the Kufa Gallery, London) but I would also develop another strand of work that was based on objects. In this way I tried to develop a new relationship between photography, paint and drawing. It wasn't a conscious move, arising from an ideological or theoretical position, but was the result of a meeting of many forces. This made me want to pare away at the image and find a human trace that I could portray directly, imbued with the texture of the city.

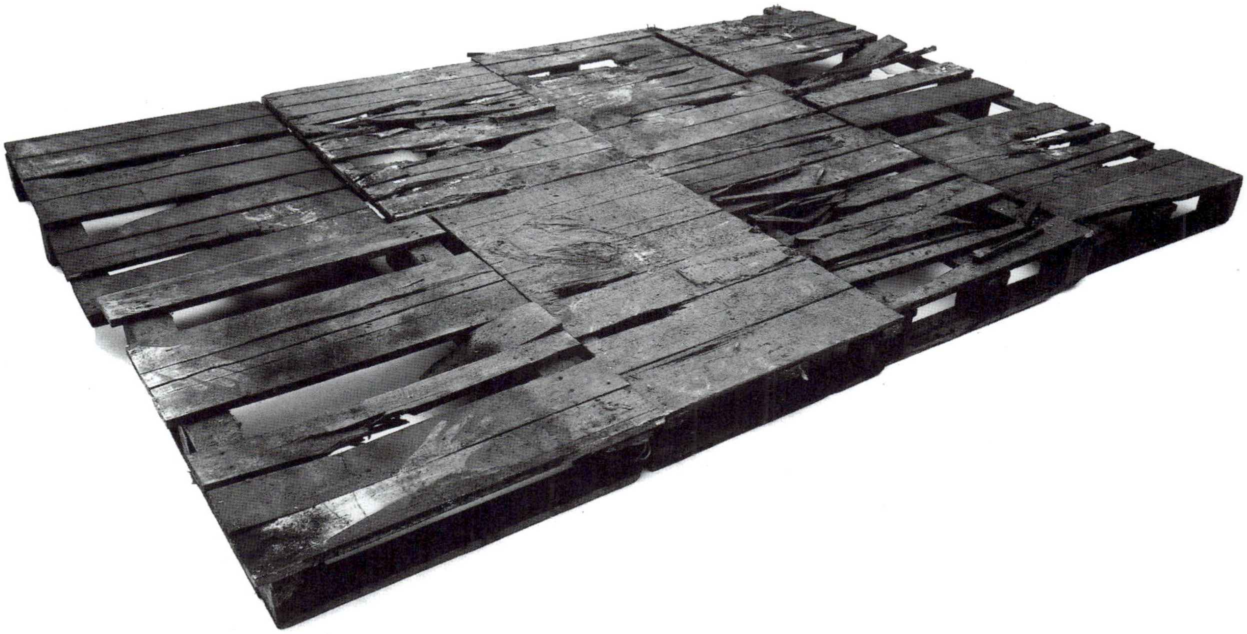

Above left
Working with a hatchet on *43 Pallets*, 1989

Above right
The Guardian/14 June 1991
Cover of supplement on the Gulf crisis on the eve of the Gulf war

Below
Mother/1966/oil, ink and pastel on canvas board

Opposite left
New World Order/1991/photomontage
Based on President Bush's call for a 'new world order', this photomontage was used as a poster by the Committee to Stop War in the Gulf

Opposite right
Sand Glass/1991/photomontage
The photomontage was made after President Bush said that time was running out for a settlement in the Gulf. The sand going through the glass is burying the emblem of the United Nations

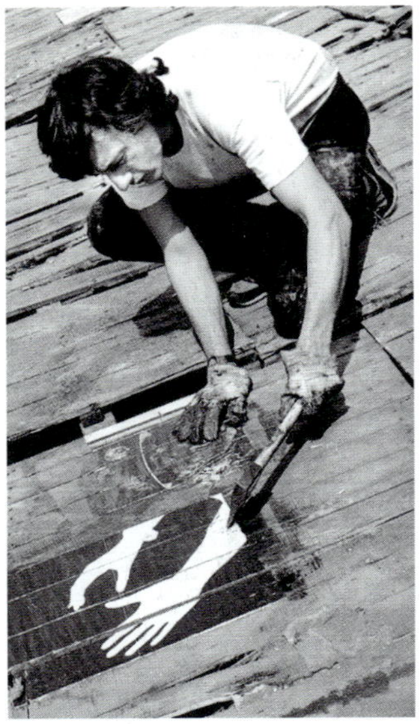

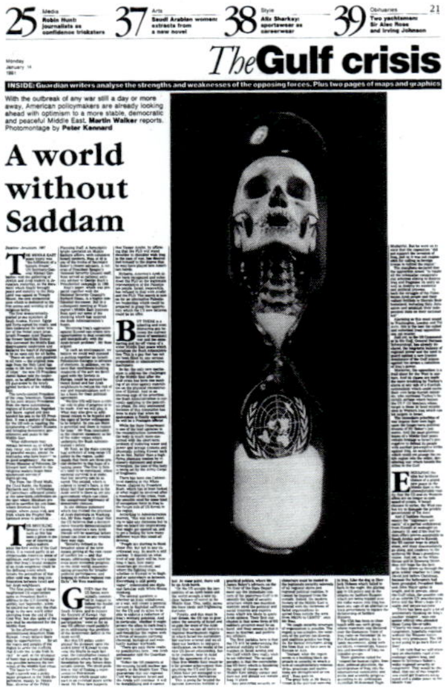

25 Media Robin Hunt: journalists as confidence tricksters 37 Arts Saudi Arabian women: extracts from a new novel 38 Style Alix Sharkey: sportswear as careerwear 39 Obituaries Two yachtsmen: Sir Alec Rose and Irving Johnson 21

Monday January 14 1991

The **Gulf crisis**

INSIDE: Guardian writers analyse the strengths and weaknesses of the opposing forces. Plus two pages of maps and graphics

With the outbreak of any war still a day or more away, American policymakers are already looking ahead with optimism to a more stable, democratic and peaceful Middle East. **Martin Walker** reports. Photomontage by **Peter Kennard**

A world without Saddam

At this time, my mother discovered that she had cancer, from which she died the following year. I went to see her almost every day for six months as she went through various treatments. I relived my childhood with her as we talked of old times. Like a lot of women of her generation, she had to give up her job when she had children. In the ensuing isolation involved in doing all the daily child care she often appeared very anxious about me and my brother. Looking back now, I think of her as suffering anxiety about life itself. Having cancer in a strange way made her calmer; all her strength came through, and in her dying months we got closer. Closer to how things had been in my childhood.

I worked on the pallets during this period. The original impetus had been a commission from a magazine to make some montages on homelessness. I went out with a camera but found I couldn't photograph homeless people on the street. I went to the roundabout near Waterloo station, under which lots of homeless people were living. I looked at the materials of homelessness – the cardboard, newspapers, or anything else that offered protection. I saw that a number of people were sleeping on wooden pallets that they'd taken from around the small factories in the area. I dropped the magazine commission, and decided to make work that would try to embody the experience of homeless people, through physical means rather than through the dialectical methods of photomontage.

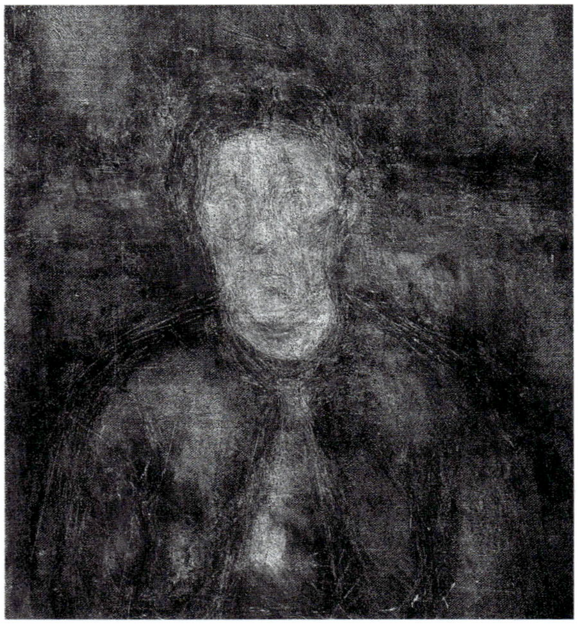

I picked up pallets from around north London and worked into them with paint. Onto them I stuck magazine clippings of photos of faces, gradually evolving a method of making the human image part of the wooden support. This involved enlarging images of faces and hands onto photodocument paper, and sticking them to pallets so that through the addition of paint the edges of the photographs became invisible. After that, in order to realise the effect of the human image as the trace of someone who might have slept on the pallet, I sieved household dust onto the image. Friends donated their used Hoover bags, and the dust became integral to the image. I smashed up some of the pallets with an axe, faces becoming fragmented in the shards of the wood. In 1999 in my book *Domesday Book* I tried to describe the pallets:

Imprinted through sweat
Unsettled dust hugs
Skin

On pallets –
Faces,
Frozen in transit

Like boxes of flesh,
Fork-lifted onto pallets
Off the public shelves.

Contact printed
Autopsies
Of the bodies' emulsion.

'All isolated cases'
Forcibly removed
From the civic glare.

Eyes, ears, etc.
Caked in blood,
Turin Shrouds of the written off.

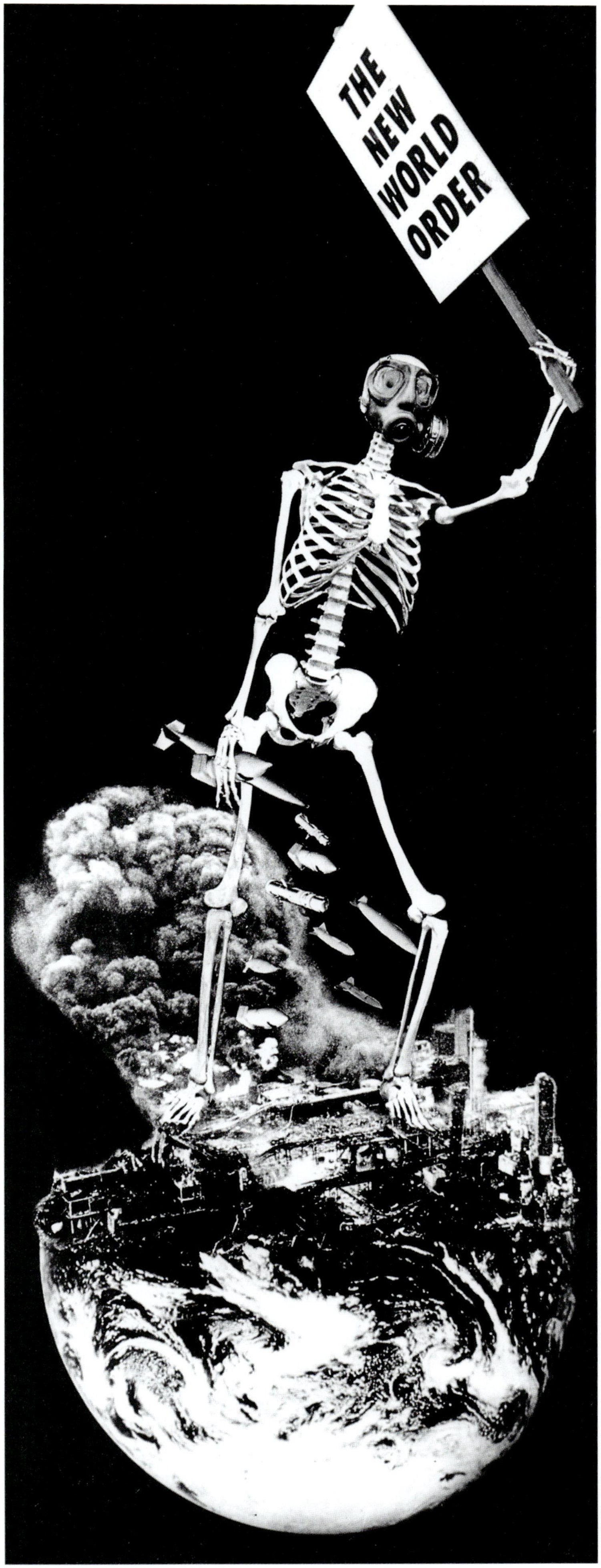
THE
NEW
WORLD
ORDER

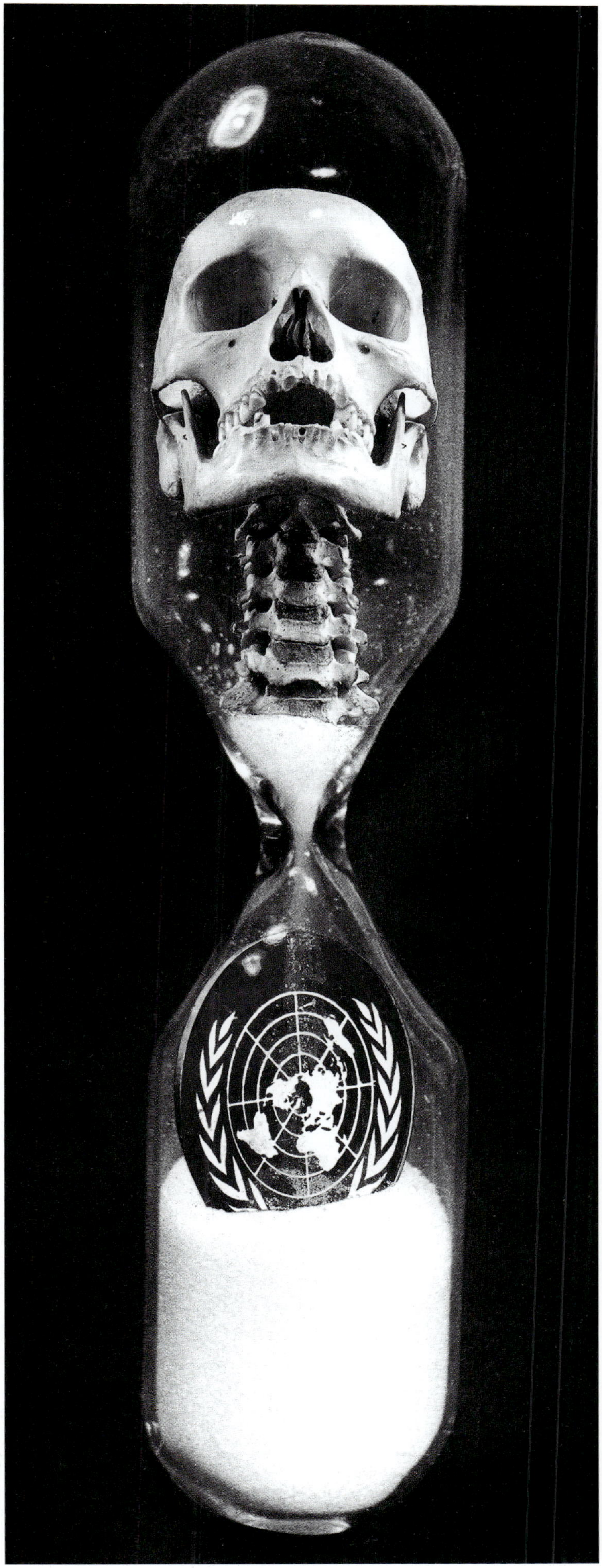

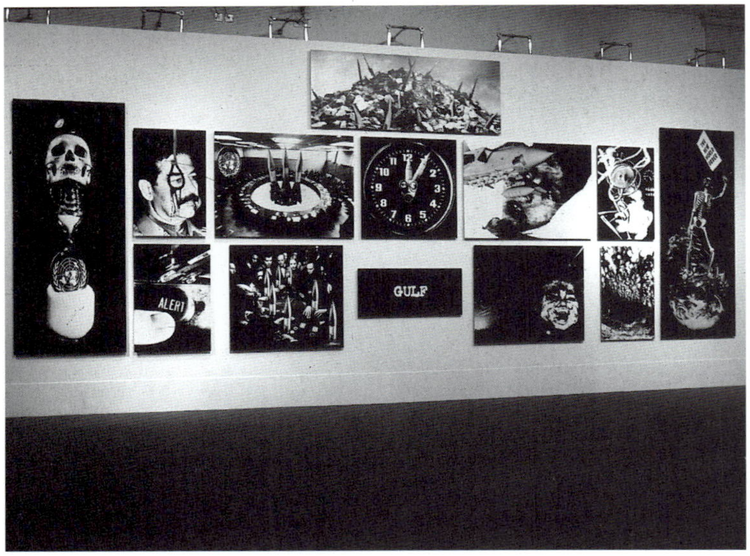

Left
Gulf/1991/photo-mural/(13 silver prints)
Installation, Manchester City Art Gallery, 1991

Below
Pallet 6/1989/dust, oil, acrylic and photograph on wood

Opposite above
Pallet 16/1990/dust, oil, acrylic and photograph on wood

Opposite below
Pallet 12/1989/dust, oil, acrylic and photograph on wood

The pallets marked an important break from my previous work and I think it was the unconscious confluence of the events I have tried to describe that led to their making. The transience and fragility of the final images, some almost invisible in the dust, does symbolise the way we pass by homeless people, trying not to see them. It does symbolise the way people are moved like objects on pallets around cities if they have no homes, but it also relates to the face of my mother, lying in bed becoming more and more fragile. From being an active presence, her being became a trace of that presence. The shock of when she stopped breathing will never leave me.

Archive B: Pallets 2

I first showed one of the pallets in the Whitechapel Open exhibition in 1988 and it was bought by the Saatchi Collection.There was an enormous contradiction in this for me as Saatchi's was the agency that produced the advertising campaign for the Conservative party that helped put Margaret Thatcher in power. It was her party's policies that created the vast rise in homelessness, that pushed people onto the streets with utter ruthlessness. Of course, any artist could issue a list of potential buyers who they will not sell work to, but how long would it stretch? Art-buying money is often not clean money. It's the surplus accrued from the world stock markets; the artist who makes objects feeds on that surplus. It's one of the main reasons why I spent 20 years making photomontages that exist through their reproduction rather than as valuable commodities. But now I am making objects again, the work is validated by the gallery, and that means commerce. If, as an artist, one produces one-off objects one exists within this contradiction.

Archive B: Pallets 3

As the pallets built up in number I had to find a new place to store them (Archive B). The removals firm that I hired to move them thought they were moving them all to the local dump. All they saw was a pile of dusty, smashed-up pallets piled up in the street ready to go into the van. They had returned to their original state. At the other extreme, when one of the pallets was shown at the Pompidou Centre, Paris in the exhibition *Invention d'un Art* in 1989, it arrived back in London in an enormous packing case containing layers of archival packing made from a variety of obscure materials. Encased in the middle, cosseted, was my smashed up pallet.

Archive B: Pallets 4

In 1990 I had a show of the pallets at Gimpel Fils, London. It consisted of a construction of 43 pallets butted up to each other flat against the wall. As the viewer moved along them, faces and hands

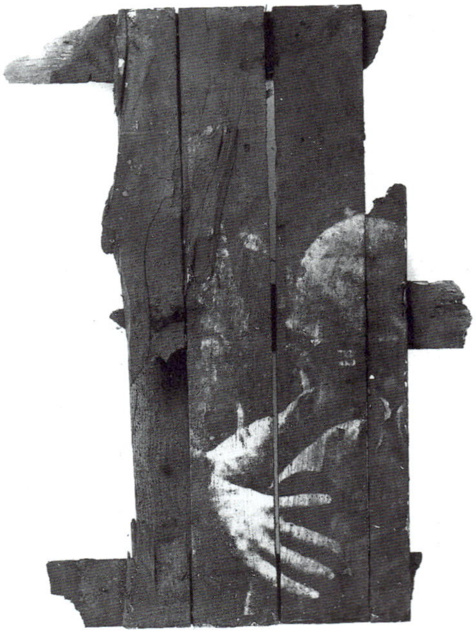

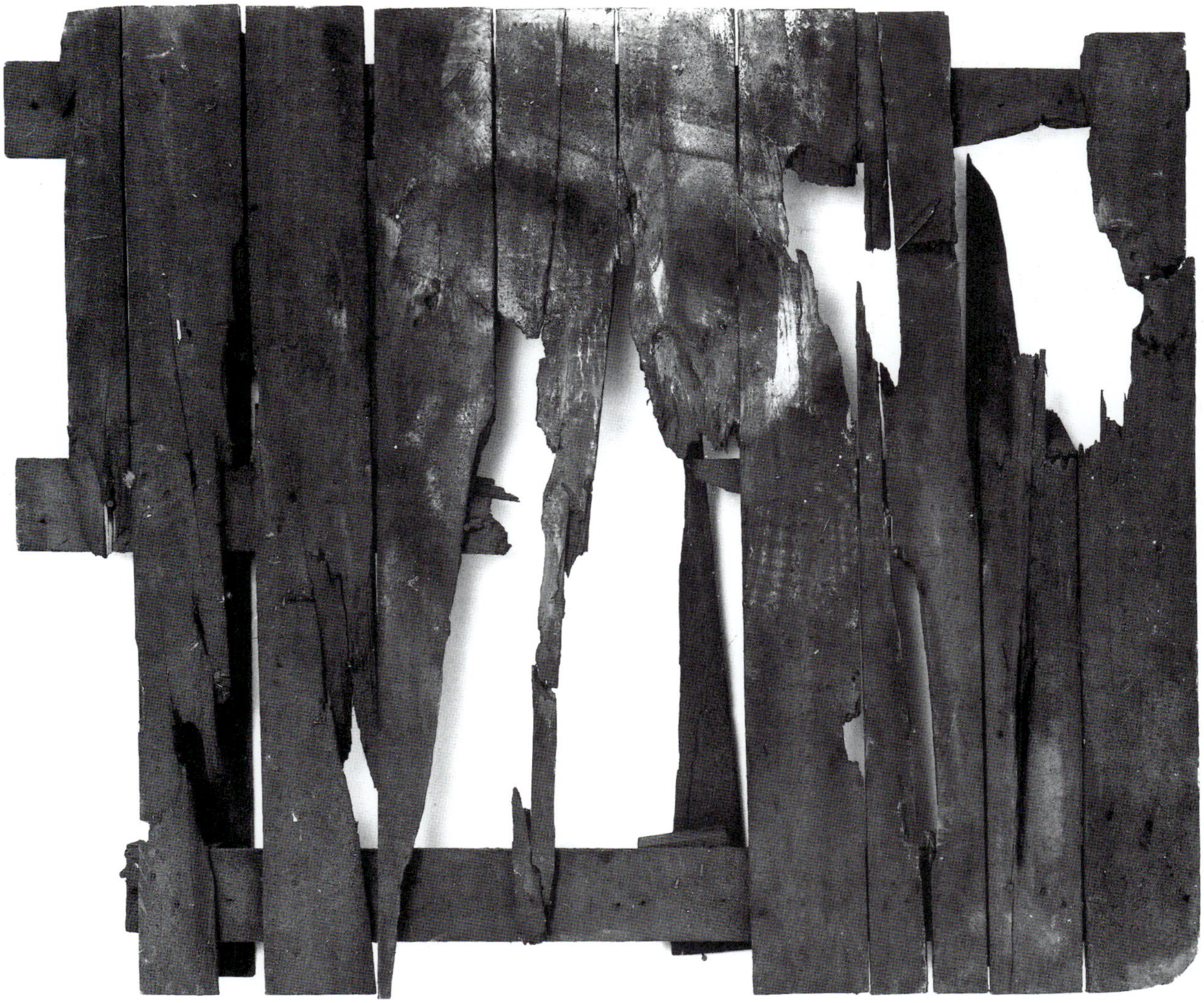

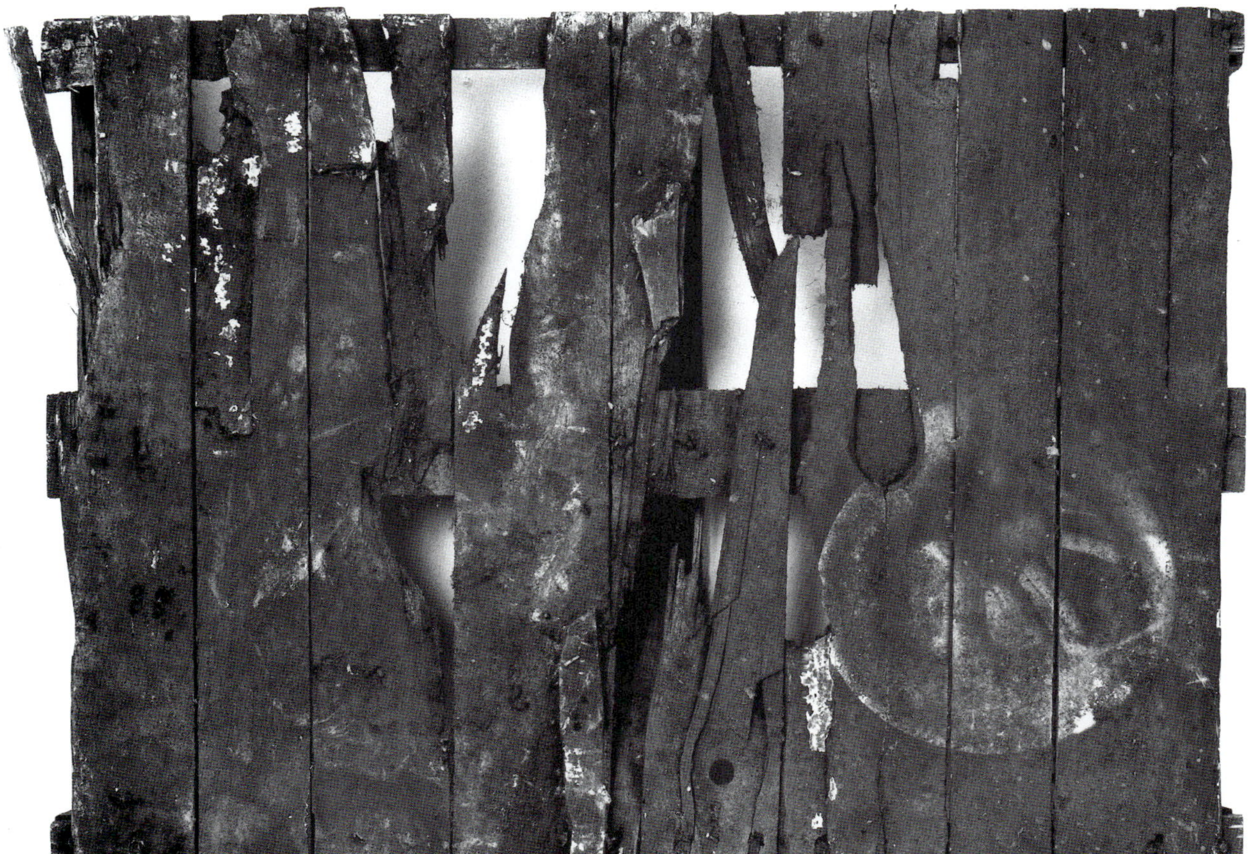

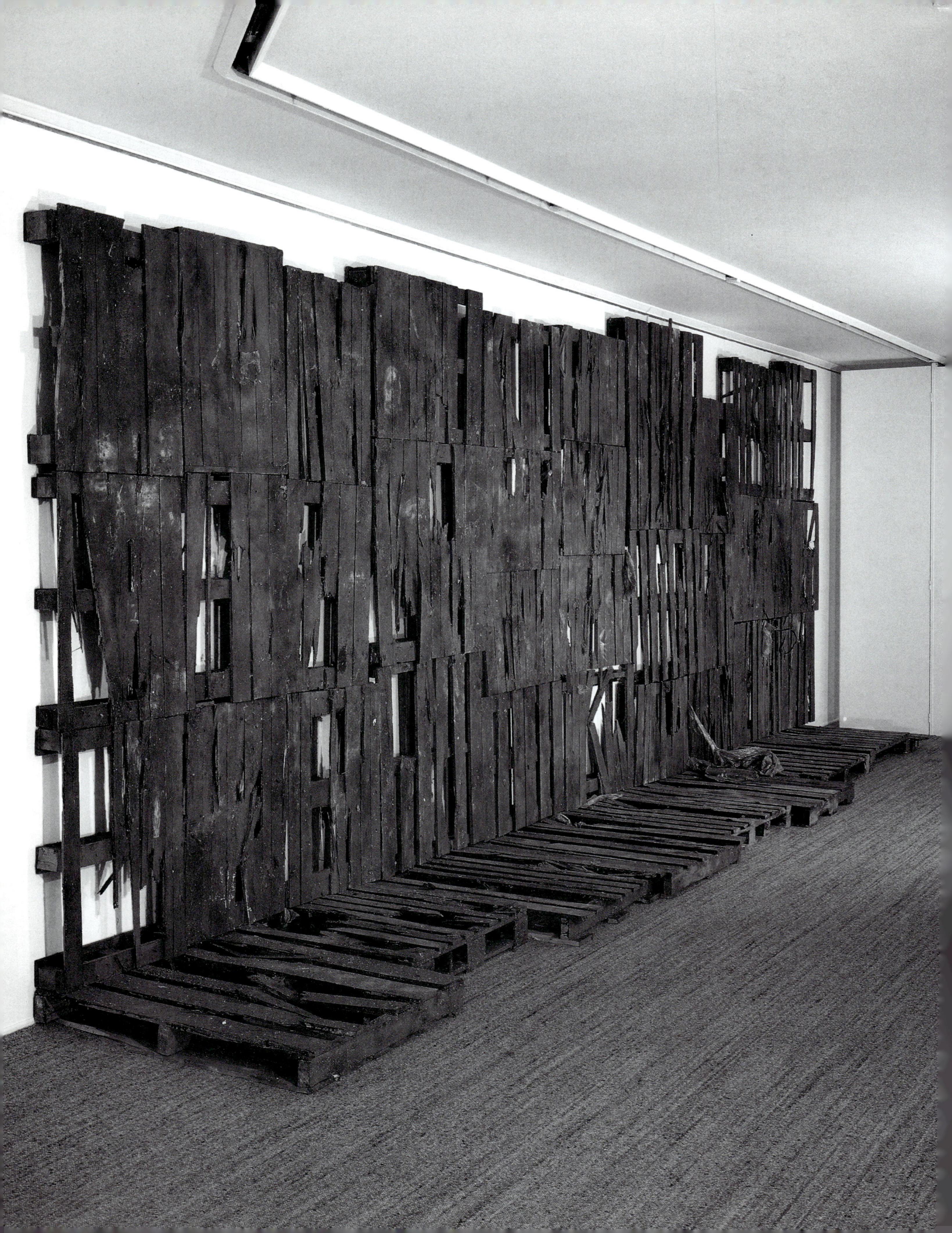

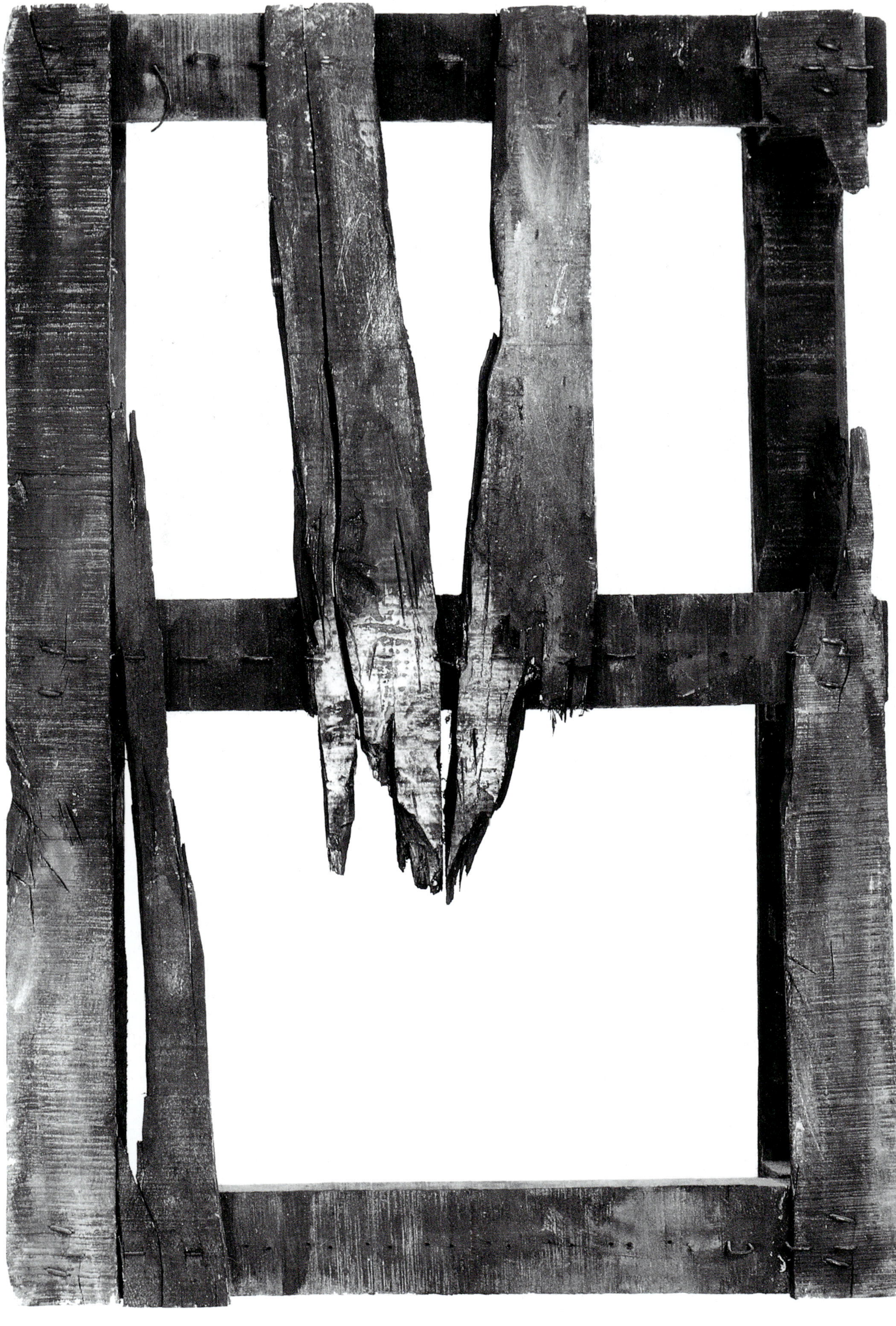

Previous page left
43 Pallets/1988–90/dust, oil, acrylic and photographs on wood
Installation, Gimpel Fils, London in solo show *Images for the End of the Century*, 1990. This coincided with an exhibition of the same name at the Imperial War Museum and *Images for the End of the Century* (Pluto Press, 1990)

Previous page right
Pallet 15/1990/dust, oil, acrylic and photograph on wood

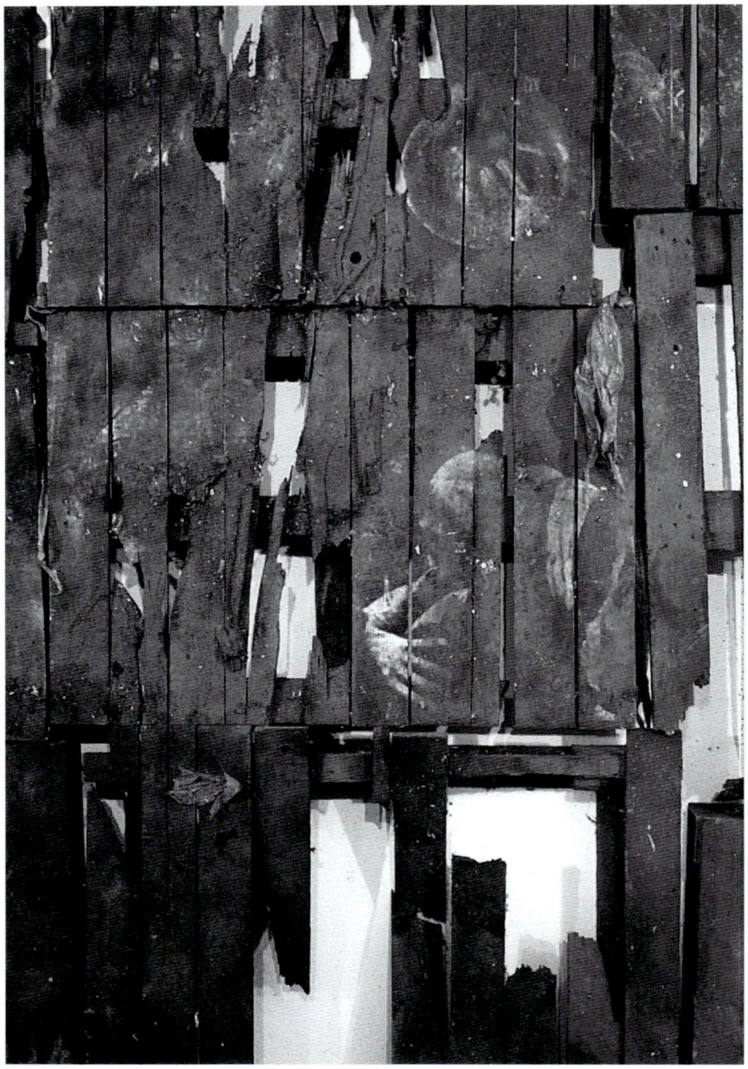

gradually came into vision. On what at first appeared to be merely a wall of smashed pallets were traces of humanity which gradually inched their way into the spectators' consciousness. Passing by the images became a mirror of how we pass by the reality of homelessness in the street.

At the same time as this exhibition, I had a show at the Imperial War Museum, London of my photomontages on disarmament. Both shows were called *Images for the End of the Century*. At the Imperial War Museum, in order to get to my show, the visitor had to walk through the main gallery with its gleaming missiles, tanks and guns. I intended my work to be the antidote when you finally got to it. I realised through this conjunction of two shows of very different work in the same city that it was okay to continue different methods of working at the same time. I've never thought of my work as an 'intervention' (a word that is often bandied about in left art circles). It suggests being outside of the experience that you depict. I am not homeless, but this studio – where I'm writing – leads through a passage onto the street where people are. I have not experienced the horror of Kosovo or East Timor, but I am a citizen in a country whose actions are globally tied up with what's happening in those countries. From childhood, like everyone else, I have interiorised the society we live in. To me it's about making work as a citizen. It's not about being a 'political artist', in the sense that Morandi is not

Working away from the confines of the darkroom and the precision that photomontage demands proved to be an enormous release, a total anarchic breakdown of all the carefulness I'd had to acquire. Especially working on '43 Pallets', which took up all the available space behind my home forcing me to work on the flat, composing at random if at all, free to make something that resonated on different levels; the images, those 'traces of reality', merging into the splintered misshapen objects, virtually disappearing under the dust I poured over it all.

Cv/interview/November 1990

Opposite
43 Pallets/1990 (detail)
Showing the incorporation of *Pallet 6* into the installation

Below
Installation shot from solo show *Images for the End of the Century* at the Imperial War Museum, 1990

named as a 'bottle artist'. The naming is an attempt to neutralise the specificity of the subject in a particular work. It's a way of saying it's all just politics. My practice as an artist is to take as the subject what's happening in the world, to act as a witness, a reporter who through joining images can report back on the hows and whys of struggle. Then comes the question of audiences, context, methods of reaching out beyond the places designated for experiencing art. Developing forms that slide from the gallery back into the street, and vice versa. I believe that there is no right or wrong place to show my work, be it the gallery, the newspaper, the book, the net or the placard. I don't work in a vacuum. It is what is happening politically at any particular time that affects how the work gets out into the world.

Archive B: Pallets 5

The pallets are now my raw material. They are piled up in Archive B and are part of the lorry load that I take out and put together in different configurations with other objects in different places. They are like words to be constructed into sentences. With other sentences they make paragraphs.

Archive B: London – a map of voices

I look up through the slats of the pallets, out of the window, onto London Fields. I remember the day, five years ago, a few days after my father had died. I was in here, messing around, not able to concentrate, and went for a walk. I can't remember deciding to go; I just went. I walked and walked across London, to where I was born and spent my childhood. It was as if I was being pulled back to where I had spent most time with my dad. I hadn't been back to Maida Vale for years, and subconsciously I think I needed to experience the pavements, bricked walkways and the cracks in the concrete of my childhood. I know every step of the area so well; it's embedded in me like a map of my childhood. Being back there, I found I could live through my relationship with my dad in my mind; the sense of loss could be represented materially through these streets and buildings.

A map of London is the closest I can come to a map of my own experience and struggles as an artist. I don't drive a car; bus numbers represent different times in my life: 16, 260, 60 to school, then 28, 31 to art school and so on. When I have to state my nationality on a form, I put 'Londoner'. The texture of different parts of the city is imbued in my work. I have rarely represented the city directly, but each workroom and archive I have inhabited is a conglomeration of the city. At night, in the lit room where I work, I look out over the darkness of London and the city seems to whisper innumerable messages from my personal history.

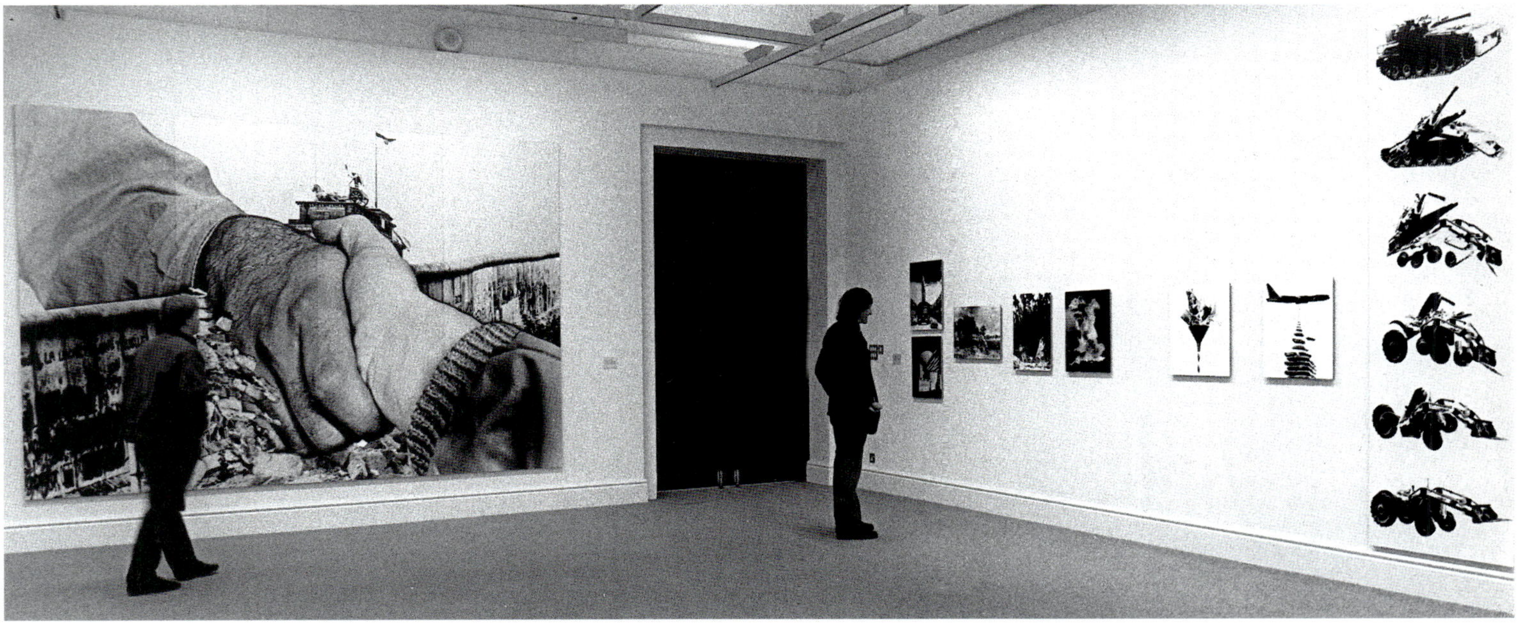

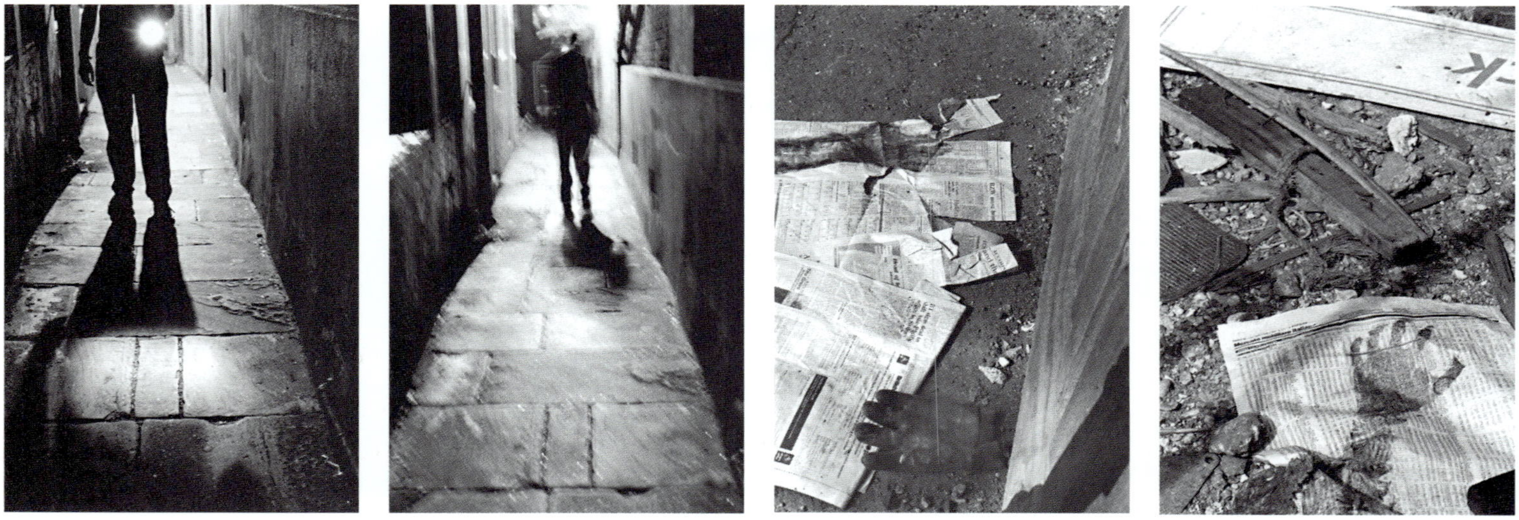

Below
From an Abandoned Alley/1995/silver prints
From a sequence of 15 photographs originating in an alley in north London

From different rooms spanning 30 years, I have looked out from my desk and tried to picture life beyond the city. I haven't travelled to all of the countries that I've made work about. I sit at a desk and work from images coming in from anywhere in the world. The photojournalist goes out and takes the pictures; I sit in a room with the tools of my trade and try to pummel these pictures into revealing invisible connections, disconnecting them from direct representation into statement and argument. Although, compared to a photojournalist, I'm grounded and stuck at my safe desk or in my darkroom under safelight, I still feel that my subject has to be made up from events from around the world. The peoples of the world are here now in London. In Stoke Newington, where I live, I hear fragments of countless languages when I wander the streets.

I'm Jewish; the movements of my parents' families across the globe ended up in London via eastern Europe. I have scant details, but I've always felt connected to eastern and central Europe, and I have a sense of London as a microcosm of a larger city that spreads out through the Baltic states to Russia. What is most important to me about London is that its population is composed of a mix of people from across the world. It is a multi-racial and multi-cultural city. This is the key to the spirit of London, and it is this world culture that is at the root of my work. The split between art and politics is a giant chasm in English culture. It doesn't exist in the same way in other countries. I have always believed that my work needed to make explicit the link between art and politics. To me, to grapple with political reality through art is as natural as breathing. Being Jewish, albeit from non-religious parents, has given me a sense of the diaspora as a condition for the greater part of humanity. The twentieth century was the century of forced movements of people; people trudging or falling by the wayside; carrying old mattresses and a few battered bags. People pushed around by the movements of history. I've had a privileged existence, but my forebears arrived here in a state of exile, and I've internalised that exile and then externalised it through my work.

When I walk the streets of London, I feel connected to the voices of those that don't fit in the official story of the city. Just 300 yards from where I live, James O'Brien, the Chartist leader, is buried in Abney Park Cemetery. Thousands of dissident voices echo through these streets. This is a time when voices against ... are almost smothered by voices for ... It's this sense of being connected to these dissident voices that keeps me going.

Archive B: London – the Switch Room

From 1974 to 1977, I had a tangible experience of the city as a cackle of voices. Though the voices going through my ears were mostly far from dissident – apart from those who were complaining about

By breaking down elements in photographs, cutting them up and reconstituting them, a critical narrative on opposing futures can be presented visually. The resultant images are not documentary mirrors (although some of my work only exists as a result of the bravery of documentary photographers who go out into the world while I sit in a room trying to make sense of the images that they bring back), but visual maps of human choice.

Images for the End of the Century/1990

the service they received from me – becoming a night telephone operator was a whole new point of departure for me. Living on thin air had finally become intolerable. So I got a full-time job following a long period of unemployment. In the interview for the job they misread my form and asked me why I had been working on and off for the Department of Health and Social Security for so long. I had to tell them I hadn't been working *for* the Social Security, I'd been *on* it. Somehow I managed to pass the exams that took place eight weeks into the job, and became qualified to do something useful for the first – and last – time in my life.

In the day, I worked in a studio off Chalk Farm, and at night in the Finchley Road telephone exchange. The shifts were 6pm to 11pm, with one or two 13-hour shifts a week. The disciplinary code of the Post Office at that time was byzantine, based on the rigours of army life. I was constantly being given 'Informal oral reprimands' in written form, and 'Formal written reprimands' in vocal form, and every other combination imaginable. We sat in the 'switch room', a rich collection of failed actors, ex-BBC alcoholics and aspiring young workers, using ancient equipment, controlling the 'phones of a large area of north and central London. We answered 999 calls and burglar alarms which when triggered came straight through to the exchange, often overlaid by the voice of the burglar saying he was just testing his alarm. We did wake-up calls and normal operator calls, often answering what sounded like angry Viennese analysts in the Finchley Road or Hampstead who blamed us for every one of their failed attempts to use the telephone. We also controlled the Soho area, and got innumerable calls from male punters, often tourists, who'd been fleeced and were trouserless in W1. Through the long night, a vivid picture built up of a city miscommunicating. To survive the long nights being overseen by a supervisor in a glass box in the middle of the switch room – a living panopticon – I responded to the calls subjectively. If someone rang through in a friendly way, I let them phone for free (sometimes to Australia for an hour!) and if someone was rude, I plugged up their line with *Dial a-Disc* for 15 minutes. Callers were always complaining to the supervisor about my mumbling, claiming I was drunk or stoned. More often it was exhaustion, trying to make work in the day, and doing the 'phones at night – although we did sometimes get stoned during breaks on the long shifts on the roof of the exchange, where we had a few dope plants growing. I got involved with the Post Office and Engineering Workers' Union, becoming the branch representative, and transformed the union noticeboard with an array of Rodchenko-like arrows, pointing out complaints and various political rallies that were going on. In the end, the union claimed that the noticeboard could not advertise political activities, and I redoubled the revolutionary graphics, with the red arrows

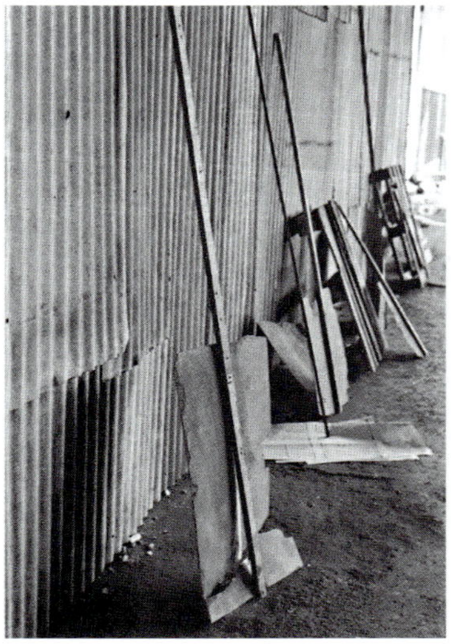

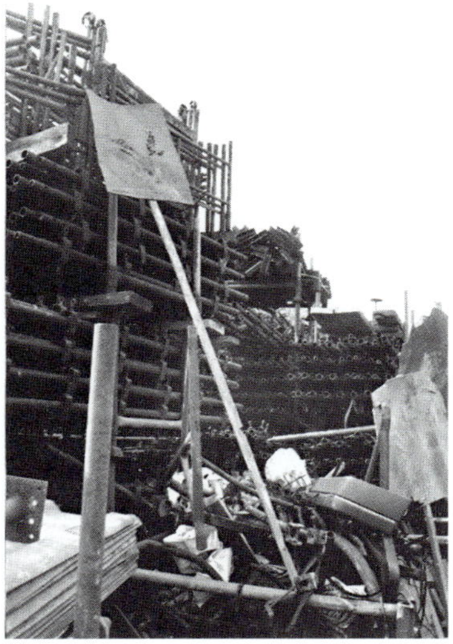

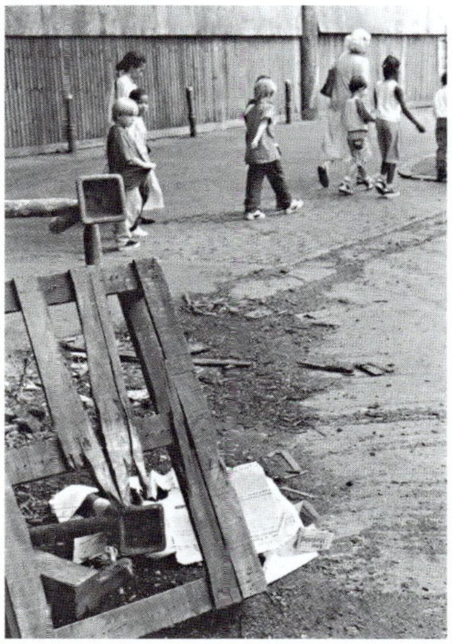

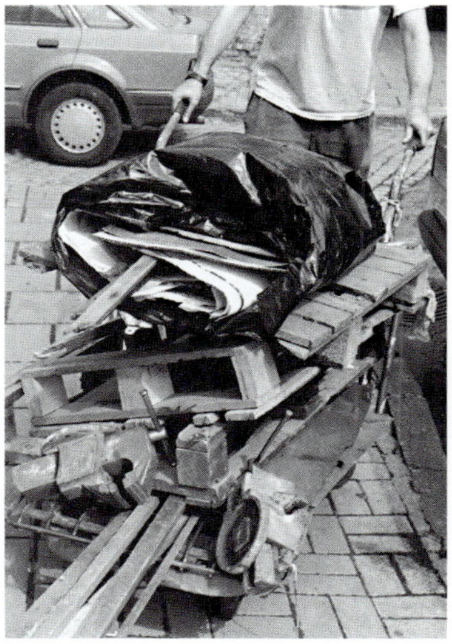

Below
CND posters, flyposted in Hackney, London, 1981

Opposite
Broken Missile/1980/photomontage

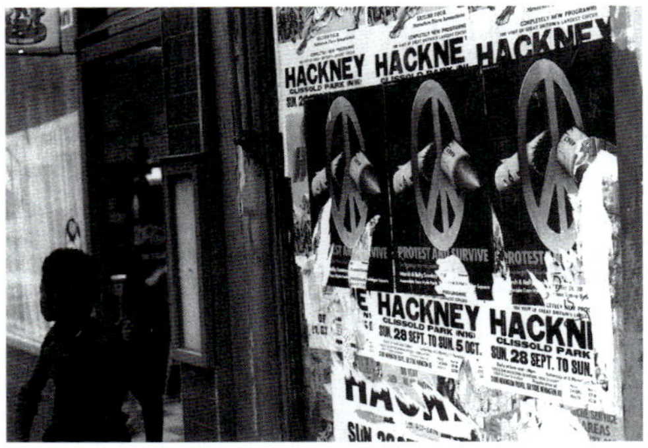

pointing at advice on how to look after your pets and where to get cheap dry-cleaning. The management then thought that this was encoded exhortation to revolt, direct from the Stasi, and banned the noticeboard altogether. We were not a strong trade union branch and after one particularly gruelling 13-hour shift I snapped, and went to see Peter de Francia, who was professor of painting at the Royal College of Art, London, to apply to do an MA. Even though my application was late, I was eventually taken on later that year.

The 'switch room' stands out in my memory as a jangling nerve centre always on the point of overload and collapse. It was as if the chaos of London was passing through my brain via the headset. The pre-digital technology now seems from another age, but the feel of those long nights in that strange hall of voices gave me another view of the London night as a multi-layered cacophony of voices, desperate not to be cut off.

Archive B: London – from rooms to streets

My map of London is a map of attempts to work my art into the social fabric of everyday life. Other than the switch room, it is a picture of small, ramshackle spaces where people have got together through believing that things could be changed. I remember in 1979 going to a tiny office in Great Queen Street where the Campaign for Nuclear Disarmament (CND) was based. It was there that I showed Bruce Kent and a few others my photomontages and said I'd like to do work for nuclear disarmament. I had become disturbed by the fact that the burgeoning anti-nuclear campaign was using undoctored images of nuclear bombs and missiles, merely adding their own slogan. This was also the time when Athena posters were selling a poster of an air-brushed mushroom cloud which was deemed to be an acceptable image to put up on bedroom walls. I still have the page from their catalogue which illustrates the poster, next to two American pick-up trucks, all listed under 'The Twentieth Century: Power and Energy'. My elder son once came home with a book called *Discover the World of Weapons*. On its cover was the photo of an enormous missile pointing skywards at the title. The whole book was designed with psychedelic 1960s graphics. This was considered suitable reading matter for eight year olds. And they called *us* insane. I felt that these images had to be broken, had to be taken out of the supposedly rational discourse in which they could become domestic decoration.

The headquarters of CND were so cramped that movement had to be strategic. I remember I had to lay my work on the floor, causing total snarl-up for human traffic. From that space, in the early 1980s an enormous movement for disarmament grew. I remember the early discussions I had there about re-invigorating the CND symbol, leaving the office and then going back a day or so later with very

The point of my work is to use easily recognisable iconic images, but to render them unacceptable. To break down the image of the all-powerful missile, in order to represent the power of the millions of people who are actually trying to break them. After breaking them, to show new possibilities emerging in the cracks and splintered fragments of the old reality.

Images for the End of the Century/1990

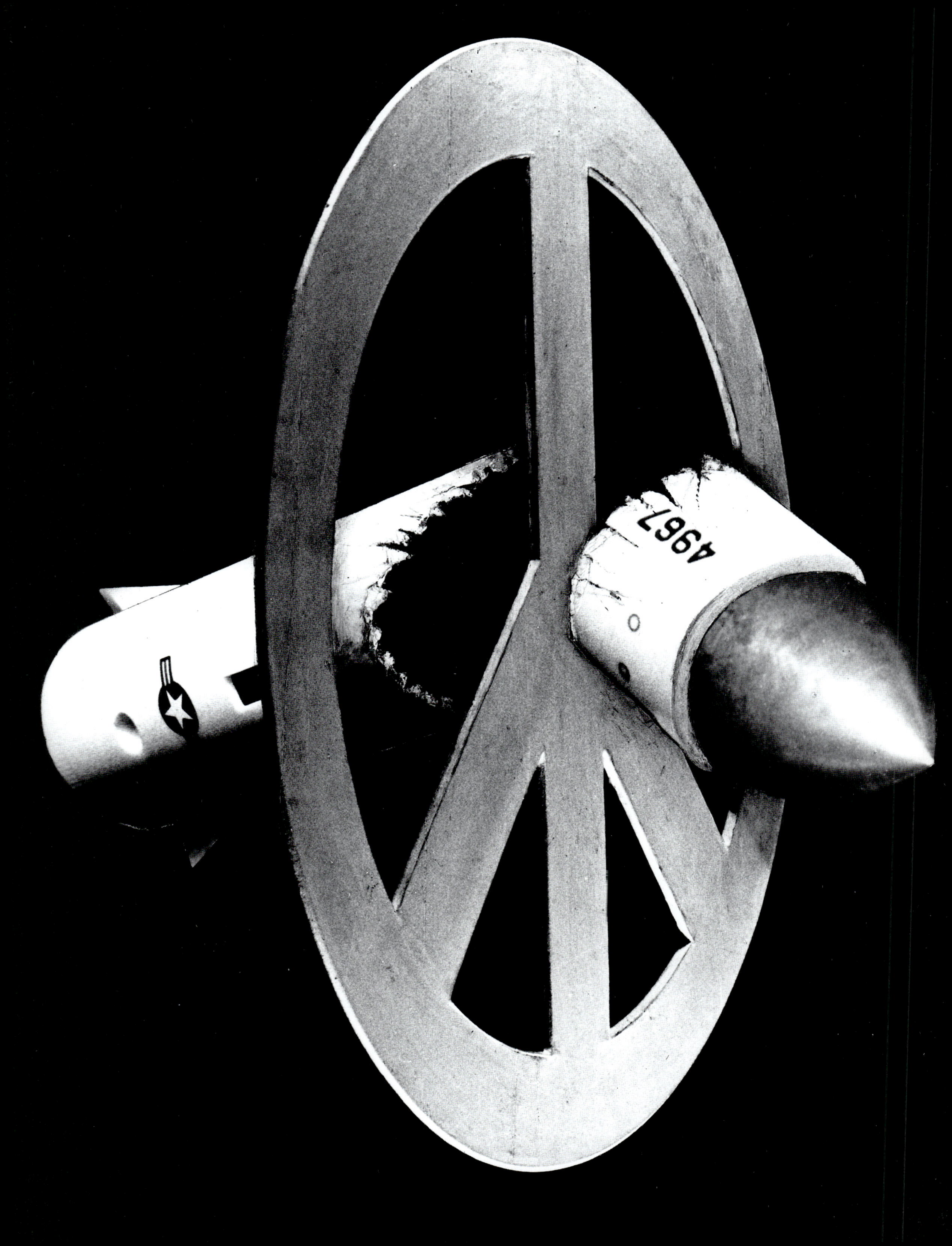
4967

Right
Front page of *The Sunday Times*, 25 October 1981, showing *Broken Missile* on placards

Below
A poster of *Broken Missile* taped to the fence of Greenham Common by a protester, 1982

Opposite
CND demonstration in London, 1982

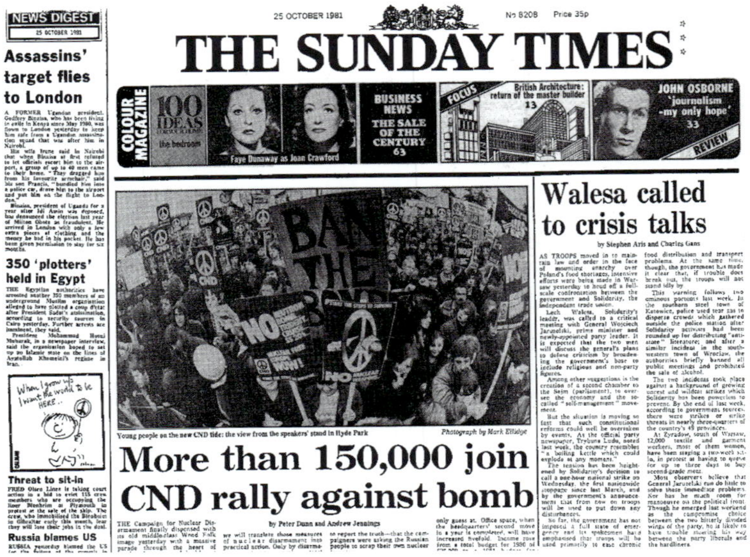
NEWS DIGEST
25 OCTOBER 1981

Assassins' target flies to London

350 'plotters' held in Egypt

Threat to sit-in

Russia blames US

25 OCTOBER 1981 No 8208 Price 35p

THE SUNDAY TIMES

COLOUR MAGAZINE
100 IDEAS
Faye Dunaway as Joan Crawford
BUSINESS NEWS
THE SALE OF THE CENTURY 63
FOCUS
British Architecture: return of the master builder 13
JOHN OSBORNE 'journalism -my only hope' 33
REVIEW

Walesa called to crisis talks

Young people on the new CND tide: the view from the speakers' stand in Hyde Park
Photograph by Mark Ellidge

More than 150,000 join CND rally against bomb

by Peter Dunn and Andrew Jennings

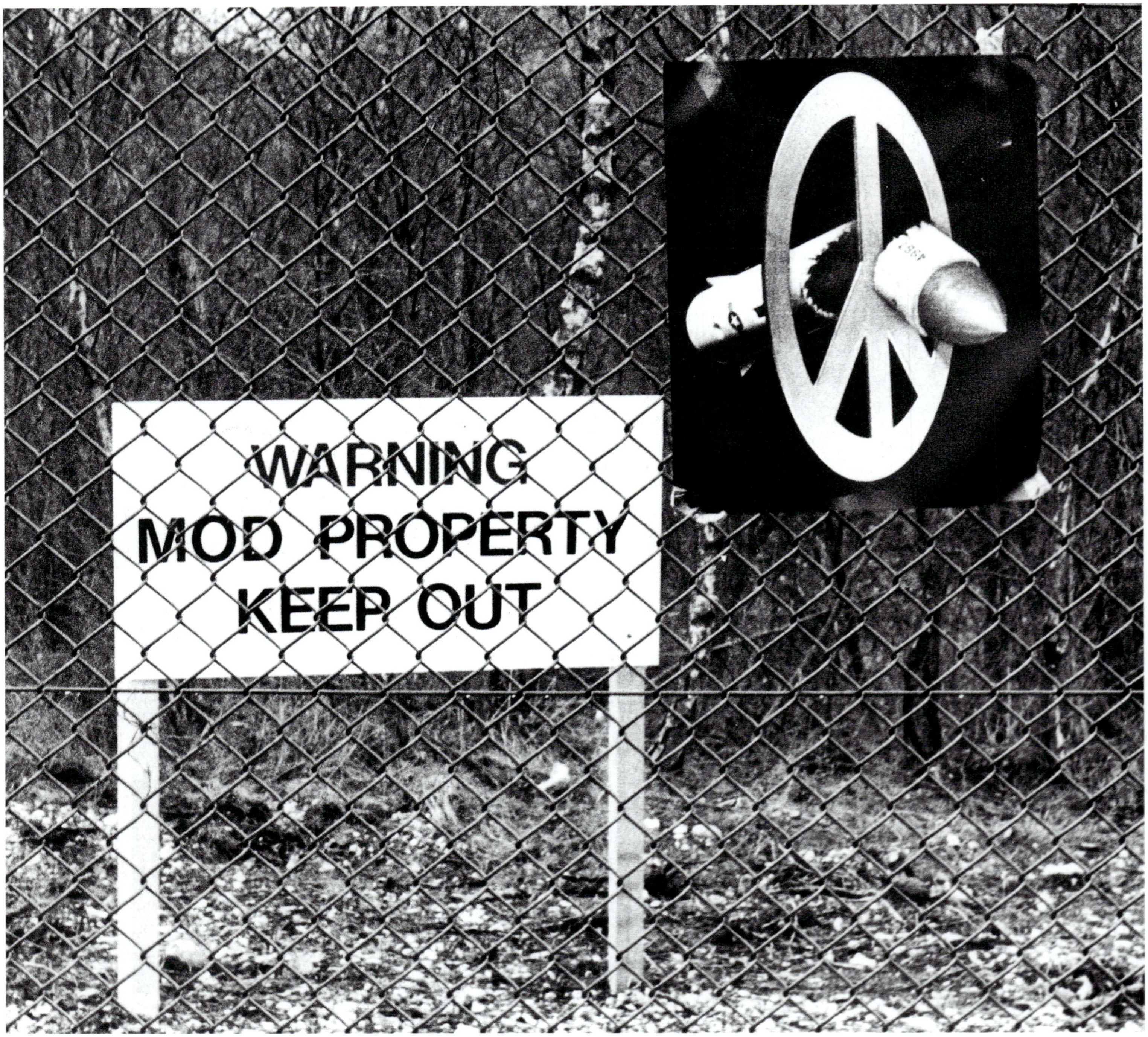

The nuclear industry has not revealed its destructive potential to the documentary camera since we saw photographs of the victims of the bombing of Hiroshima. A photograph in today's paper about Britain's 'defence' system is now likely to be illustrated by Cruise missiles looking like friendly little aircraft placed next to a picture of the defence minister. His bland face would not reveal that another part of the social services was being destroyed in this country to pay for a weapons system which was aimed at destroying the people of another country.

Undercurrents/February 1982

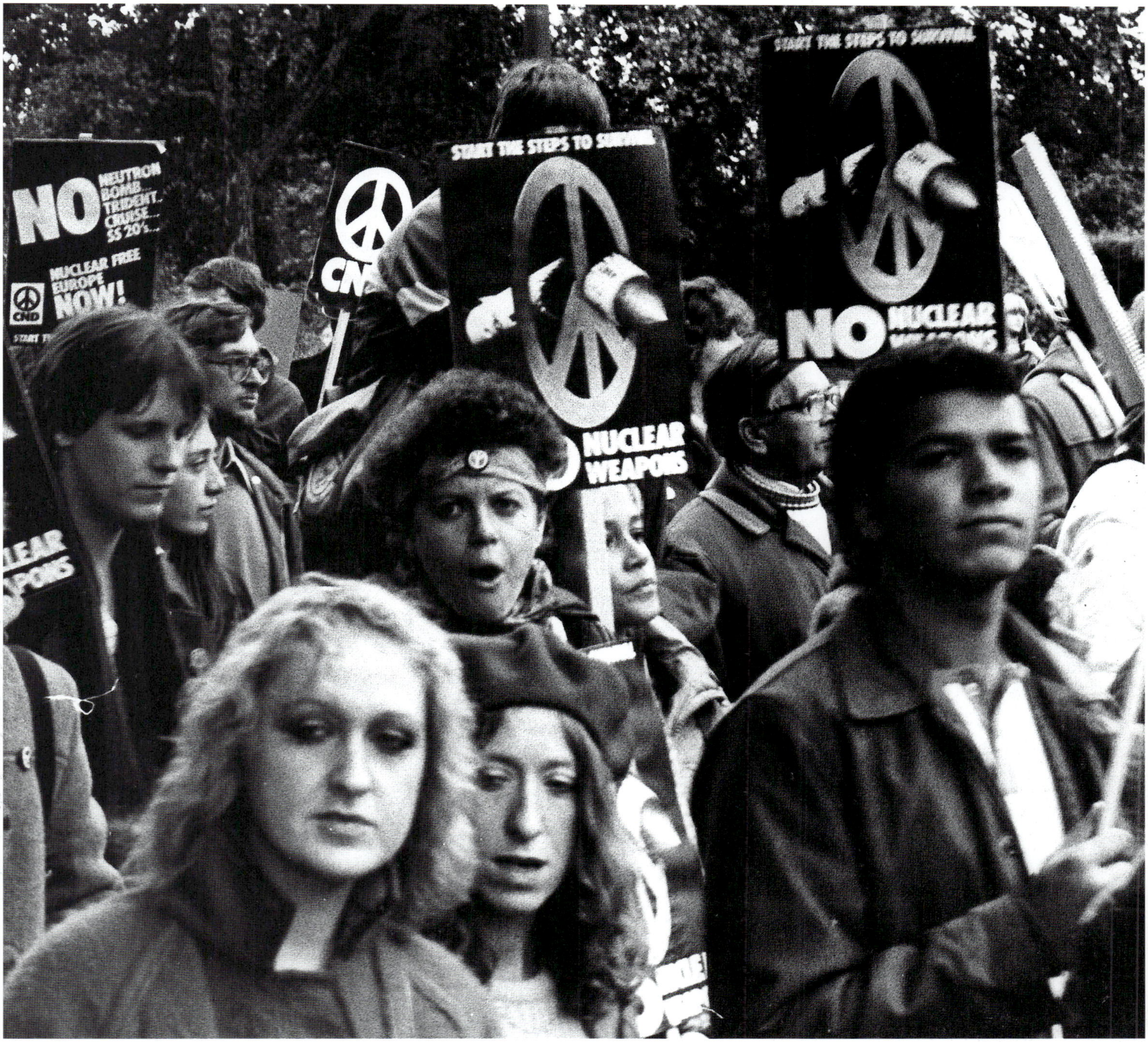

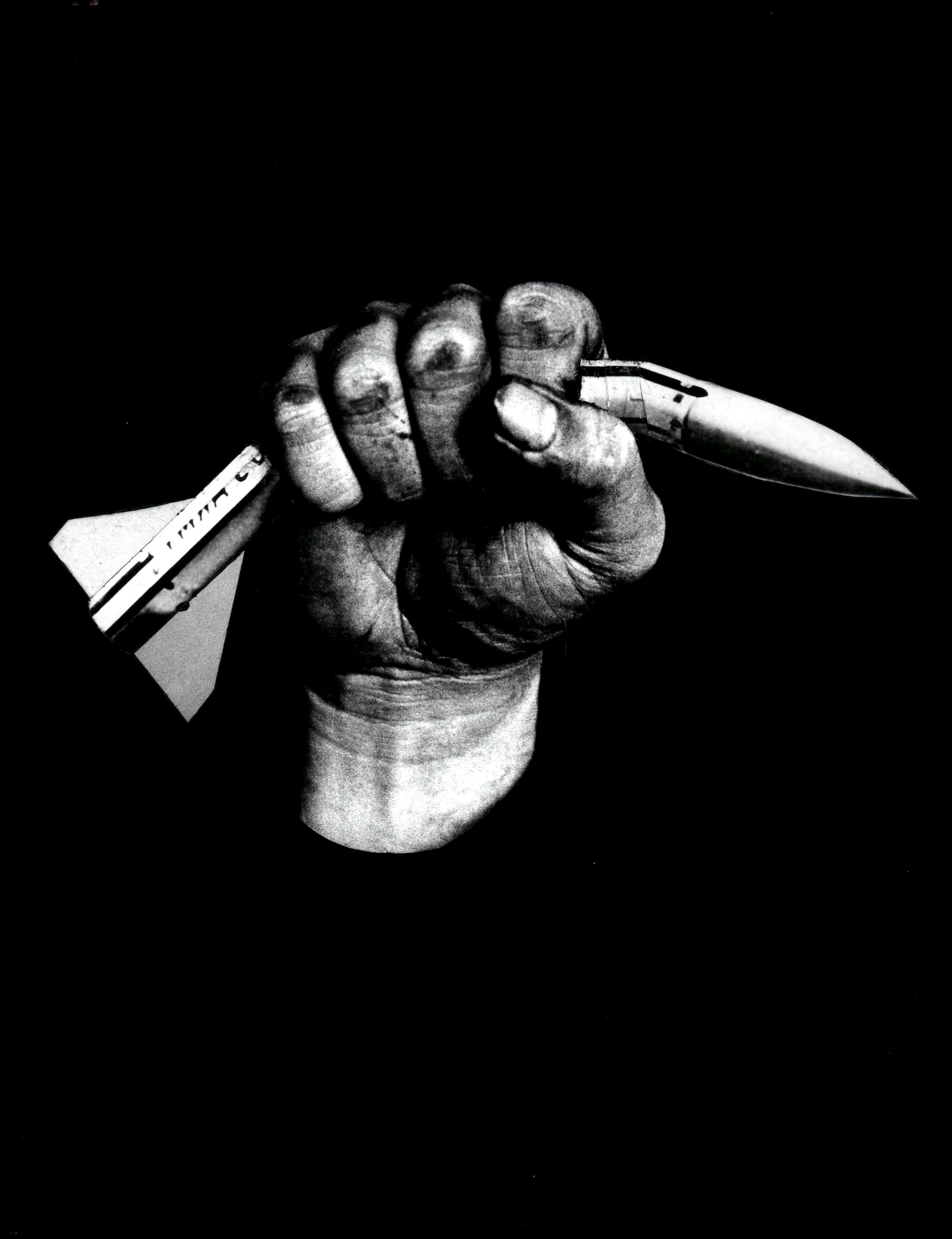

On Sunday, at the UN Open Day, it was great to see so many people young and old, from across the globe, reacting to and discussing my exhibition. I personally talked to people from a great many countries and the usual language problems did not seem to matter as the images spoke to them across language barriers. I will always remember one old Japanese man looking at one of my photomontages of a fist breaking a missile who raised his own fist as if mirroring the image and smiled to himself.

United Nations Conference on Art and Disarmament/1989

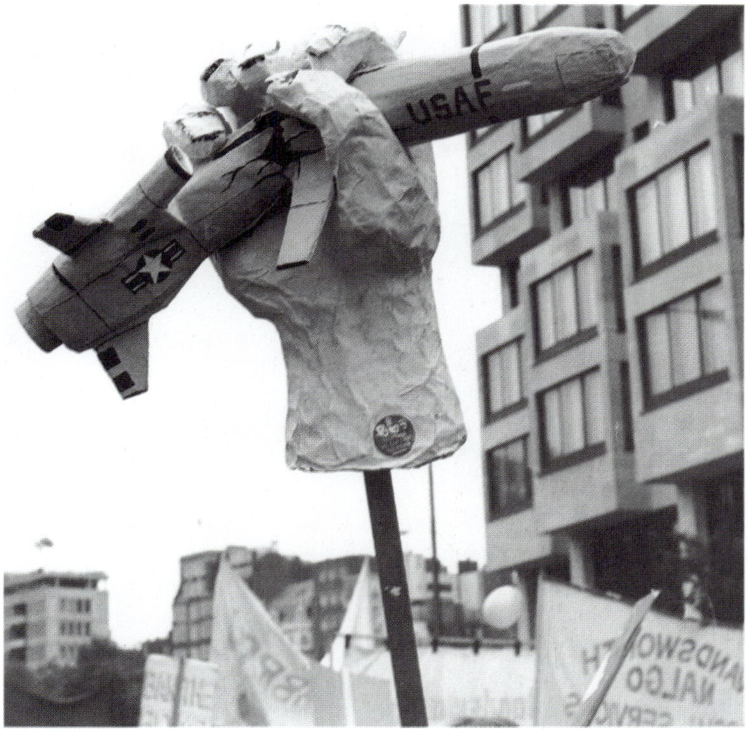

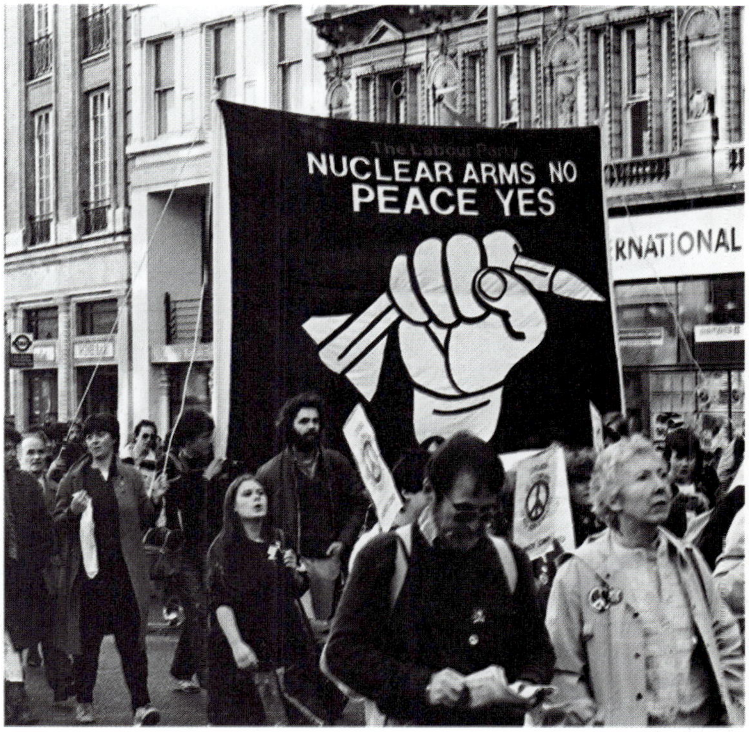

Opposite
Crushed Missile/1980/photomontage
Commissioned by the Labour Party as their anti-nuclear symbol

Above left
Anti-nuclear demonstration in 1981 showing a three-dimensional version of *Crushed Missile* made by protesters

Above right
Demonstration in London, 1982, showing Labour Party banner made from a drawing based on the photomontage *Crushed Missile*

I believe that the image of objects that we oppose should be broken up, shattered by opposing imagery. We must find key images enabling us to prise open and reveal the hidden mechanisms of oppressive regimes.

Artery/1980

Below
Anatomy Lesson/1980/photomontage
First used as a cover for 'State of the Nation' (*Camerawork*, July 1980)

Opposite above left
Warhead/1983/photomontage (rough)
Ideas are developed by trial and error, cutting and sticking prints made in the darkroom. This rough later became the basis for *Warhead 2* and *Warhead 5*

Opposite above right
Warhead 5/1986/photomontage
Produced as one of a set of nine photomontages used as chapter openers in the *Gaia Peace Atlas* (Doubleday, 1988)

Opposite below left
Warhead 2/1983/photomontage

Opposite below right
Protest and Survive/1981/photomontage
The skeleton is reading a copy of the government pamphlet *Protect and Survive*, (HMSO, 1980) which offers guidelines of how to act in the event of a nuclear war

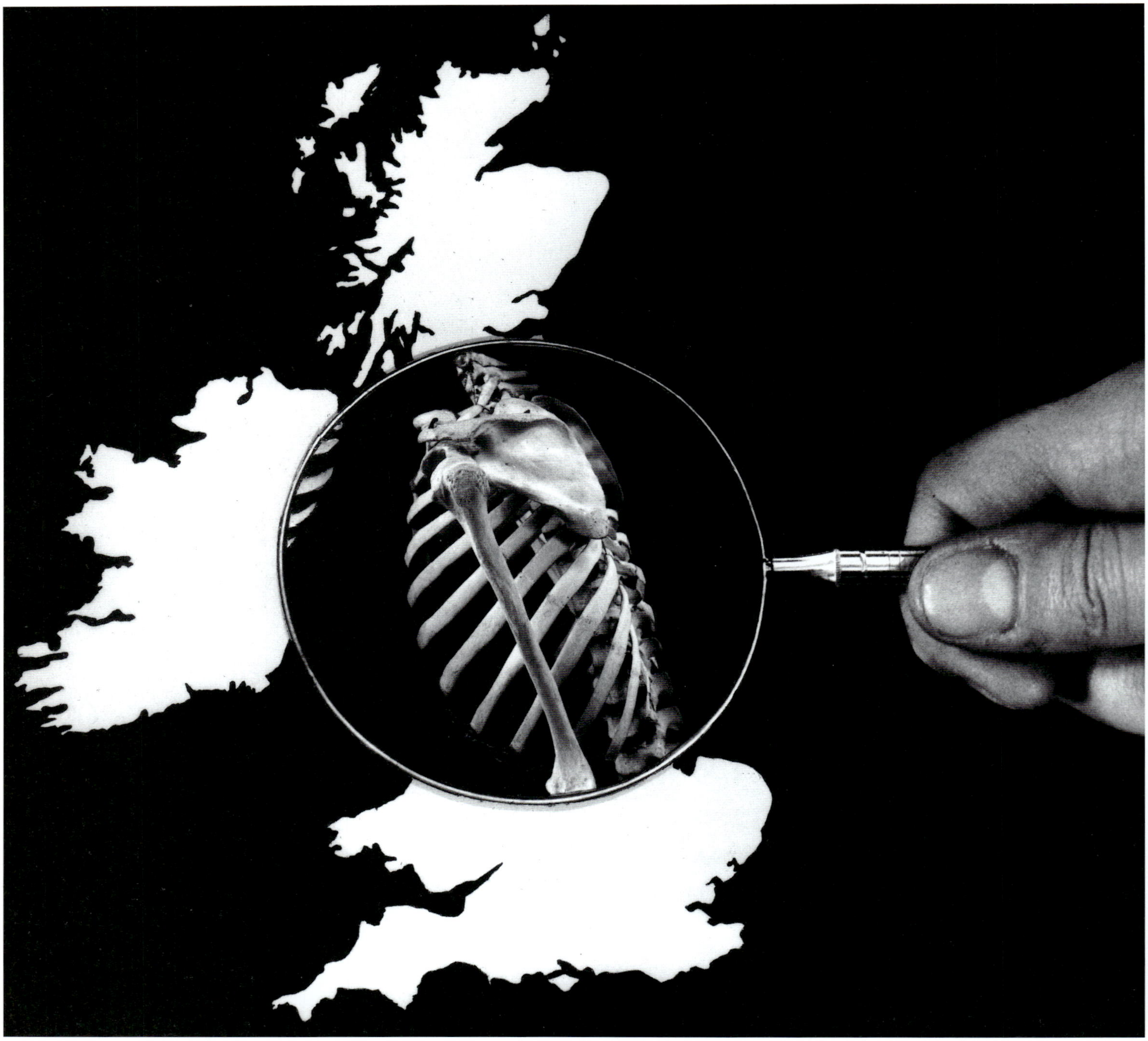

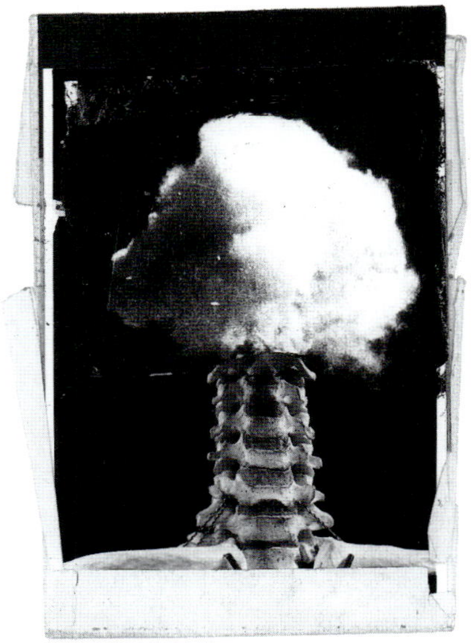

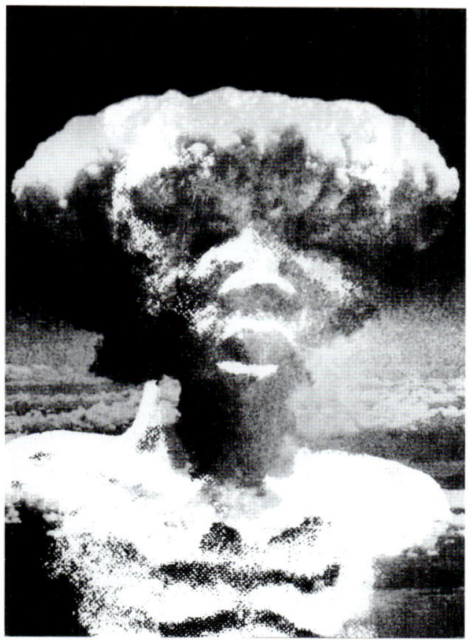

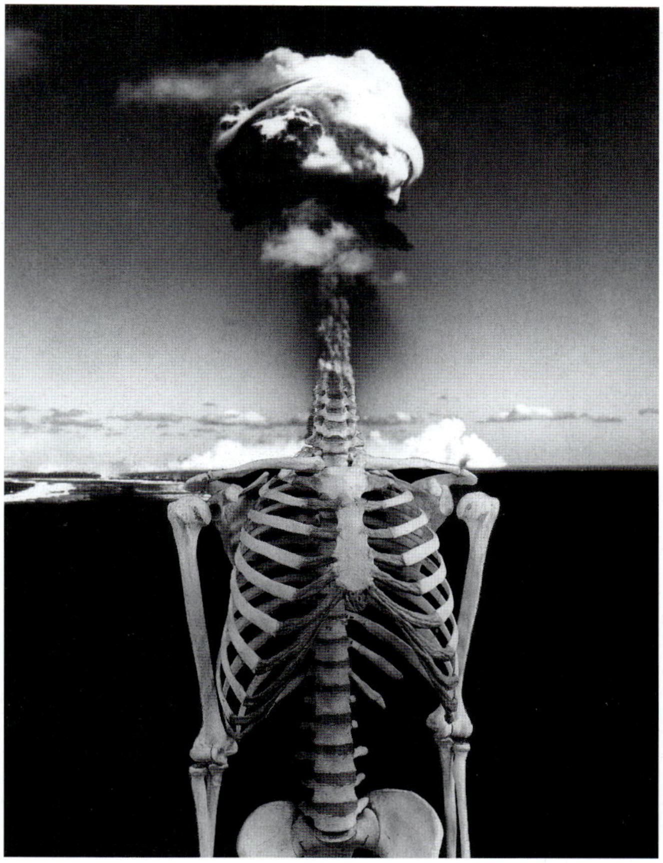

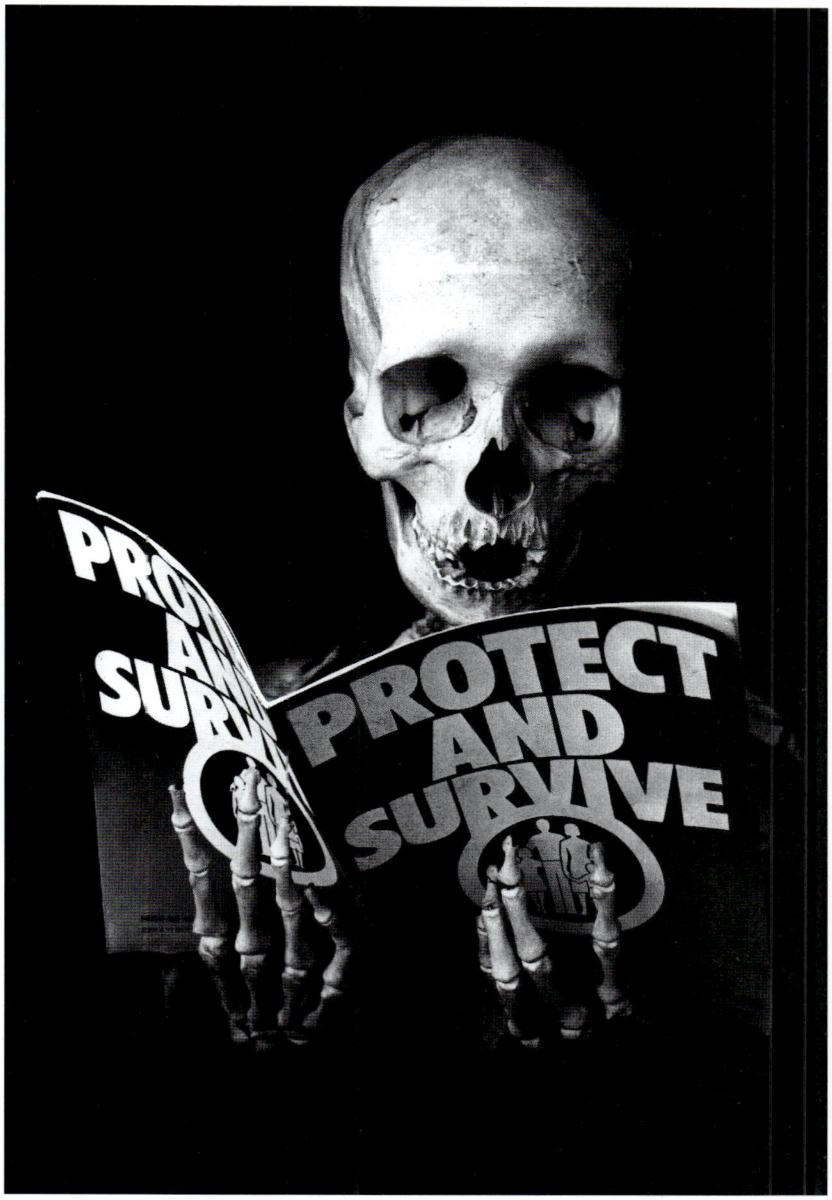
PROTECT
AND
SURVIVE

Left and right
Placards/1993–95 (details)
Vices hold up the placards, some of which have live microphones attached for anyone to speak into during the show

Opposite and overleaf
Placards/1993–95/dust, oil, chalk and charcoal on photographs, cardboard and wood

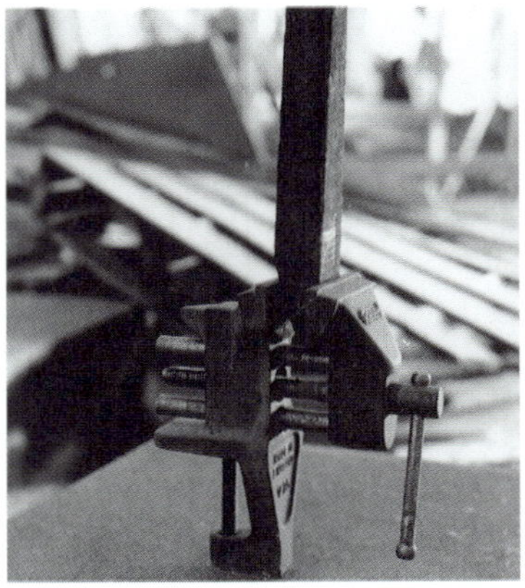

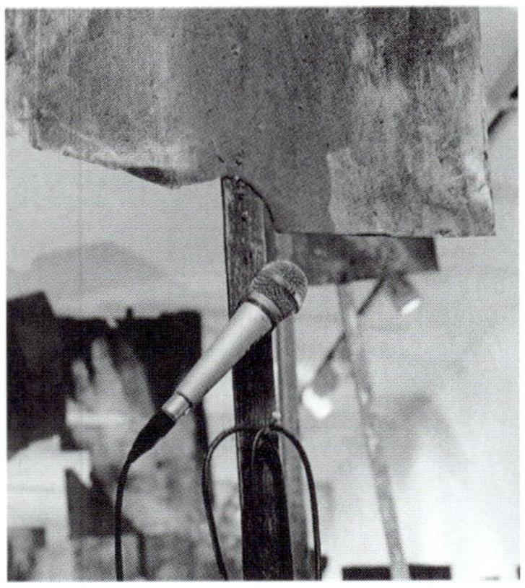

tatty roughs that I'd made deconstructing the symbol so that in the end it started looking like an ad for British Rail. Each attempt failed until I made a cardboard peace symbol which I photographed from different angles and broke the image of a missile on it as if on a wheel. At first that still didn't seem to work as the missile was too flat and unthreatening. So I went to what appeared to be the missile department in Hamley's toy shop, bought a plastic missile, smashed it up with a hammer and photographed the debris. This finally became the image. On Saturday 24 October 1981 I got on a 73 bus with my partner Judy and young son Daniel and went to Hyde Park. There were thousands of people on an enormous demonstration for nuclear disarmament who were holding up *Broken Missile* on placards as well as another image I'd made for the Labour party, *Crushed Missile*. People had also made their own versions of both images in papier mâché or sewn them onto banners and many children had made drawings of them. Through my work I had been able to provide visual representation of the madness of the nuclear arms race that could be used and re-interpreted by many of the thousands of people who campaigned against nuclear weapons.

London changed for me in the years of CND. The photomontages I made for the disarmament movement were out in the street, stuck on walls, up in town halls, on badges and in newspapers. I could spot my work around the city being used in campaigns rather than only being shown to people in galleries. The photomontages began to be used in campaigns across the world. I saw pictures of a mural in Australia, a photograph in a Soviet newspaper and a poster on a wall in Japan that had all used the photomontages. Through the collision of a visual technique I had developed over ten years, and a mass movement, I was able to produce a public art that developed its own momentum through anti-nuclear networks. The images had become placards for the street.

Archive B: Placards
A pile of battered looking placards is leaning against the wall. They were made 15 years after the placards that used my images on disarmament marches. They represent a different vision of the street as a site for struggle and are part of an installation of placards in ruins. I made the first ones in 1993. Held up by rusty metal vices they have images on them of hands – as if the hands of the campaigner had evacuated onto the placard itself. These hands are tearing at the cardboard of the placard, as if tearing at their own representation. The placards look as if they were dug up, archaeological remains of a long gone street protest. Covered in dust and grime, they appear as a desperate grasping against social

anæsthesia. They are not programmatic in any way. I made them as a personal response to events at the time. Now, comparing the two sets of placards, those for CND and those made 15 years later, they do represent a change in the political, and through that my personal, landscape. These placards are shown in galleries. In the street they would become indistinguishable from the street. As with the pallets, I have tried to build into them the textures of the street, as if its grime and dust were sucked onto their surface. The result is contradictory. By taking on the surface wear and tear of everyday life, they become a representation of struggle rather than the visual elements *in a struggle* as in the case of the CND placards. I wrote about these placards in *Domesday Book*:

Hands –
My hands?
Your hands?

Taut under pressure
Miming the hands
Of the carrier,

Slither up sticks
Onto placards
Amputated into image.

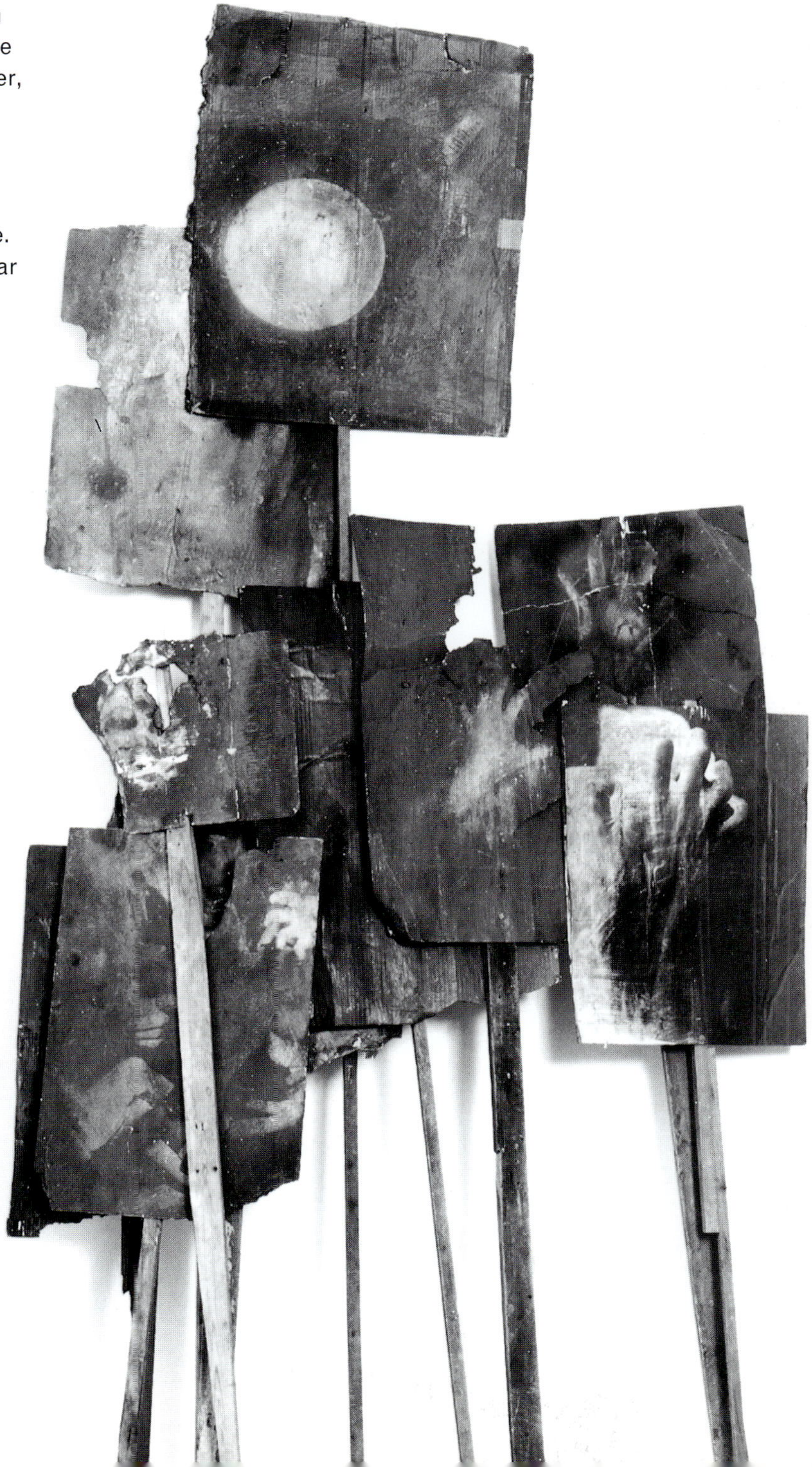

A phrase spoken recently by Dr Hiroshi Nakajima, director-general of the World Health Organisation, has been haunting me. He said that for less than one billion dollars – the cost of twenty modern military planes – the world could control the illness which kills eleven million children in the developing world every year. That connection between starvation and military spending is usually concealed in our society. We know that such an equation, or something similar, is a basic facet of the modern world, but we learn to live with it. Well, I believe it is up to the artist to try and make that equation impossible to live with. The artist must find ways to picture its obscenity. Only the artist can attempt to bring together images that society tries desperately to keep apart and make the connections in which we are all implicated. Artists can act as early warning systems to the plight of the globe.

United Nations Conference on Art and Disarmament/1989

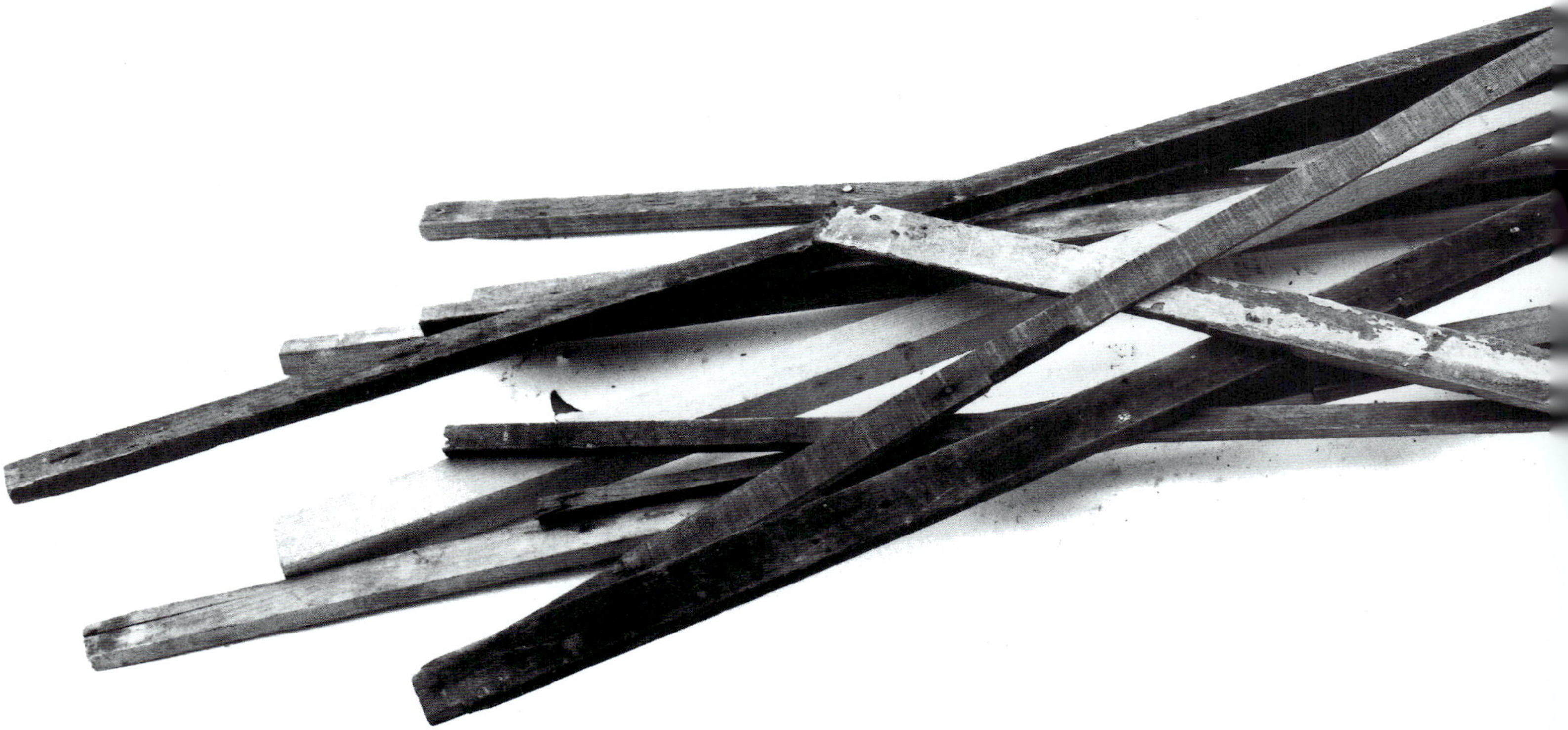

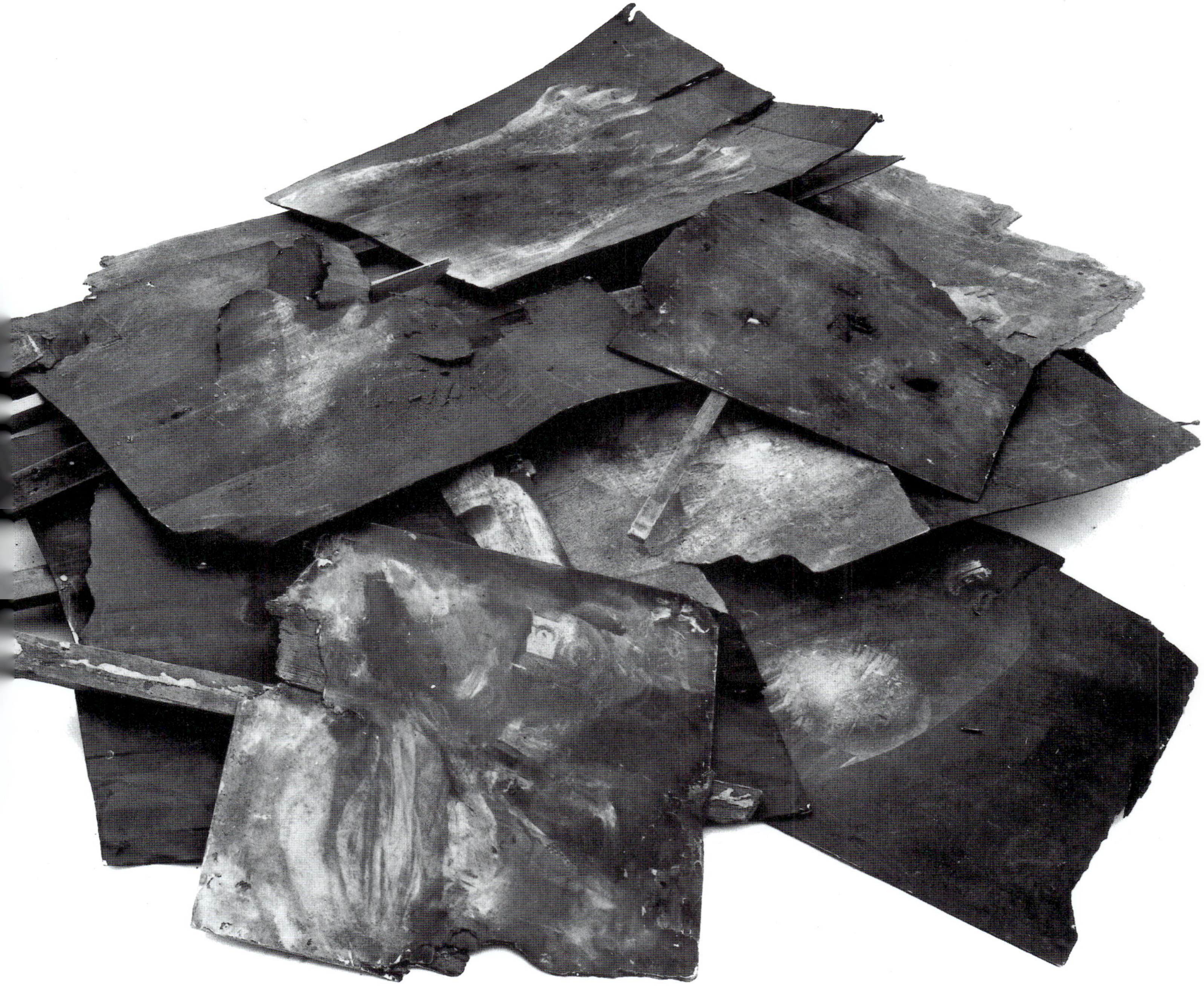

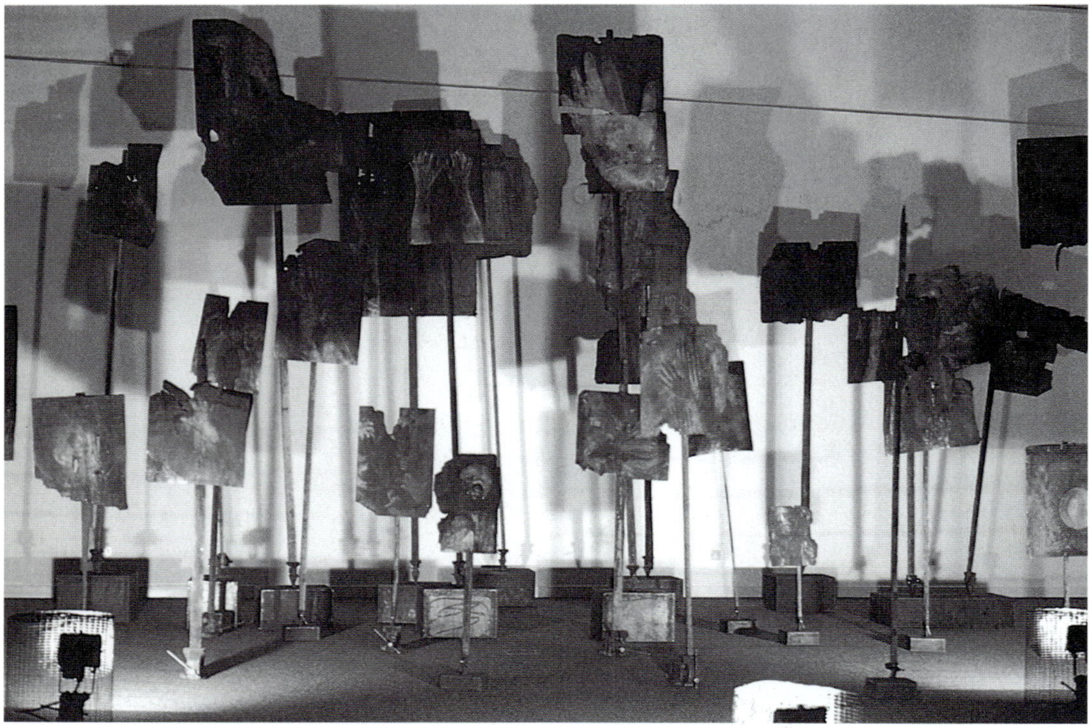

Left
Placards/1993–95/mixed media
Installation, Rijksmuseum Twenthe, Holland, during the *Foto Biennale Enschede*, 1995

Opposite left
Placards/1993–95/mixed media
Installation, Cambridge Darkroom, 1995, solo show, *From an Abandoned Alley*

Opposite right
Placards/1993–95/mixed media
Installation, Bluecoat Gallery, Liverpool, 1996, solo show, *Unwords*

The specific qualities of paint and various other materials is something which I used to enjoy and have repressed for 20 years, because I felt it was important to make work which was bound up with political movements. Now I have got to find a new way to get work across. Working with cardboard, paint and dust is less repressive for me at the moment than working with montage.

Creative Camera/interview/June–July 1995

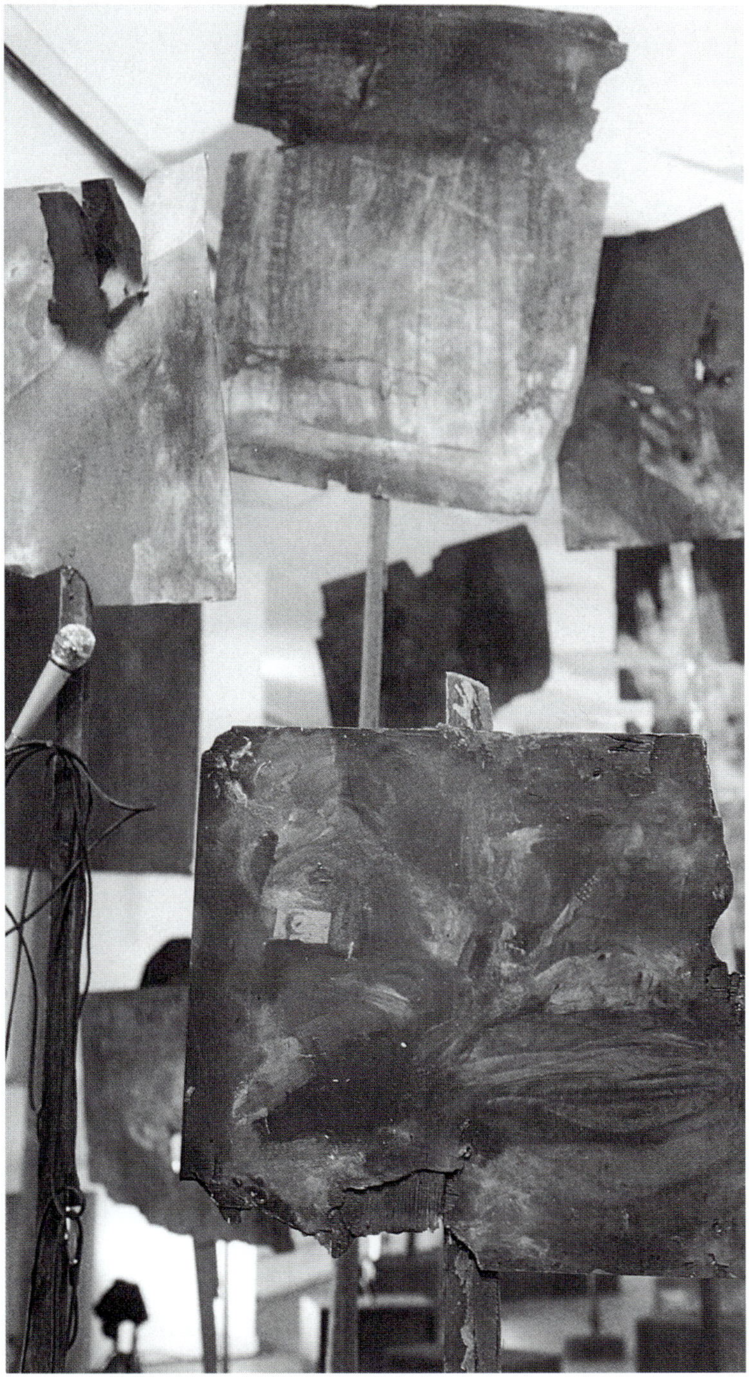

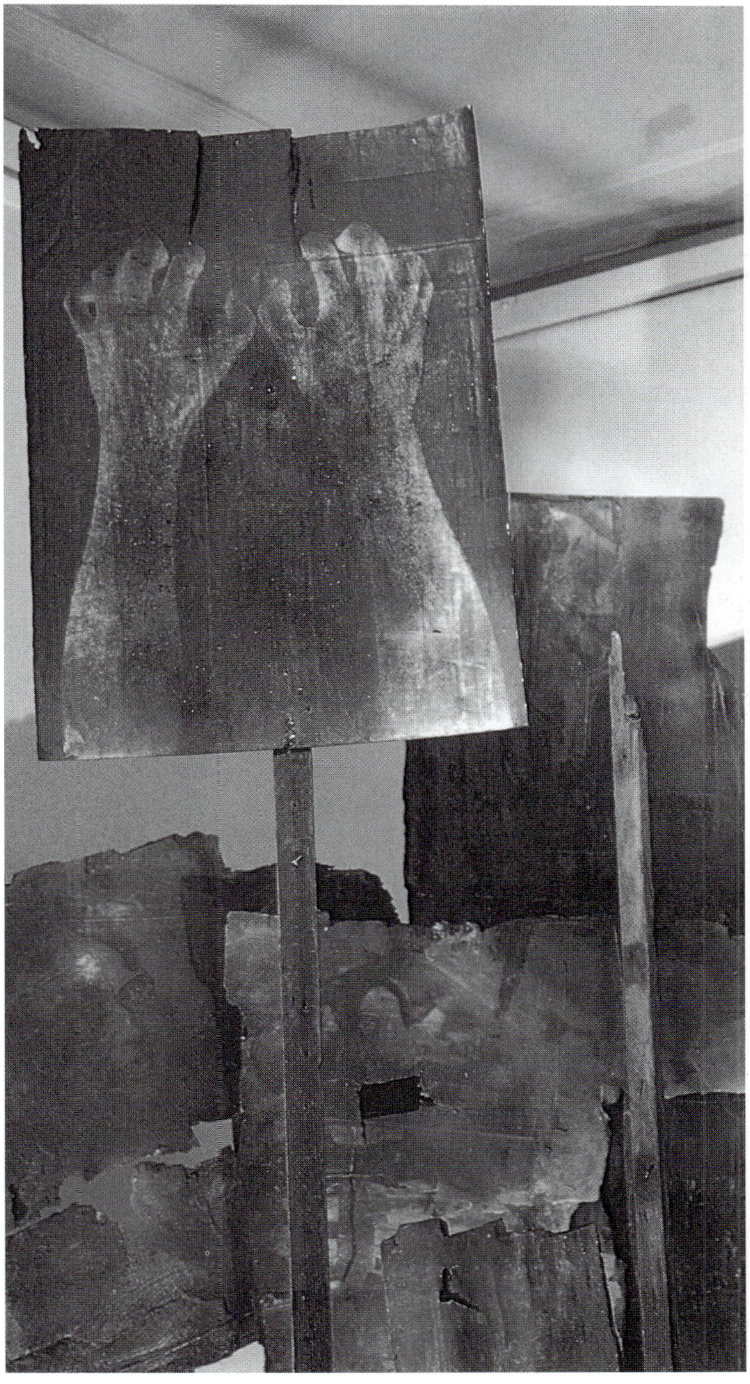

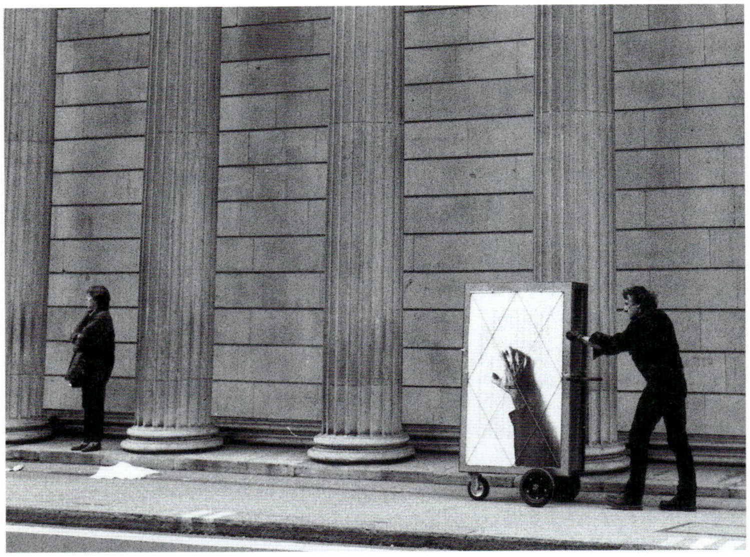

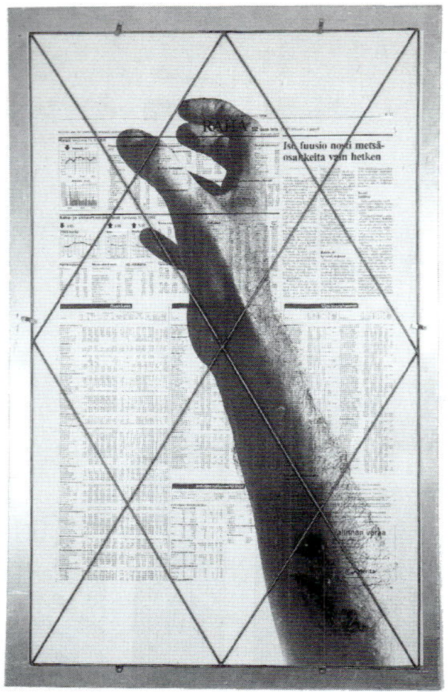

Archive B: Street vehicles, street people

Recently, to reactivate my sense of direct involvement in the streets of London, I have built a cart – *News Truck* – which is parked here in Archive B. When I was a child, the rag-and-bone men used to come round every week pushing carts. They had ingenious mechanisms for holding unwieldy objects attached to them. The carts built by homeless people to push their belongings through the streets are similarly built with extraordinary ingenuity. They appear to be totally of the city, but are also an indictment of the city. From the inventions of the Russian constructivists making mobile agit-prop, through to Krzysztof Wodiczko with his homeless vehicles, the idea of the mobile street vehicle that can sustain a life as well as represent that life has been a constant strand in many artists' work this century. Joseph Beuys's battered VW van with sledges spewing out the back is a rich symbol of the relationship between social movements and basic human needs. The literature of the city, from Henry Mayhew through to Baudelaire and Walter Benjamin, has also represented those who are forced to live by their wits on the street as somehow being emblematic of the city.

When I saw the rag-and-bone men as a kid, they seemed to me to contain the actual grit and flux of the street. When I was a little older, I used to see the newspaper seller who stood outside Maida Vale underground station every day on my way to school. Nearly 40 years later I have an absolutely clear picture of him. He had one wooden fruit box upright, with another lying horizontally on top containing the *Star*, *Evening News* and the *Evening Standard* folded inside. He shouted out what I guess was an amalgamation of those three papers' names; it came out as 'Sauceny'. He was a small man, very self-contained. I remember his shape, totally of a piece: head, shoulders, legs, all merging together under a large, threadbare coat tied up with a piece of cord, his squat frame topped off with a brown cap. Resting against the fruit box was the battered metal news-screen covered by a grille where he put the headline sheets that were delivered with his papers. He had an extraordinary presence. Only some of the images of the characters in Beckett's later plays come near to my memory of his presence. I think the use of the news-screens in my work goes back to his image.

News Truck has ten giant news-screens which are carried inside it, plus one on either side. It is a rapid response vehicle which I can wheel out to the financial heart of London whenever there is a shudder on the stock market. I push it from Archive B in London Fields through Kingsland Road, down past Liverpool Street to the Stock Exchange. I then take out the screens and lean them against the Stock Exchange wall. Each image is of a financial page from one of the world's newspapers, with a hand in front of it. The hand is grasping at the paper or turning around, as if grasping at air. I stand

My prints are portable, unfinished, they can be put up indoors, outdoors, on hoardings, they can be used and got rid of–
They are cheap, they are about us in a cheap situation–
They are fragments in Newseum, a News Flop-House, visual headlines from the Clearing House Unclassified–
They about received commands obeyed–
They are nothing if they cannot for a split second make you think why we do what we do to our flesh on our planet.

Art and Artists/December 1973

Opposite left
Pushing *News Truck* through the City of London, 1998

Opposite right
News-Screen/1997/carbon toner, charcoal on paper with metal

Right and far right
News You Missed/1970
Live performance in the theatre at the Institute of Contemporary Arts, London, during solo exhibition, *News You Missed*, 1970

Below left and right
News You Missed/1972
Street performance in the shopping centre in Harlow New Town while artist in residence at Harlow Playhouse. People were invited to write their own headlines on newsbills, which were then shown in news-screens

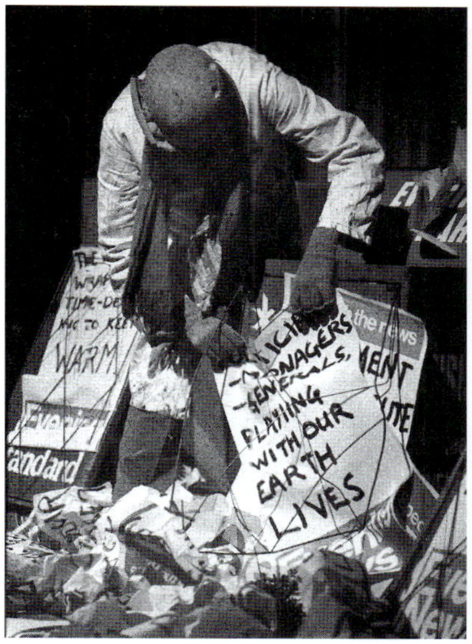

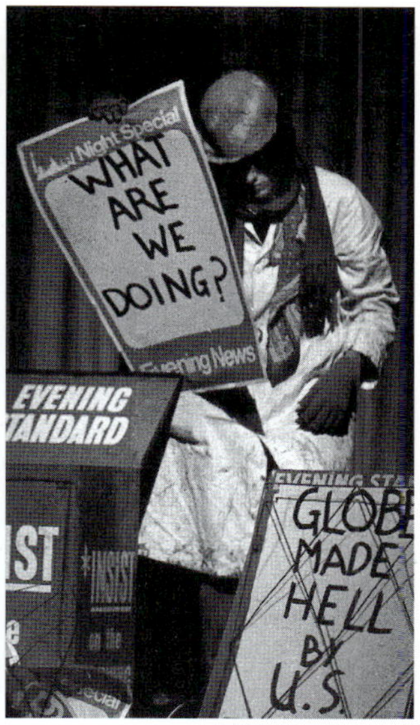

by the side of the screens, by the truck, and offer no leaflets or explanations. But I do talk to anyone passing by who wants to discuss the work. Some people think I must be selling something, advertising something. Others think I must be mad. But it leads to many intense discussions with passers-by on the uncontrolled power of the free market, some very supportive comments from city workers, and some hostile comments from passing stockbrokers. A couple of stockbrokers have actually thought it was art made especially for them. Stockbroker art! It's a way to engage in debate, in the actual environment where the transactions are going on.

Archive B: News bills

I first used the news-screen in 1971 when I was artist in residence at Sussex University. I used the actual screens that I'd taken off the streets and I made images as a kind of visual headline which I then put in them. In 1972, when I was artist in residence in Harlow New Town, I had blank sheets with the words *Evening News* (a now defunct evening paper) printed on them. I took them out onto the street and asked people to use them to write their own headlines. Some people wrote what they'd had for breakfast, others responded to the news of the day, others with their fears for the future. The different responses were placed in the screens side by side, public and private events playing off each other. It was an attempt to let people speak for themselves, and because the headlines – hand-written as they were (and still are) – were a form everyone knew and understood, people quickly cottoned on to the process without feeling intimidated.

In 1970 I had an exhibition, *News You Missed*, at the Institute of Contemporary Arts (ICA), London. I also performed in the ICA theatre as a manic newspaper seller changing as many headline sheets, which were strewn over the stage, as I could in 20 minutes. I wore a newspaperman's white coat and a waistcoat underneath which had pockets full of debris, dust and litter. The idea was that, as I rushed around changing news-bills, the debris would drop out from under the coat, and the texture and atmosphere of the street would thus emanate from me. Later I began making a short British Film Institute funded film sequence of the same event being enacted on the streets of Holborn. This was part of a film script that I wrote about a newspaperman in London.

At this time my connection to the street became a kind of quasi-mystical over-identification with the texture and material of the city. I was losing my sense of where I ended and the street began; my edges were dissolving into the city, and I had some kind of breakdown. Its distinct nature is hazy in my memory, but for a few months I had to separate myself from the environment I was sinking into. I never completed the film.

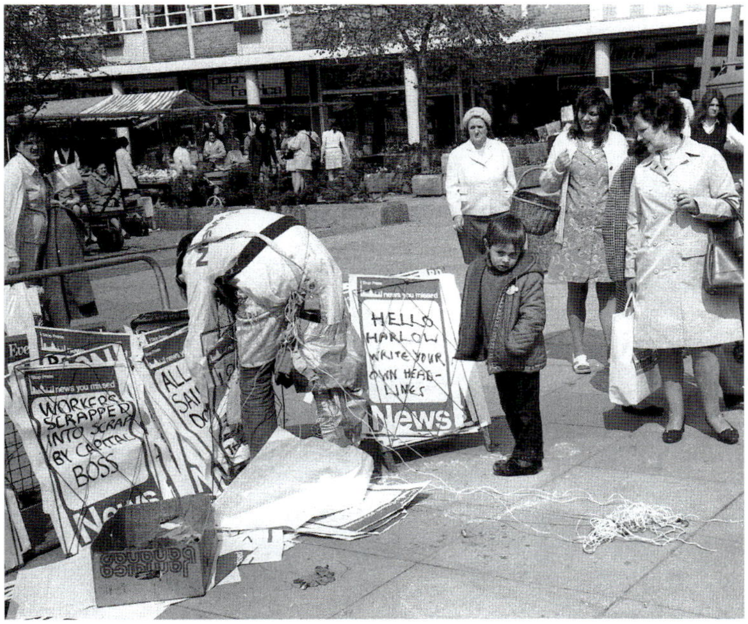

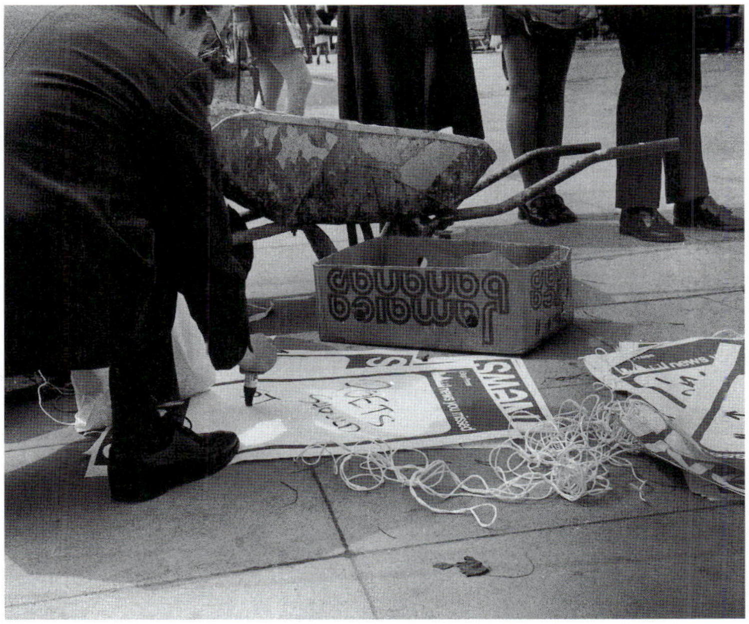

Below
Domesday 8/1999/photomontage
From *Domesday Book* (Manchester University Press, 1999)

Opposite
Domesday 5/1999/photomontage
From *Domesday Book* (Manchester University Press, 1999)

Archive A: London flashed up

I pick up a copy of *Domesday Book* from the top of a pile. In it I've tried to recapture the texture of our time using the idea of the Millennium Dome as an empty screen onto which to project images about the twentieth century. The book is a kind of summation of my experience of living in London. By using poetry and images I've tried to pull together my personal life and the political events that I've lived through. The Thames runs through the poem like an artery, as it does through so much poetry on London. Now, at Greenwich, we have the Millennium Dome with the river running right next to its gigantic empty heart pumping out lies with logos attached. In *Domesday Book*, I wrote about security lights illuminating a hidden history of the century, a history that is untold in the Dome.

One of my strongest experiences when I wander the streets of London now is of security lights with movement detectors on auto-switch lighting up when I get in the way of their beams. I like wandering in alleyways, around the backs of municipal buildings, derelict industrialised areas, places that have their backs turned, that reveal themselves from their least public side. I remember in my teens walking around these kinds of places in London with my great friend Al Rees, now a film historian and writer, fuelled on the images of London from T S Eliot's *The Wasteland*, and on William Blake's *Songs of Innocence and Experience*. Some of these places are what are known today as non-spaces, the city spaces left as by-products of commerce, through which the wind blows and the kids smash up. When I was a student at Byam Shaw, it was in just such a place, behind the shops of Notting Hill Gate that I kissed the first girl I was in love with, amongst the cardboard boxes and rotting vegetables.

It is these places, as well as the more obvious fortresses of the rich or insecure that now light up all over the city as I pass by. But the light is its opposite. It's not there to illuminate what I'm looking at, but to illuminate me looking. It's light to stop me looking, to burst in my face, to blind me and make me go away. This is the new illumination of London. Light, that renders the wanderer the intruder. What in Dickens's day was 'lighting up time', enabling people to see the city at night, is now 'lighting down time'. In the flash of security lights we are being watched in the city on CCTV screens. Recorded by cameras we cannot see in the glare.

Out of Archives A/B: 30 November 1999

Today I was out of the archives at Gimpel Fils where I was putting up my installation. It's my take on the Millennium Dome. A torn umbrella stretched out on wire over a pile of pallets. Hidden amongst the pallets are speakers with my voice endlessly repeating the word 'speak'. A security light on auto-switch is activated when someone comes near. The flash of light illuminates the dust and

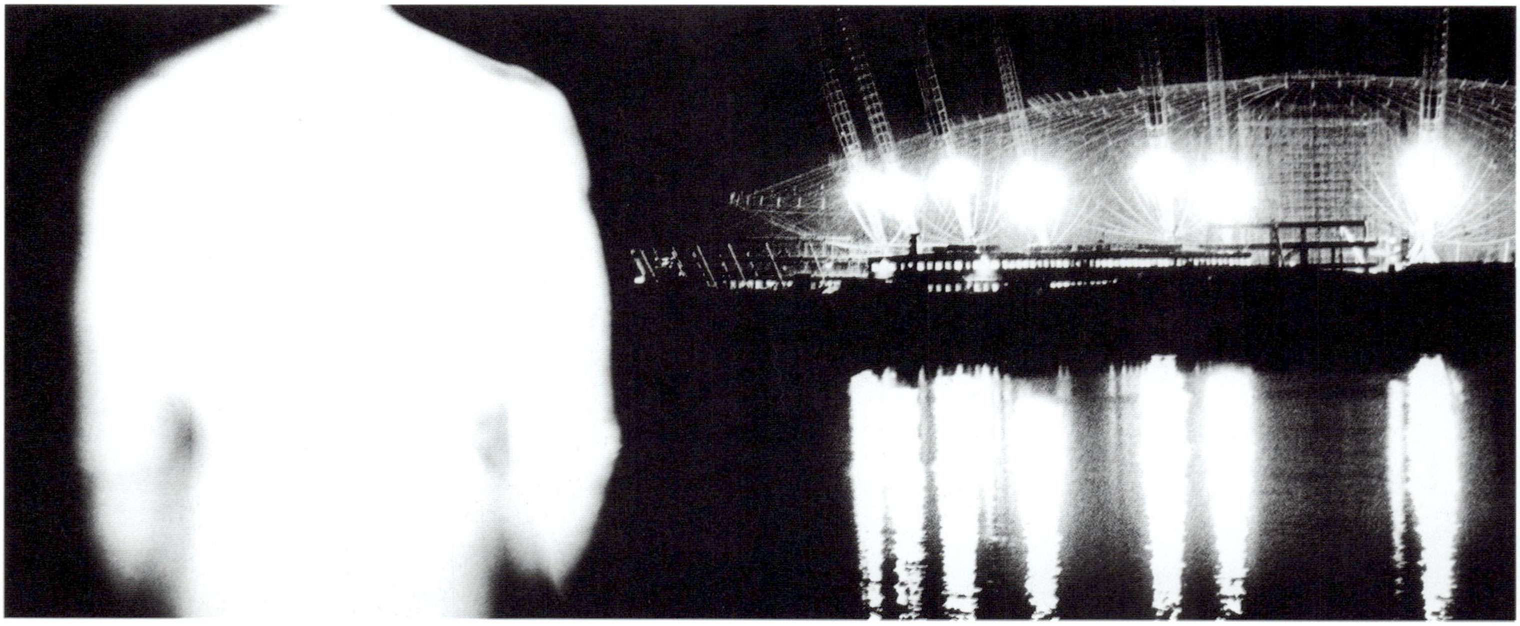

At midnight 2000, the light from the Millenium Dome will not be glinting on a nurse's night shift, a huddled body in a doorway, an asylum seeker, the victim of a NATO bombing or the disabled and poor, but on Tony Blair's teeth.

The *Guardian*/31 December 1999

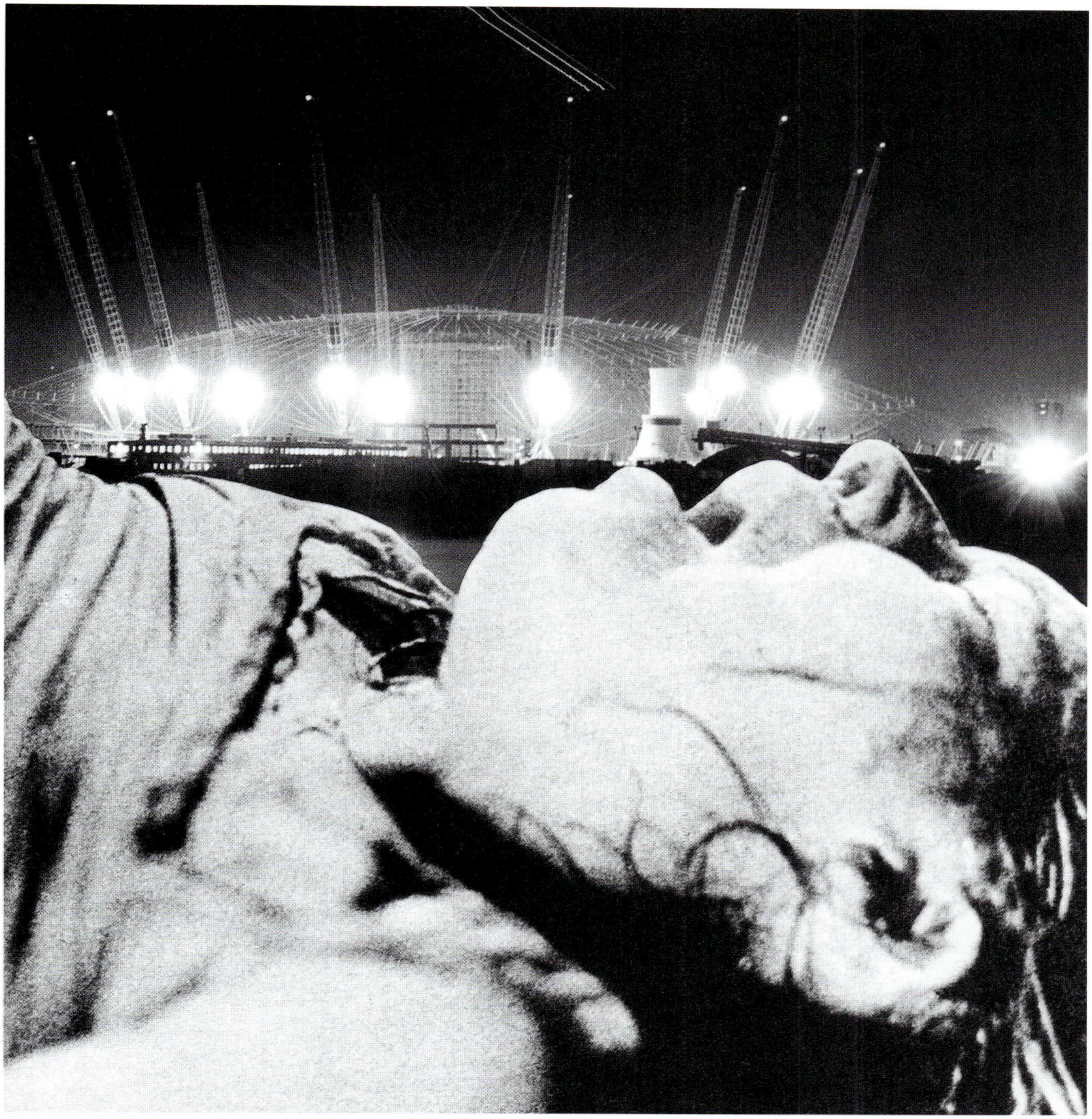

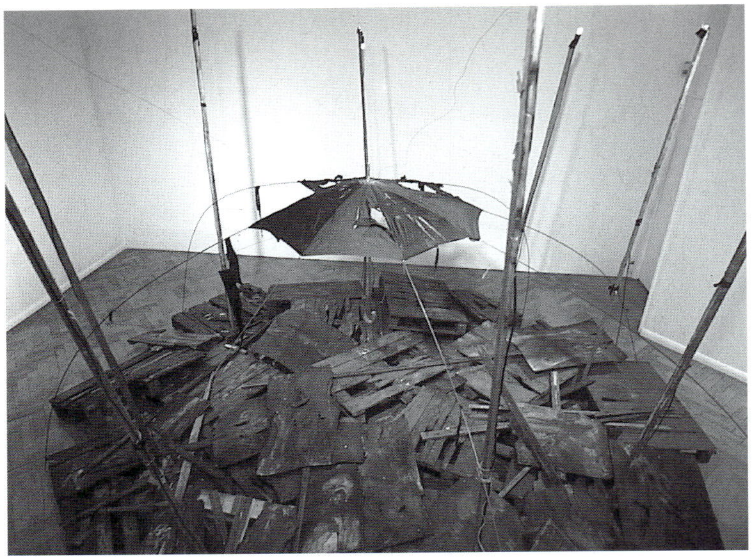

Left
People's Dome/1999/mixed media
Installation, Gimpel Fils, London, 1999, solo exhibition, *Domesday*

Opposite
With Judy in 1971 during solo exhibition *Printevents* while artist in residence at Gardner Arts Centre, Sussex University

fragments of pallet and the umbrella which gives no protection. This is my *People's Dome*, a tatty impoverished representation of the twentieth century. A three-dimensional reply to the logo strewn version down in Greenwich which I wrote about in *Domesday Book* as 'leaving the mute mute'.

Now, after putting up my dome for the first time, I realise how I'm trying more and more in my work to let the actual materials speak. In my latest images it's human skin itself which becomes saturated with the world in the same way that the rips of the umbrella speak of human rips. I read last night in *The Arcades Project* by Walter Benjamin, that 'I will merely show. I shall purloin no valuables, appropriate no ingenious formulations. But the rags, the refuse – these I will not inventory but allow, in the only way possible, to come into their own; by making use of them.' This takes me back to a quote from *Let Us Now Praise Famous Men* by James Agee and Walter Evans which I used as an epigraph for my book *Images for the End of the Century*: 'If I could do it, I'd do no writing at all here. It would be photographs; the rest would be fragments of cloth, bits of cotton, lumps of earth, records of speech, pieces of wood and iron, phials of odours, plates of food and of excrement.'

I want to make the actual stuff speak. But not speak with nostalgia. Nor anaesthetise decay. I can't do it yet. Laying down the material isn't enough for me as it still only refers to itself. But I'm trying to simplify the means, trying to allow the stuff to be, trying to let it exist. Finding a formulation that will allow stuff to speak of itself and also beyond itself. My dystopian dome is another stab in the dark.

Archive A: Beginnings and endings

I pull a copy of *Camerawork* dated July 1978 off the pile, there is a short obituary of Ian Stern on the back cover. I knew Ian from childhood and we had remained great friends. At the age of 30 he committed suicide. In a short space of time he had produced some remarkable work both as a documentary photographer and as a filmmaker. The first photographic printing that I did in a dark-room was in my late teens with Ian, under Broadcasting House in Portland Place, the headquarters of the BBC, where he had recently become a trainee cameraman. We experimented with photograms and double exposing negatives and it was the long discussions and arguments with him that kindled in us both the need to make art. His parents had always wanted him to be respectable and at first he went into accountancy, but hated it. It was later that he joined the BBC. In 1967 he made a short film using my drawings and paintings, cut to a Miles Davis *Sketches of Spain* soundtrack. In August 1968 we showed this film in the basement of the Arts Laboratory in Drury Lane. The Arts Lab was an extraordinary place where artists and

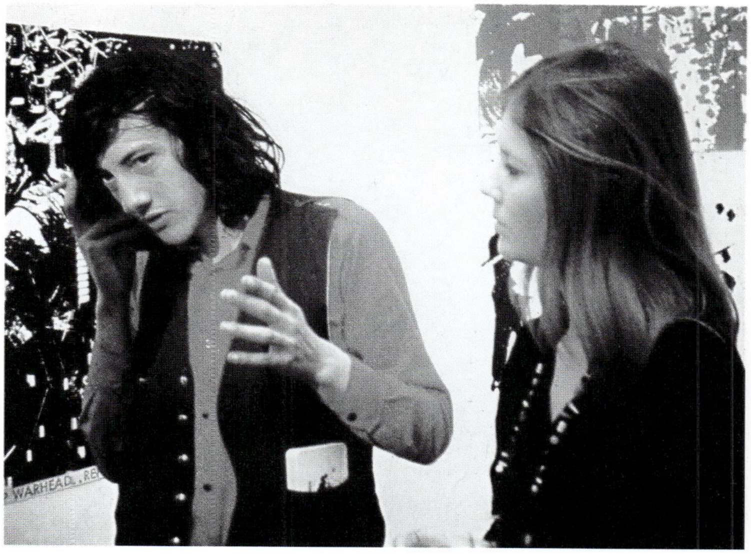

film-makers could drop in, show their work and generally hang out. I first saw films such as *Un Chien Andalou*, *Battleship Potemkin* and *The Man with the Movie Camera* at the Arts Lab.

It was there, after we had shown our film, that I met Judy who was a student nurse at the Middlesex Hospital and we fell in love. In her life as a student nurse she had to deal with the actual experience of life and death whereas for me, an art student at the Slade, I was just beginning to make work dealing with actual events happening in the world. Meeting Judy gave me insight into people's real suffering and her experiences through the years working in the health service dealing with the impact of poverty and deprivation has imbued my understanding of what my own work should be about. Judy supported me through our early days of living and working in one small room when we lived hand to mouth and we are still together. We have been through many ups and downs, breaks and reconciliations and have had two children. We both, through our work, have attempted to deal with the impact of inequality on people's lives. In our youth we were both directly involved in the organised left whereas today we have a much more ramshackle and spontaneous approach to dealing with social and political realities. Her belief in what I do has been very important to me. When making work has been tough going she's been there to talk it through and make things appear less intractable.

The births of our sons, Daniel in 1979 and Matthew in 1983, gave me a focus and further impetus for my work in many ways that are impossible to articulate. But I know that the excitement and joy of bringing up the kids with Judy intensified my resolve to make work that engaged with flesh and blood issues. The incredible love I feel for our own children involuntarily increases my empathy for all the families desperately trying to protect their children from the scourge of war and famine. It's not intellectual identification, it's gut feeling ...

My friend Ian, in his last years, became more and more overwhelmed by his experience of war. As a BBC cameraman he went to the USA and filmed the body bags of US servicemen coming back from Vietnam. For him, it was seeing too much too young that began to disturb his ability to make sense of things. He was always a passionate but uneasy man. He ended his days in the psychiatric ward of the Royal Free Hospital labelled schizophrenic and being overdosed on anti-depressants.

I remember one day in 1978 I tried to ring him from a pay-phone in the Royal College of Art, where I was a student, but lost the money and couldn't get through. A few days later I heard from his parents that he had disappeared from hospital. Judy and I spent days looking for him around all our old haunts, the cafes and bookshops in the area. We showed people his photo and asked if they'd seen

We are in the middle as flesh vacuum-cleaners for our own inventions which come to us from the factory performing in ways their packaging never mentioned and their inventor never envisaged. The products cannot be named. They have irrational life in their own right aiming their wares straight at the bull's eye of the soft target. The products implode simultaneously like a film played backwards constantly changing their form creating ambiguous objects which are on the edge of being recognisable. They then let us wonder if that is a migrating swallow on the radar screen or an approaching missile and let us decide.

Generation Newspeak/1968

What does a photograph of a computer tell us? Not that our personal histories are recorded on disk and that one database can relay information to another. How can we 'picture' the 'Disappeared' – people who are torn from their houses at night and rendered invisible by authoritarian regimes? What does a photograph of a nuclear power station tell us? Not that its radioactive emissions can cause birth deformaties.

Images for the End of the Century/1990

him. Six days later we heard that his body had been found in Highgate pond. I think of that lost 'phone call – if only ... I think of what he could have done if his passionate intensity had not been so raw that the world seemed to hit him under the skin and leave him defenceless.

Archive A: Working together 1

In the same issue of *Camerawork* as Ian's obituary is a piece written by photographer Jenny Matthews who I met at this time. Jenny has remained true to the idea of the documentary photographer as witness to the oppression and resistance of people across the world, especially women in the aftermath of war. She works for a number of charities and often goes to war-torn countries after the other photographers have left, getting a deeper picture of how people pick up the pieces of their lives, photographing them as survivors rather than victims.

Jenny has been vital to the development of my work allowing me to use the photographs she has taken around the world. Some of the faces used in my installation *Reading Room* are based on her photographs. She also takes pictures of my exhibitions and street events. Through working with a photographer whose work is in accordance with my own, I have been able to direct my images into areas which I could not have done had I been working alone. An example are my most recent images which have shown the financial pages from newspapers imprinted on my body, as if no part of our being is untouched by the power of market forces. My own body becomes a stand-in for the people around the world who are violated by the consequences of the obscene scramble for the fast buck.

Collaboration is a key element in my work. I have worked with writers, designers, politicians, photographers, craftsmen, curators and editors. It's through working closely with skilled people in all these areas that a project comes to fruition. It's like a scaled-down version of making a film. Without them all, and without countless friends who have helped on projects, I could not have made my work. There are many who go unnamed but not forgotten in these pages.

Archive A: Working together 2

Turning to another page in the same issue of *Camerawork* is an article on 'A Document on Chile' which was an exhibition, first shown in 1978, of my photomontages with an accompanying text by Ric Sissons. At that time I was involved with Half Moon Photography Workshop which was a collective of mainly documentary photographers who produced touring exhibitions and *Camerawork* magazine. The exhibitions were laminated in

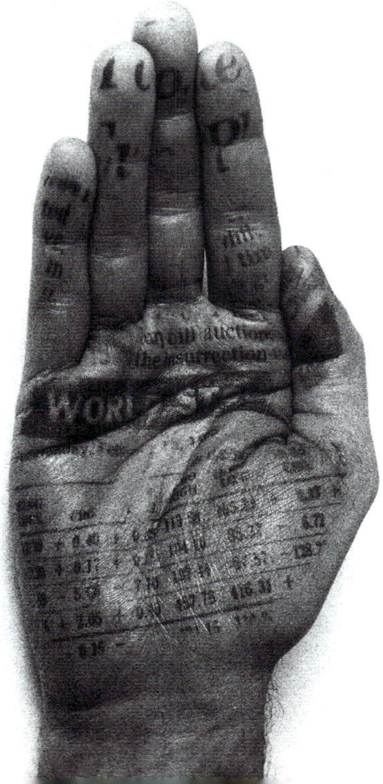

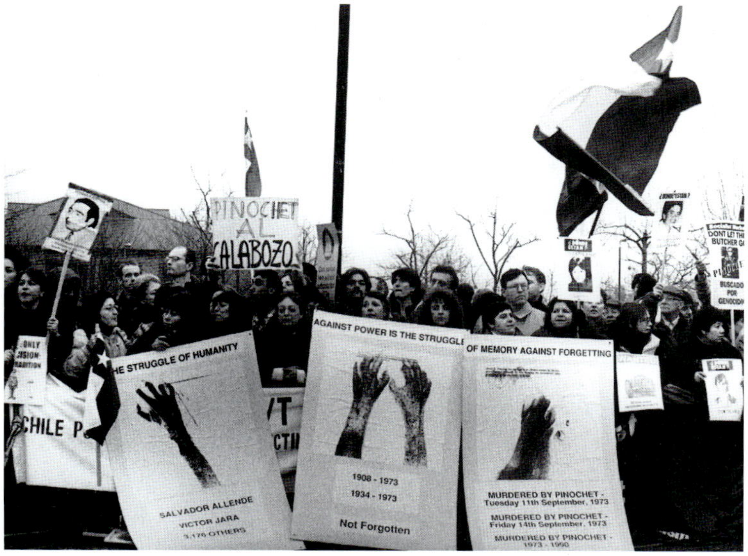

Opposite
Skin 15/2000/silver print

Left
11 December 1998: Images from *Unwords* being used on placards by demonstrators protesting against General Pinochet during his appearance at Belmarsh Magistrates Court in south London. He had to answer the extradition arrest warrant served on him at the request of the Spanish authorities

Below
Disappeared Prisoners/1978/photomontage and text
Image and text from *A Document on Chile*, a Half Moon travelling exhibition shown here as it was reproduced in *Camerawork*

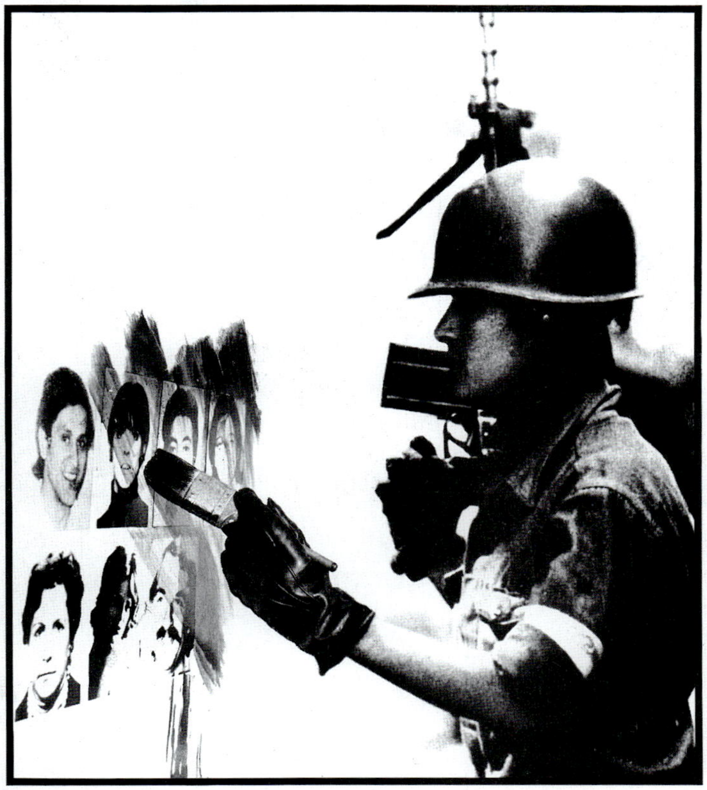
CAMERAWORK 7

'DISAPPEARED PRISONERS'
Top row, left to right: Jose Fidel Flores Perez, Jacqueline Del Carmen Binfa Contreras, Ugarte Roman Marta, Perevia Plaza Reinalda.
Bottom row, left to right: Rosa Elena Morales, Mamia Angelica Andreoli Bravo, Juan Canales.

" 'The disappeared prisoners' is the name we give to members of our families who have been taken from our homes, in front of our eyes, or in their work places, colleges and universities, with eye witnesses or strong proof of their detention. The people who detained them were members of the military intelligence service. They are being held in secret and all our efforts, such as writs of habeas corpus, affidavits of kidnapping, and letters and interviews with Government officials, have been flung back in our faces with the following answer: 'This person has never been detained'. There are variations such as: 'He has left the country', 'He has gone into hiding', 'He has been kidnapped by a band of extremists', and so forth."

Committee of the Families of Disappeared Prisoners, Santiago, June 1975.

Photo-montage and text by Peter Kennard and Ric Sissons.

plastic with holes in the corners for pins. They were put in purpose-built boxes so that they could be sent very cheaply by Red Star to anywhere in the country. Our exhibition on Chile tried to explain the recent history of the country through the presidency of Allende to the military coup of 1973. It was the first time that I had worked in collaboration with a writer. We worked in a reciprocal way, either I made specific images for his text or he wrote around the subject matter of my images.

The strength of the *Camerawork* exhibitions was that they could be put up in community centres, shops, town halls, places that were not designed as art galleries. Because they were laminated and unframed they became sources of information as well as æsthetic objects. Ric and I later collaborated, with documentary photographer, Mike Abrahams on an exhibition *No Nuclear Weapons* in 1980. In this show there was a three-way meshing of documentary photography, photomontage and writing. Ric and I produced a pamphlet called *No Nuclear Weapons* published by Pluto Press and CND. It was sold for one pound – as cheaply as possible – and thousands of copies were sold from stalls on demonstrations as well as from bookshops. An exception to this was the Arts Council bookshop which refused to stock it as they deemed it to be too political. I asked them why they stocked John Heartfield catalogues and they replied that that was legitimate because it

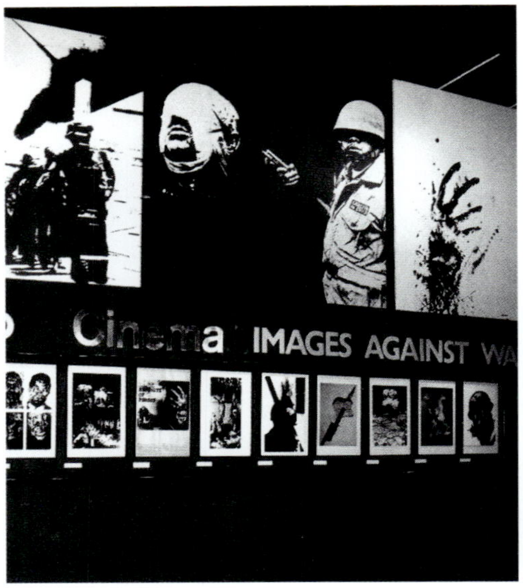

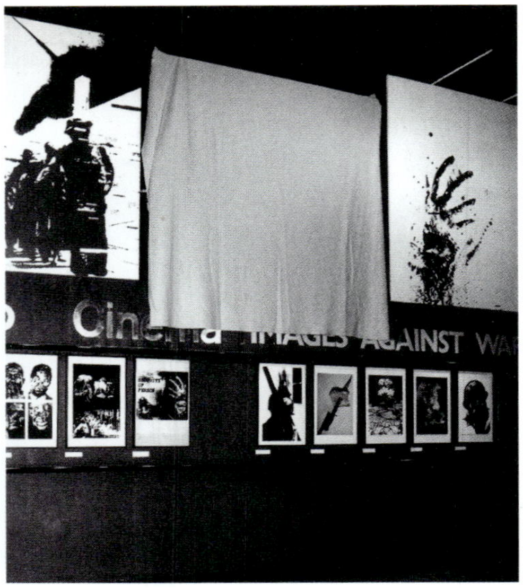

was art history. The Arts Council's literature director, as reported in the *Guardian* on 2 January 1982 told their reporter, 'I know of no change in circumstances which would make it likely that the decision might be reversed, and I suggest, unacceptable though you may find this, that you leave matters as they stand.'

Archive B: Blanket censorship

Under a pile of posters I notice a strange memento of my exhibition *Peter Kennard: Images Against War 1965–1985* at the Barbican Arts Centre in 1985. It's a moth-eaten grey blanket. I had just hung a small retrospective exhibition of my work to coincide with a group of plays, *War Plays*, by Edward Bond. On the night before the opening of the show the then director of the Barbican Arts Centre, Henry Wrong suddenly appeared and demanded that two of the works should be removed forthwith. The pictures in question were *Santiago Stadium 1* and *Santiago Stadium 3*. They were images of the bloody repression following the Pinochet coup in Chile. The director said that a high-ranking Chilean official was coming to the Barbican the next day for a special meeting with British bankers. This meeting was to take place in the auditorium adjacent to my exhibition and the director felt that the official might be upset by my work. Arguments ensued. The end result was that the smaller picture in question was unscrewed from the wall and the larger one, which couldn't be taken down in time, was covered with the grey blanket for the duration of his visit.

On 17 July 1985 the London *Evening Standard* reported:

> 'Peter Kennard's exhibition, *Images Against War*, at the Barbican Centre should perhaps be retitled. Images Against Censorship might not be too wide off the mark. When it reopened to the public this morning a grey blanket covered one painting and there was a vacant space where another work hung until 36 hours ago. That was when the Barbican management suddenly turned all coy. Two of Kennard's pieces show Chilean soldiers in aggressive stance ... "We hope to accommodate the artist. It's his exhibition. We don't exercise censorship," was the remarkable way the woman at the Centre put it.'

Archive B: Attempts at censorship

Near the blanket is a large mounted photograph of Michael Howard. It was used in my installation, *Home*, at the Sassoon Gallery in Folkestone,1995. Michael Howard was at the time Conservative MP for Folkestone and Home Secretary. The photograph of his face is seen to turn away from piles of disintegrating placards and pallets. Howard's constituency agent, Michael Buxton, came to the exhibition and tried to have the show removed. He was reported as

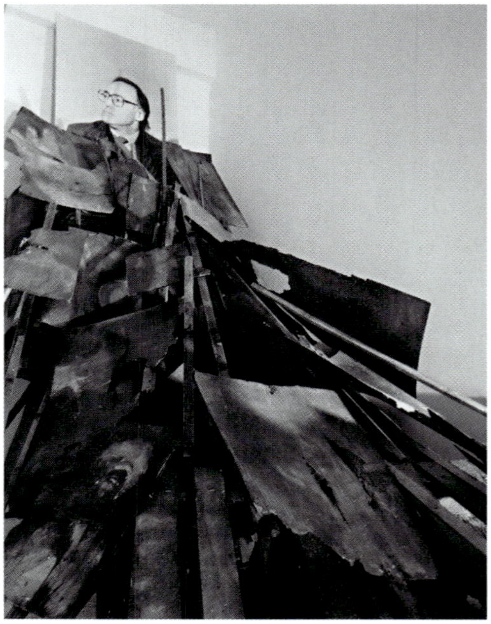

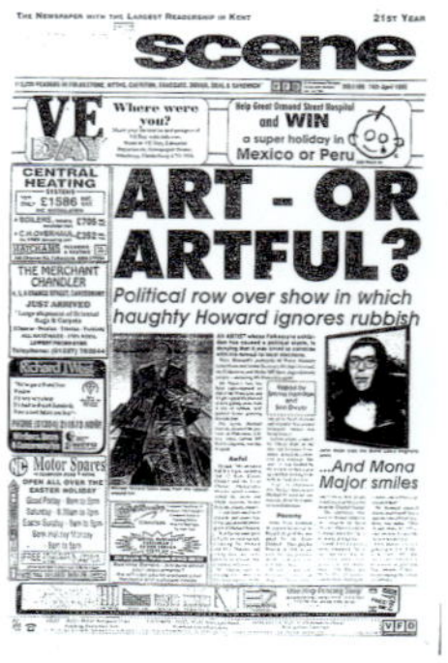
The Newspaper with the Largest Readership in Kent
21st Year
scene
VE DAY
Where were you?
Help Great Ormond Street Hospital and WIN a super holiday in Mexico or Peru
CENTRAL HEATING
£1586
THE MERCHANT CHANDLER
JUST ARRIVED
Motor Spares
OPEN ALL OVER THE EASTER HOLIDAY
ART - OR ARTFUL?
Political row over show in which haughty Howard ignores rubbish
...And Mona Major smiles

Above left
Installation shot of exhibition *Peter Kennard: Images Against War 1965–1985* at the Barbican Arts Centre on the morning of 16 July 1985

Above right
Installation shot on the afternoon of 16 July 1985, showing one work concealed by a blanket and a gap where another work was removed from the wall

Below left
Home/1995/mixed media
Installation, Sassoon Gallery, Folkestone showing photograph of the then Home Secretary, Michael Howard, in the background

Below right
Front page of *Scene*, 14 April 1995. Local paper reporting on the row over the exhibition *Home*

For me, getting the work out into the world and used is as important as its production. My images are not only reports on events and possibilities but become part of those events themselves when they are used by people campaigning for change.

Images for the End of the Century/1990

saying that 'the exhibition is clearly political and it is not right that council tax payers' money and a public building should be used for this'. The county council defended the show and it remained up. It was later shown at the Dazed and Confused gallery, London in 1996.

Archive A: Pre-censorship

A letter from an Arts Council trainee dated 19 December 1997. I won't name the trainee who wrote it or the gallery it was sent from as she had not yet learned that these delicate matters are best not put in writing. I had been invited to put forward a project for the public space outside this major public gallery in London. Before I had even come up with a specific idea for a project they had second thoughts. I quote:

> '... having spoken with the "powers that be" at the ... gallery, I fear that this project may not be the best place for an overtly political artist. The indication was that "controversial" work may be at risk of censorship and I feel it would be unfair to ask you to invest in a project when this is a possible outcome.'

Censored – to save me from the awful experience of being censored!

Archive A: On the buses

I find on the pile a battered catalogue from my degree show at the Slade. When I was at the Slade in the late 1960s the orthodoxies of modernism were still being perpetrated. Modern art was a bus driven by Cézanne with Matisse as the conductor and Jackson Pollock as the drunken passenger. Clement Greenberg was the inspector whose eye you tried to avoid as he came up the aisle in case you had bought the wrong ticket. On leaving the Slade this was the only bus to get on, and if you didn't make it you would wait at the bus stop forever. As novelist Ken Kesey said at the time, in a different context, 'you were either on the bus or you were off'. An even worse fate was to enter one of those buses driven by foreign 'marxists' who would drive you away from the womb of Artland WC1 into a land of grey basements and 'ordinary' people, definitely a wrong turning. Against all the odds, to find a way to relate my growing political commitment to my art, I got on the wrong bus and found the driver was John Heartfield. His work was distinctly off limits in England at the time and hardly appeared in official histories of modern art. At this time I looked hard at the work of Heartfield, Rodchenko and Hannah Höch. I was especially affected by Heartfield's montage *Millions Stand Behind Me*. In 1932, Hitler said 'Millions stand behind me'. A few weeks later Heartfield put these words on a magazine cover with a photograph of a huge,

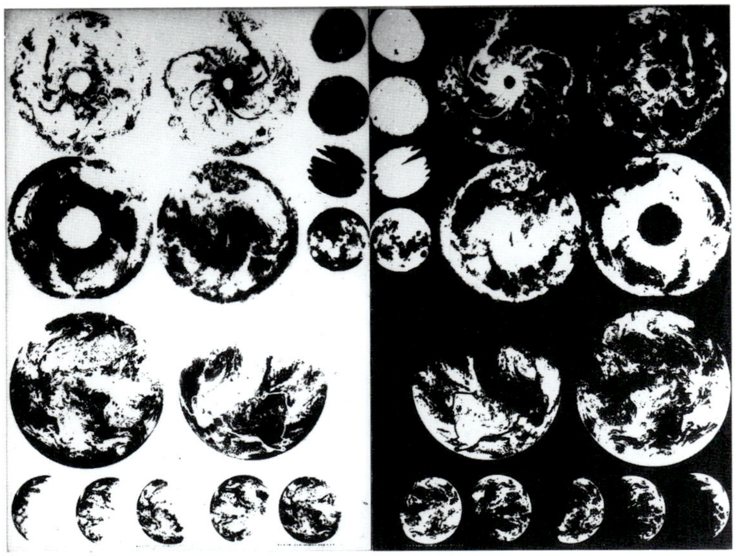

Left
Dictionary: Positive Earth–Negative Earth/ 1969/photomontage
One of the 40 double-page spreads from the visual dictionary of images that was used as a source book for future work

Below
Walter Benjamin/1990/photomontage
Through its use of multiple Mona Lisas and text, the photomontage refers both to Benjamin's essay *The Work of Art in the Age of Mechanical Reproduction* and to his revolutionary politics

Opposite, clockwise from top left
Stop 16/1971/oil and printers ink on canvas
Stop 13/1970/oil and printers ink on canvas
Stop 19/1972/oil and printers ink on canvas
Stop 6/1969/oil and printers ink on canvas

anonymous businessman putting money into Hitler's saluting hand. The meaning of Hitler's words had been destroyed by Heartfield's image. The millions became money, and with the addition of the words 'The meaning of the Hitler salute: little man asks for big gifts' the authority of Hitler's image was also destroyed. Heartfield demonstrated that the artist could develop a visual language of opposition by using familiar images in new contexts.

Archive A: Generation Newspeak/STOP

After leaving the Slade I tried to get my work out in many different ways: through books, prints, street events and later, newspapers. While at the Slade, I made large dyeline prints that could be produced and sold cheaply. In 1969 I'd made a book, *Dictionary: Positive Earth–Negative Earth*, which contained hundreds of photographic images culled from magazines and newspapers. These were laid out across the pages as in a pattern book and became the basis for another book of images and series of prints, *STOP* which I continued to work on into the 1970s. The images in *STOP* were put together through sandwiching layers of negatives in the enlarger. The marks overlaid on the prints tried to relay the experience of being on a demonstration, where the mood can suddenly change and one loses focus. I was trying to represent the violence of the state and the struggle to resist it, by breaking down the photographic images into the least representational mark that could still show a human presence. I was going on anti-Vietnam demonstrations, getting involved with student sit-ins and beginning to understand the political system. I wanted to make work seeping with conflict. The ideas of Bertolt Brecht and Walter Benjamin on distanciation and dislocation were beginning to influence me. I was trying to break with ideas of realism, trying to dig into surface appearances and make work from what I'd scooped out. Through the use of photographic fragments, blots, scratches and broken lines, I was making images that I wanted people to actively engage in rather than passively empathise with. The images didn't reveal themselves immediately. The idea was that people through engaging with the images would become active participants in the struggles depicted.

To make the *STOP* pictures I used photographs of current events as well as using hundreds of acetate overlays of more abstract marks which I had originally made for my first solo show *Generation Newspeak* at St Catherine's College, Oxford in 1968. In that show I had laid the sheets of acetate on tables so that people could participate in putting them together in different combinations and clip them into stands that I had made. I also made slides of hundreds of the acetate sheets in different combinations which were then used as projections at public events. One memory I have

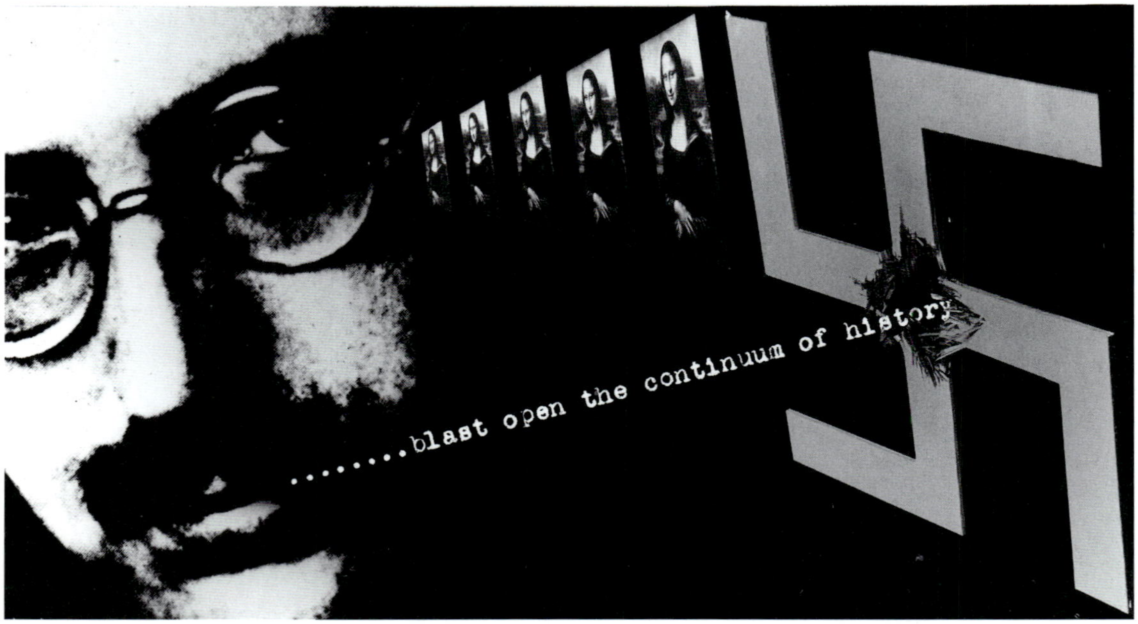

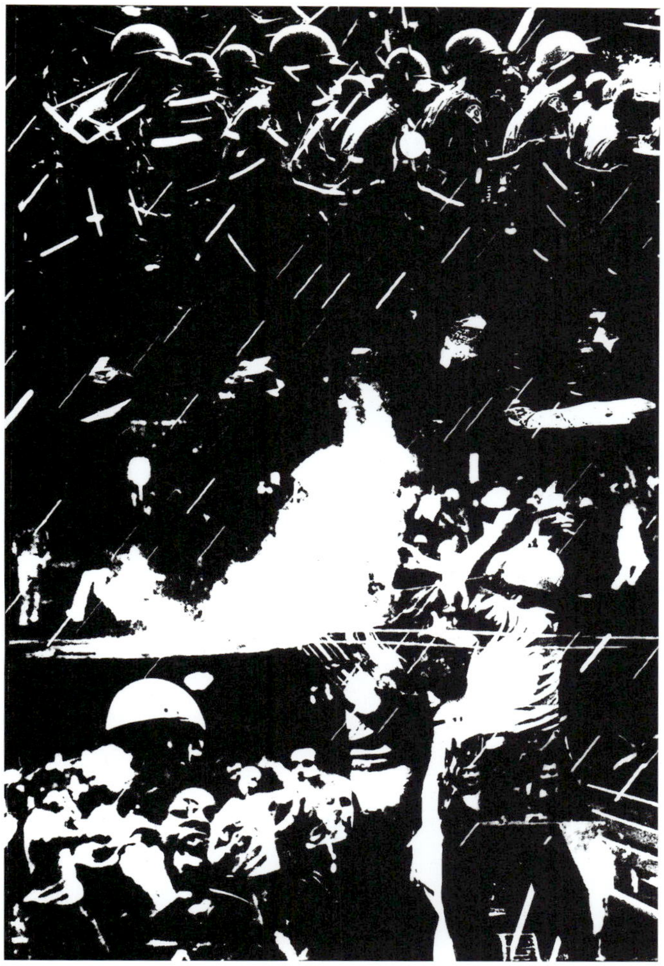
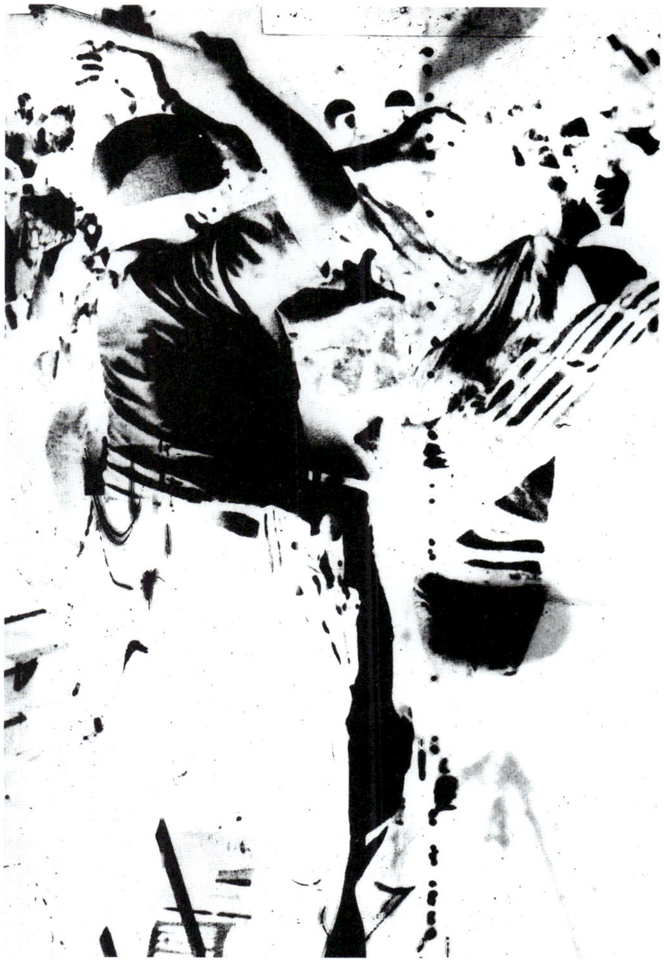
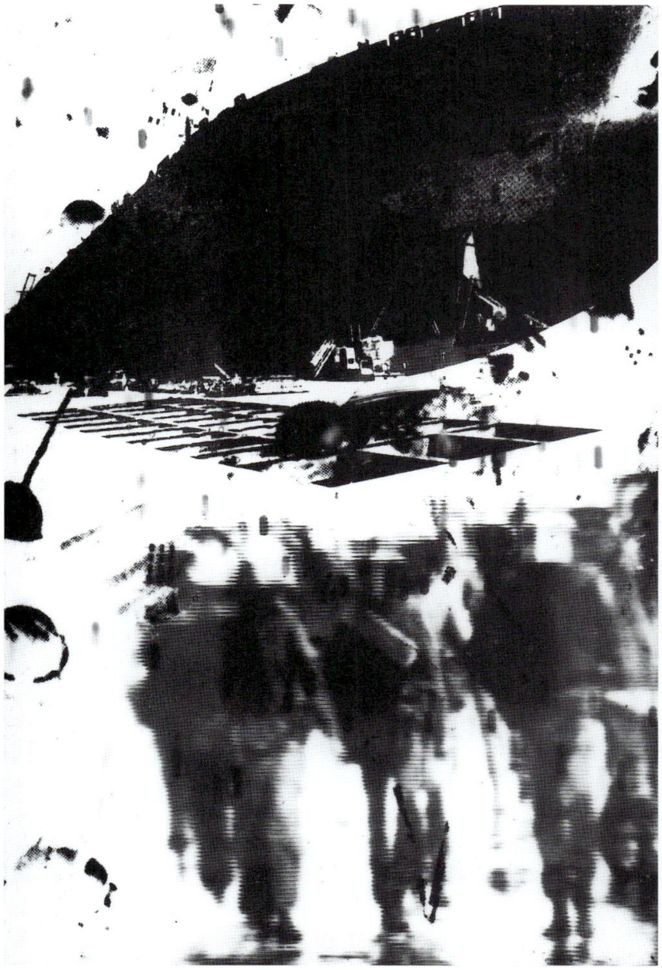
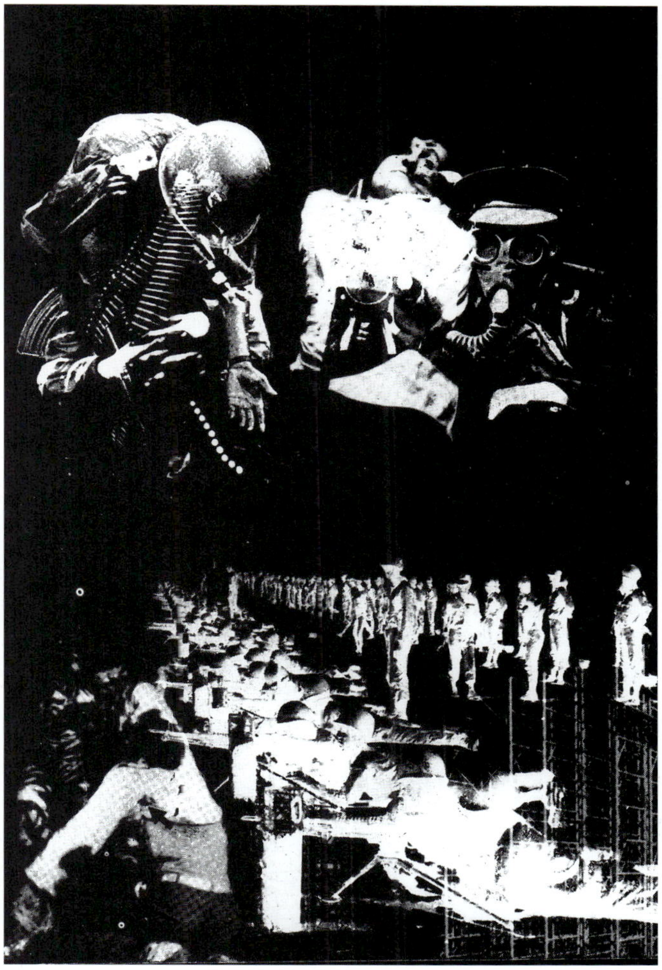

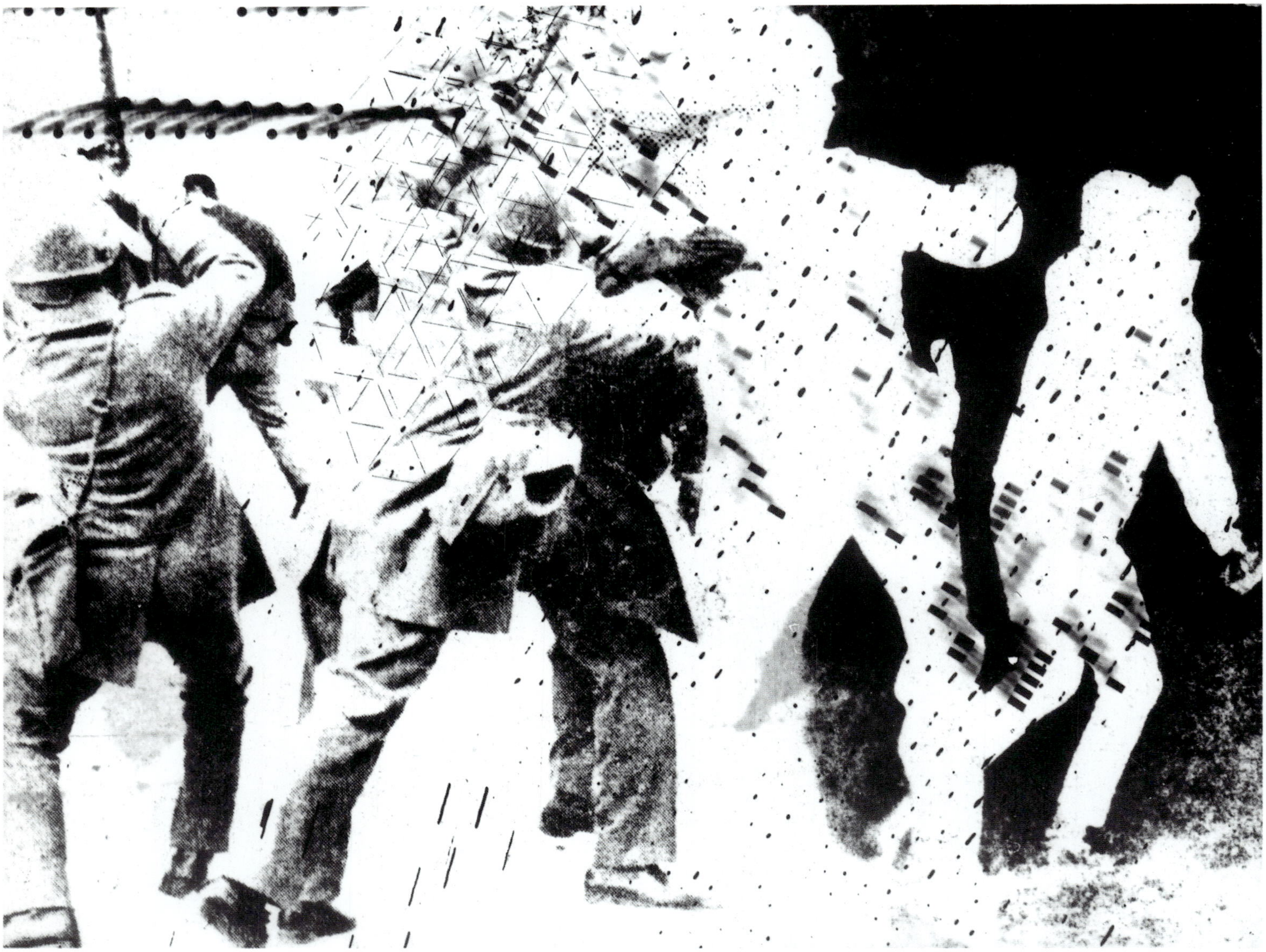

Above
Stop 24/1972/oil and printers ink on canvas

Opposite
Stop 23/1972/oil and printers ink on canvas

STOP THE STATE...STEADY STATE...STATE YOUR... STOP THE TOXIC-NERVE-GAS-NERVE...STOP OUTPUT AS HEAVE-UP...STOP KILLER LEADER, BETWEEN WHAT YOU SAY AND WHAT YOU DO LIES LIES...STOP TRASH CHILD IN THE NAME OF CHRIST CHILD...SPREAD FOOD ON A SPOON NOT ON A BAYONET...STOP THEM AND US-BETTER DEAD THAN RED...STOP G.I...STOP M.I.G... STOP MISSILE...STOP WARHEAD...REPEAT STOP WARHEAD...STOP...

Printevents/1971

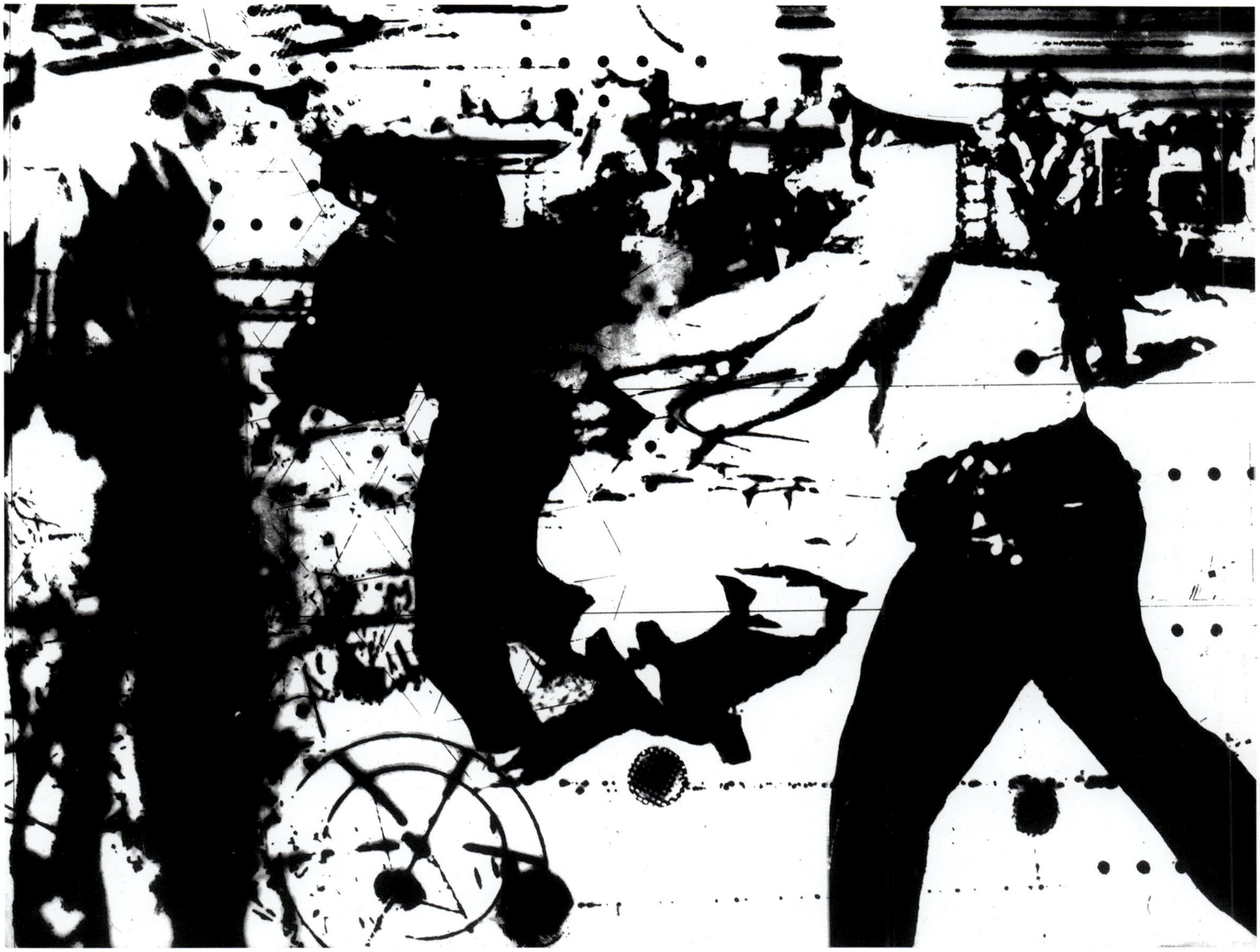

Below left
Stop 1/1969/photomontage

Below right
Stop/1971–72/oil and printers ink on canvas
Mural commissioned by London University for the Central Collegiate Building, University College, London

Opposite
Kent State/1970/dyeline print (edition of 40)
Flyposted around London after the shooting of four students by National Guardsmen at Kent State University, Ohio, USA

is of me and my friends waving projectors containing these images above our heads at a college disco and temporarily blinding anyone who danced too near the 500 watt bulb.

In 1970 I made 40 copies of a large print showing the image of a student lying in a pool of blood. He had been shot dead with three other students by National Guardsmen at Kent State University, Ohio, USA while protesting against the Vietnam war. I took the photo from the front page of the *Evening Standard*, cropped it, painted out all the inessentials and the body and blood of the student became a cruciform. With a group of fellow students I fly-posted it around London in solidarity with the American students. Because they were water-based dyelines printed in red they bled in the rain and in the end the ones that weren't pulled down became blank sheets which could, and did, become notice-boards for people's slogans and messages.

A number of the separate pictures in *STOP* were merged together in 1971 to create a 40-foot long mural commissioned for the Central Collegiate Building, University College, London where it is still on view, slightly worse for wear.

Archive A: Workers Press

A pile of *Workers Press* emerges from the chaos. In 1973 I tried to get montages published in *Workers Press* along with other left-wing publications. Unexpectedly *Workers Press* offered me a full-time job as a photomontagist. *Workers Press* was the daily paper of the Socialist Labour League just about to become the Workers Revolutionary Party. I was now able to test out my ideas concerning the artist as a communicator, making work outside the art world, in a situation where I was part of a production process rather than a lone artist. Sometimes I would make a photomontage in one day. In the morning I would go to an editorial meeting, choose a story to illustrate, make the montage, process it into the paper and see it printed at 6pm that evening. Later that evening I could often be seen in the streets and pubs of north London trying to sell copies. It was a long day.

The political excesses of the Workers Revolutionary Party gradually wore me down and I lasted a year before the daily anticipation of world revolution being just round the corner got too much. Gerry Healy, the leader of the party, also began to interfere with my work by thinking up specific images that he wanted me to produce. I remember he once asked me to illustrate his theory that the Labour party was a Trojan horse for the Tories. The montage that I made in response to this was a disaster. As I remember, it had Harold Wilson as a sad looking horse, with Edward Heath riding him. It was the type of farcical montage which always results from having ideas prescribed by over-zealous

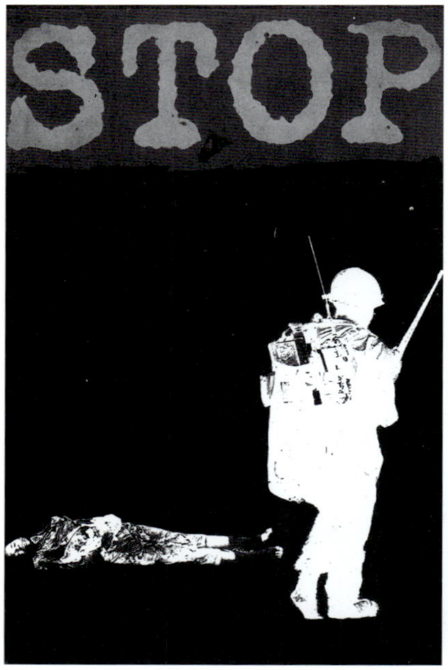

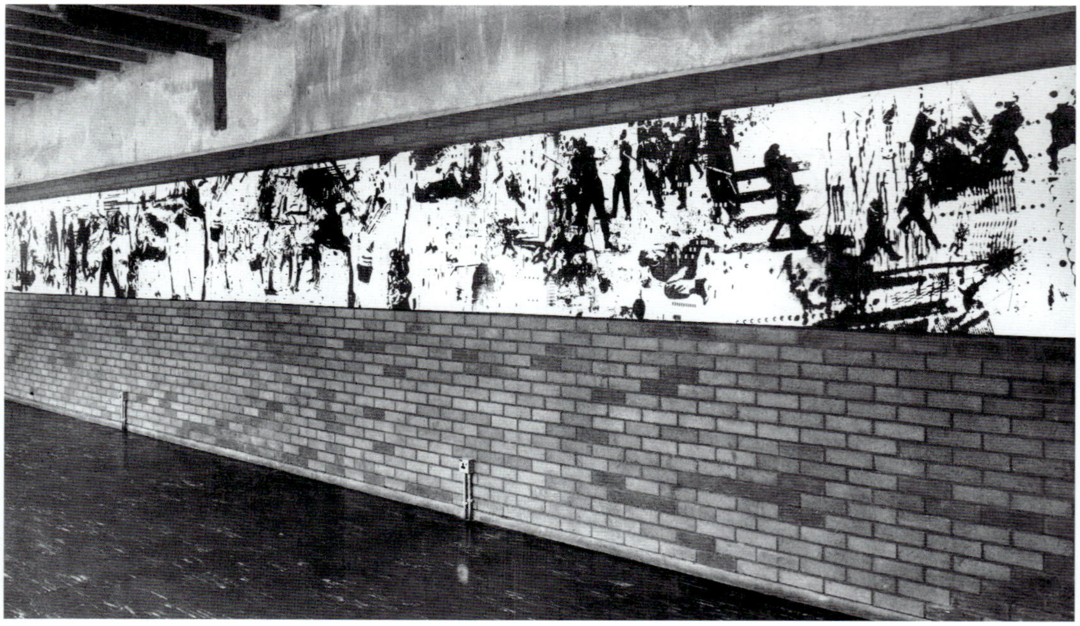

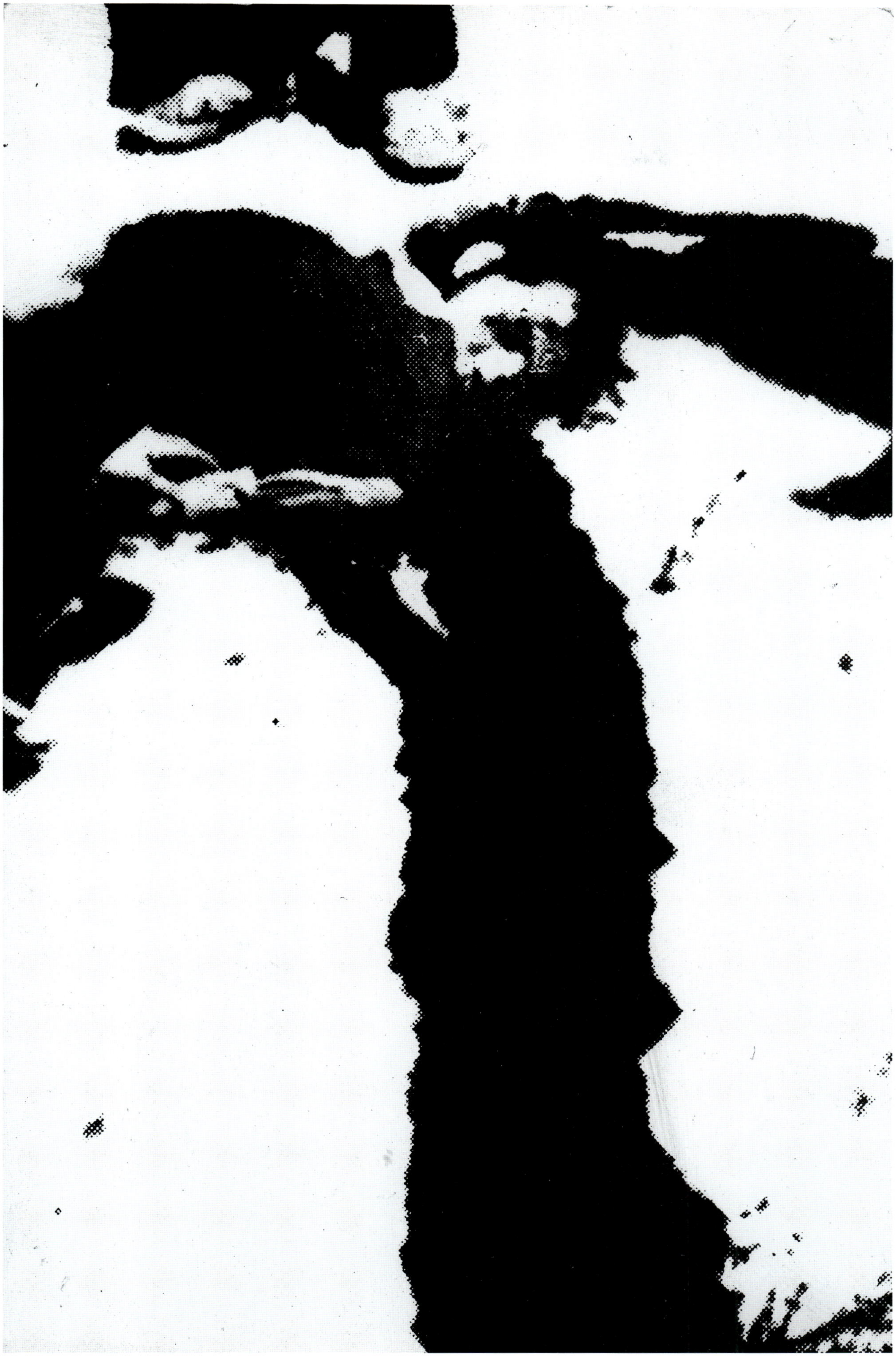

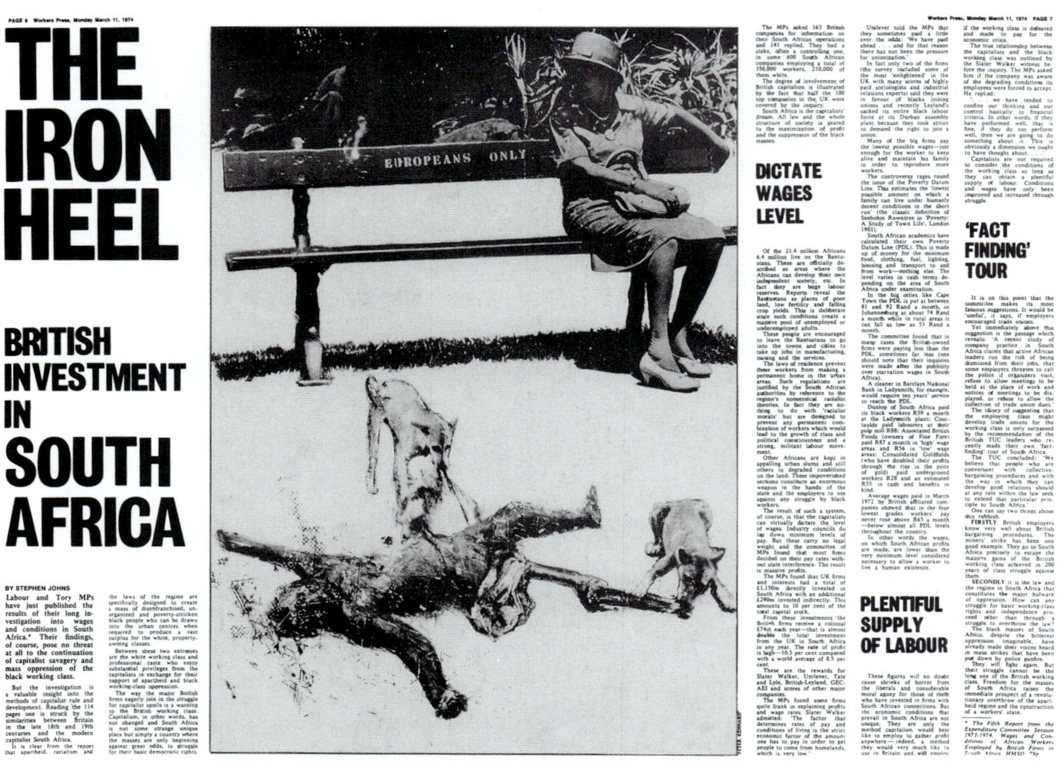

PAGE 6 Workers Press, Monday March 11, 1974

THE IRON HEEL

BRITISH INVESTMENT IN SOUTH AFRICA

BY STEPHEN JOHNS

Labour and Tory MPs have just published the results of their long investigation into wages and conditions in South Africa.* Their findings, of course, pose no threat at all to the continuation of capitalist savagery and mass oppression of the black working class.

Workers Press, Monday March 11, 1974 PAGE 7

DICTATE WAGES LEVEL

PLENTIFUL SUPPLY OF LABOUR

'FACT FINDING' TOUR

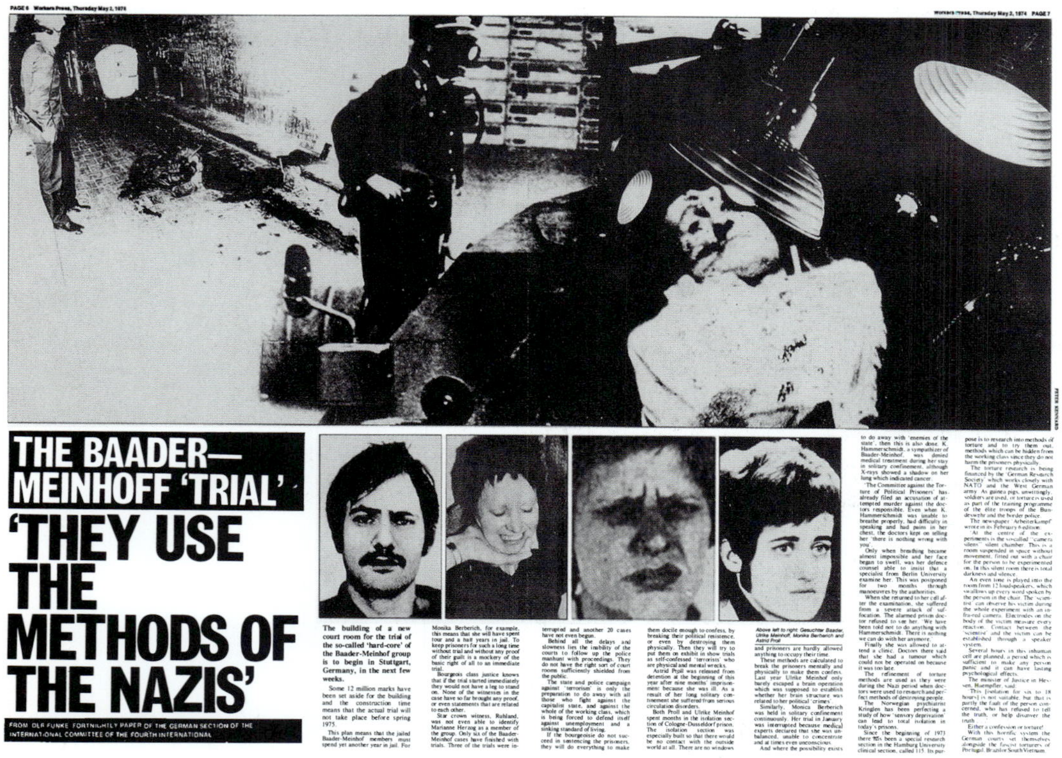

PAGE 6 Workers Press, Thursday May 2, 1974

Workers Press, Thursday May 2, 1974 PAGE 7

THE BAADER—MEINHOFF 'TRIAL'

'THEY USE THE METHODS OF THE NAZIS'

FROM DER FUNKE FORTNIGHTLY PAPER OF THE GERMAN SECTION OF THE INTERNATIONAL COMMITTEE OF THE FOURTH INTERNATIONAL

The building of a new court room for the trial of the so-called 'hard-core' of the Baader-Meinhof group is to begin in Stuttgart, Germany, in the next few weeks.

Above left
Workers Press/11 March 1974

Below left
Workers Press/2 May 1974

Opposite above
Workers Press/19 November 1973

Opposite above right
Original photomontage of image from *Workers Press*, 19 November 1973. It was made in one day, between the morning editorial meeting and going to press at 6pm. As there was no picture in the files of a scientist in a white coat, a photograph of a meat porter at Smithfield market was hastily taken instead

Opposite below
Workers Press/6 October 1973

PAGE 6 Workers Press, Monday November 19, 1973

TORTURE SCIENTISTS AT WORK

BY STEPHEN JOHNS

Torture has always been an essential part of ruling-class oppression. But it is only in recent times that it has become an experimental science of great sophistication.

The key men in the British torture system and torture research are specially selected scientists who put their knowledge of human stress at the disposal of the army and its special secret detachments.

Many are academics who mix lecturing at universities with detailed and advance research at army HQ in Lisburn, in Northern Ireland, and at the joint services intelligence centre at Ashford, Kent.

Ashford is a school for all the underground activity of the security services in Ulster and Ulster situations.

Many murderous facilities are located there, including a production line for animated female models. These are made for special firing ranges resembling Ulster streets where soldiers are given target practice.

The army was embarrassed when the local Press had printed pictures of General Sir William Jackson, the army Quartermaster, posing with one of the glamour models.

LONG BOUTS OF SENSORY DEPRIVATION

The army said the replicas were used only to make street-scenes 'more realistic'.

Elsewhere in Ashford the torture scientists are at work.

Research centres do not simply concentrate on forms of torture involving physical violence — the experts have come a long way since the scientists of the Spanish Inquisition.

Most investigations now centre on what has cynically been dubbed as 'humane' forms of torture. By this the scientists mean various forms of psychological torture often involving the subject in long bouts of sensory deprivation.

The current issue of 'World Medicine' notes that, 'despite the seemingly innocuous and even "humane" methods employed in the Northern Ireland situation, suspects after only a few days began to suffer severe mental and physical disorientation, such as could only be accomplished in the 1930s by the Stalinist KGB over a period of more than a month'.

The kind of torture was described in the Socialist Labour League Pocket Library publication 'The Ulster Dossier' (New Park Publications, 186a Clapham High Street, London, SW4 7UG, or the Paperback Centre, 28 Charlotte Street, London, W1).

Apart from the many physical attacks, Ulster internees undergo mental harassment through special interrogation methods. Men and women are kept awake forcibly for days. They are hooded and subject to a continual barrage of threats.

A report into army torture by the Compton Committee found that the hooding treatment had resulted in no long-term affects or injuries. In parliament, the then Home Secretary Reginald Maudling (he later resigned over the Poulson case) said the torture resulted in 'no permanent injury of either a mental or physical nature'.

But Robert Daly, professor of psychiatry at Cork University, reached a different conclusion after examining 20 men subjected to British army torture.

He found they showed marked symptoms of anxiety, fear and dread, as well as insomnia and startled responses. They were, he said, similar to the victims of shell-shock.

There was an early development of psychosomatic illnesses, such as peptic ulcers, headaches and buzzing in the ears.

The men who had undergone the ordeal of arrest and interrogation had, said Professor Daly, 'a diminished will to live, a generally diminished hold on life . . . Some of them said they would sooner die than face further interrogation or torture-chamber experiences'.

Most of the interrogation methods suffered by the 20 men examined by the professor were admitted by the army during the Compton Committee investigations. The government argued they did no harm.

EXPERTS USED BY MILITARY

'World Medicine' comments that such speeded-up methods of breaking down a victim are the result of military research by many scientists.

'These techniques,' says the journal, 'are taught at purpose-built intelligence centres where Service personnel are instructed in the art of interrogation in depth.' One of these is at Ashford.

'Any psychiatrist who acts as adviser there must surely ask himself why his advice is sought and how it's used.'

Of course the doctors and psychiatric experts know well how their expertise is used.

Take the case of Desmond Smith, who was arrested on August 9, 1971, when internment was introduced in Ulster. He was hooded, beaten until he had a form of epileptic fit, hung from rafters and beaten again. Eventually a doctor was bought to the scene because he had collapsed. The doctor administered an injection and told the military police to take the man to hospital.

PRISONERS ATTEMPT SUICIDE

Eventually he was examined by a specialist called Sparrow and put in a hospital bed where soldiers were allowed to disturb him in his private room.

At all stages the doctors knew the treatment Smith was subjected to, but none spoke out. One is forced to conclude they agree with these widespread methods.

The Rand Corporation has studied 2,000 torture cases in South Vietnam. CIA agent Anthony Russo said the studies were to 'assess the viability of the methods used by the US forces'.

In Germany there are plans to introduce methods of sensory deprivation as a normal feature of prison life for non-political prisoners.

In June, a new prison was opened in Preungesheim, West Germany, which make sensory deprivation the norm for all prisoners because of certain architectural features.

Every single cell window is equipped with a concrete blind. This and other devices mean prisoners can be totally cut off from all life and environment—they hear no sound, they see nothing and feel nothing. Within three days of Preungesheim's opening, two prisoners had attempted suicide.

Dr Sjef Teuns, the Dutch psychiatrist, says: 'The culprit in the contemporary system of torture is not the prison guard operating the pre-fabricated torture machine, but those who are performing basic research, being aware of the connections and the interplay out of which the methods of the system evolve and are being developed.'

In fact, casting around for guilt does not explain torture or scientists involvement in the torture system. They are the hirelings of the ruling class who use this method to break down resistance to their rule.

Workers Press, Monday November 19 1973 PAGE 7

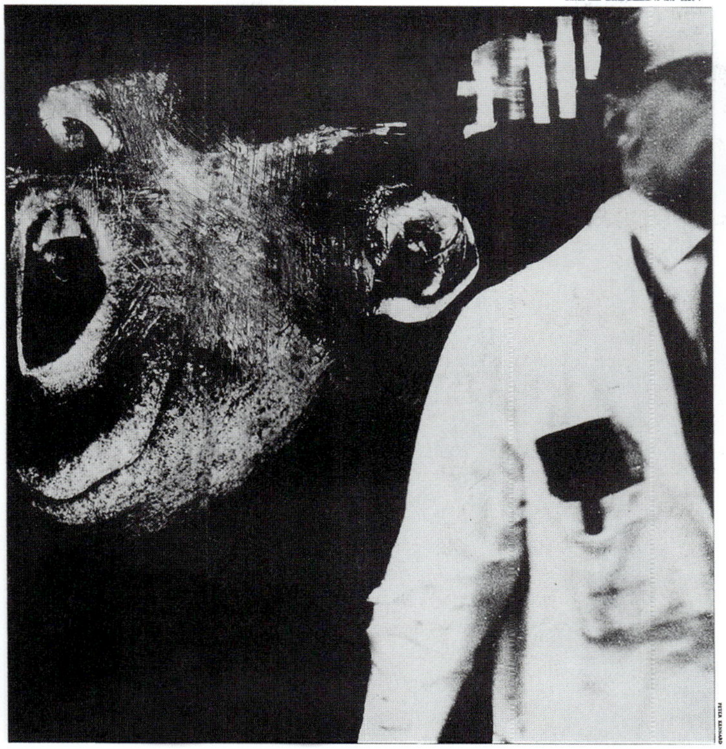

PETER KENNARD

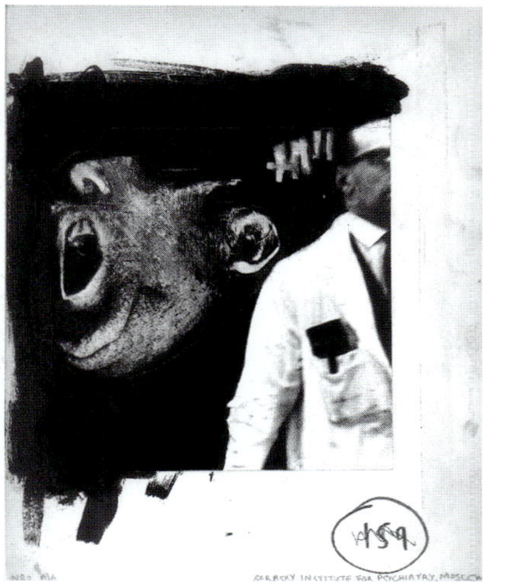

PAGE 6 Workers Press, Saturday October 6, 1973

Workers Press, Saturday October 6, 1973 PAGE 7

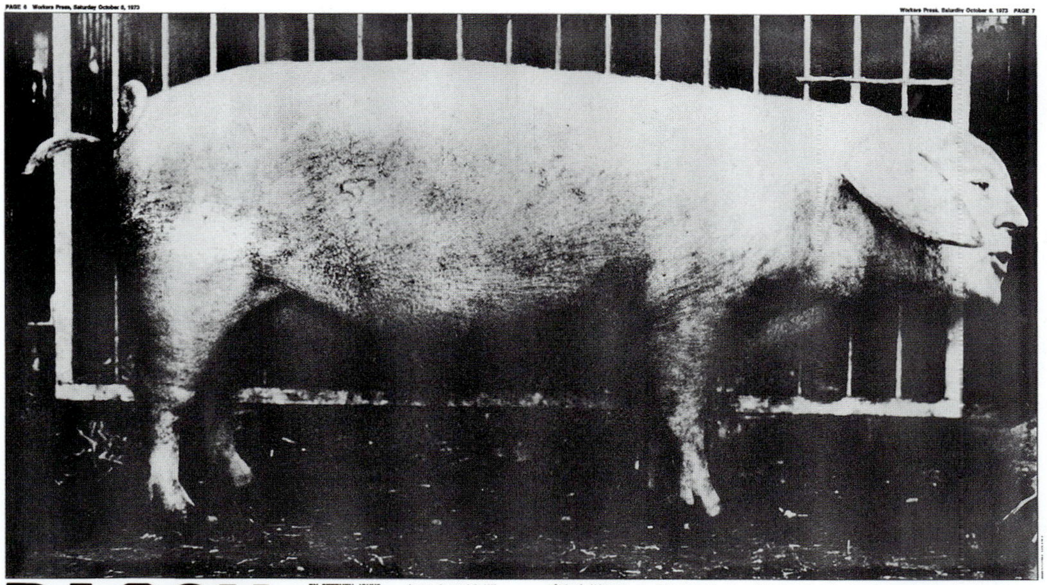

BACON THE MEAN CUT

BY STEPHEN JOHNS

The days when bacon was a good cheap meat buy are gone for ever as a trip to any supermarket will prove.

Half a pound sets the shopper back anything between 30p and 45p. Calculated in old money that is 6s to almost 10s—almost as dear as steak used to be and a breathtaking increase on the days when bacon was cheap enough for the pensioner to buy.

Bacon, once a staple food in Britain, is now a luxury. The reason is inflation and the Common Market—both a deliberate result of Tory policy.

The story of dear bacon begins in July 1970 when the newly-elected Heath government opened negotiations with the European capitalists to get into the Common Market.

Market prices were then at a level that allowed most housewives to buy as much bacon as she wanted. By 1972 they began to creep up as suppliers anticipated entry into the EEC, and in 1973, the year of the Common Market 'adventure', prices exploded.

The percentage increases from July 1970 to May 1973 are:

Collar	**up**	**65 p.c.**
Gammon	**up**	**55 p.c.**
Middle cut, smoked	**up**	**62 p.c.**
Back, smoked	**up**	**65 p.c.**
Back, unsmoked	**up**	**67 p.c.**
Streaky, smoked	**up**	**83 p.c.**

The aim of the Common Market and Tory policy is to reduce the living standards of the working class. In a number of essential food commodities like cheese, beef and milk, consumption has dropped dramatically as prices have forced the working-class buyer out of the market.

Bacon is no exception. The average consumption per household per week has dropped from 5.32 ounces in 1970 to 4.66 ounces in the first three months of this year. This is despite the fact that spending on bacon has risen, reflecting the higher prices.

In 1971, 9.32p was spent per person on bacon each week. Now the total is around 12p. These are the hard statistics that expose as an outright lie the Tory claim that living standards have improved.

The situation will get worse as long as the British working class is the prey of the Common Market—dominated by the big monopolies.

EEC regulations are designed deliberately to destroy the mechanism which helped to produce large, cheap supplies. In their place, restrictive rules apply which are designed to keep prices high.

Home-producers used to enjoy a Bacon Market Sharing Understanding. Under this, home-producers took 40 per cent of the market and the rest was shared by importers. This produced a stability which encouraged countries like Poland, Hungary and Rumania, who invested heavily in pig herds, to import cheap supplies into Britain.

These arrangements were destroyed 'at a stroke' on February 1. The result has been to make the UK market less stable and this has driven the eastern European suppliers away from the home market—which is exactly what the EEC big farming interests wanted.

The old arrangements were by no means perfect, since they existed to serve an industry run for profit. But the new regulations are far worse, reflecting, as they do, the most narrow protectionist demands of the EEC profit-makers.

The other system that was scrapped by the Common Market—this time on June 1—was the Bacon Curing (Stabilization) Scheme.

This ensured a large and fairly steady home supply of bacon meat through a mechanism which guaranteed a fixed margin over costs to the bacon curer. The government would subsidize the curer when the price over costs was less than the margin.

This system again was by no means perfect, since the subsidies and profit went into private hands. But its abolition means the working class is penalized even more. At least the subsidies are paid via taxation, which, since the rich do pay more, has a progressive element (fast disappearing under the Tory government).

In the Common Market producers are protected by high prices. And everyone pays the higher prices—from the millionaire to the man on the dole. The burden, therefore, is deliberately an unequal one.

Under EEC regulations, cheap imports are kept out. A 'sluicegate price' is fixed and on top of this a levy is fixed on all imports. This prevents imported bacon ever competing with expensive bacon within the Common Market. If the levies fail to choke off imports the price is raised until the 'foreign' bacon is higher in price than EEC bacon. The shopper foots the bill.

On top of all these nightmarish regulations there is a further way of keeping bacon costly. In the rare event that EEC prices fall of their own accord more than 8 per cent below import prices, the Agricultural Commission will step in.

Thousands of tons of bacon are bought and hoarded until the price rises. The money used for these purchases comes out of the taxpayers' pocket—dear or cheap the wage-earner will pay more for bacon in the EEC!

The levy system has naturally had a disastrous effect on the quantity of imported bacon in British shops. The figures for February this year show that when the levy on bacon exports rose to £106 a ton, 'foreign' supplies slumped to 19,600 tons. This compares with the 36,000 tons in November 1972 when there was no levy. The argument that levies simply 'even-out' supplies, therefore, is another Common Market lie.

The end result is a dramatic slump in bacon production. In 197[illegible], 13,000 tons of bacon came on to the market at £350 a ton, now about 11,000 tons come up for sale at £600 a ton. No figure better illustrates the Common Market—you eat less and pay more.

The Tory motives for launching this attack on the working class are only too plain. What is of more concern is the way the Labour opposition kept the Tories in power when 69 of their MPs voted with the government to go into the EEC.

The Jenkins band were speaking as members of the Party at the conference this week in Blackpool. This illustrates the depth of political bankruptcy in the Labour Party.

Any future socialist administration must pull out of the EEC immediately and nationalize the food industry in Britain.

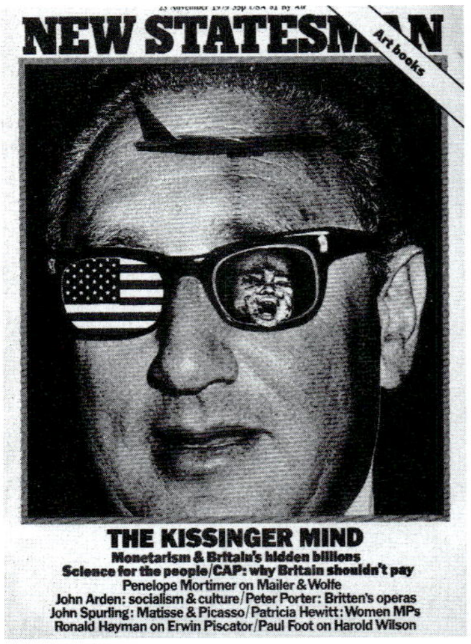

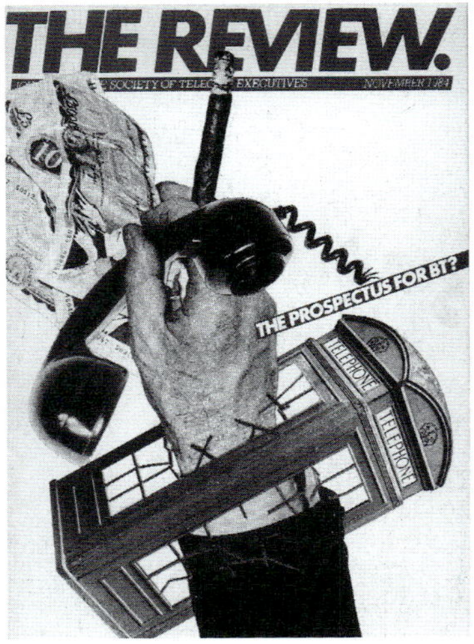

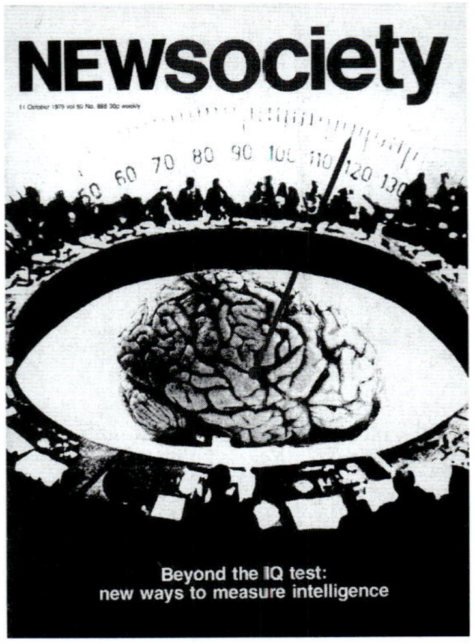

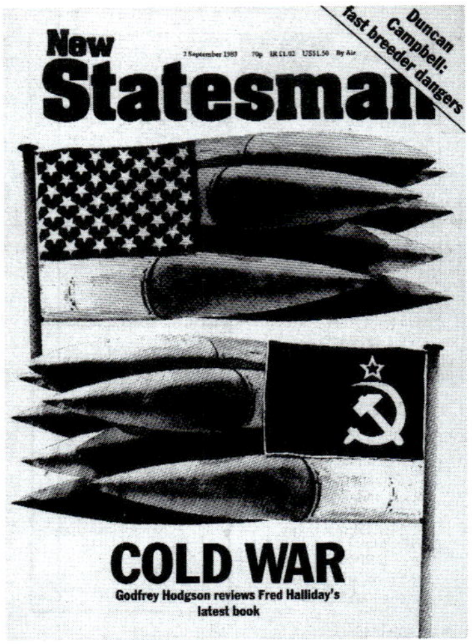

editors. In spite of all this, it was a very productive period in which I made images that got out to workers across the country. I still value and use as elements in current work images that I made at that time. It was a method of working that was closer in spirit to artists in pre-war Germany, especially John Heartfield, than to the spirit that dominated my English art education.

Archive A: Montage in print

A *New Statesman* cover of Henry Kissinger lies with piles of magazines underneath *Workers Press*. After working for *Workers Press* I started to make photomontages for a number of magazines and newspapers. It was freelance work, often illustrating articles, or making images on issues of the moment and then selling them to a paper or magazine. I also worked for a variety of campaigning organisations and charities making posters, postcards and other visual material that could be used for fundraising as well as getting the message across. Over the last 30 years I have made approximately 600 photomontages. They often began life in one publication and moved through different incarnations – galleries, posters, teeshirts, badges, postcards and placards. In this way I see them as a resource, an image bank, to be utilised in different national and international struggles. The montages go out into circulation and develop their own momentum. The authorship of the montages often gets lost as they translate into different forms, so questions of copyright are complex. I only question the use of the images uncredited (and unpaid) when they make the crossover from being used as part of a campaign against exploitation and injustice to being exploited themselves and used commercially by the mainstream media. The images turn up uncredited as posters in film or as backdrops on TV, as if they are an unauthored part of our visual landscape. It's in these cases that I try to get payment for their use. It's the fluidity of the work that is integral to its impact on the world. In August 1997 I had *News Truck* on the streets of Edinburgh during the festival. It was reported in the *Guardian* on the finance page. Many images I have made have been placed on the leader or comment pages, not the arts page.

The photomontages are critiques, statements which make it difficult for people from opposing positions to co-opt them, but it can happen. A glossy colour magazine showed my poster of *Maggie Regina* on the wall of a smart living room in one of those interminable features on houses of the rich. This image was originally made as a response to Thatcher's call for a return to Victorian values. It appeared in *Time* magazine in a feature on Thatcher's Britain and I heard rumours at the time that Thatcher herself rather approved of the image of herself as an imperial monarch.

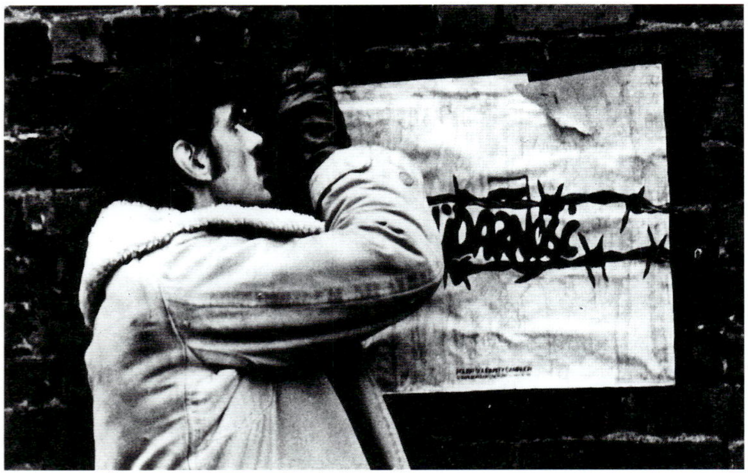
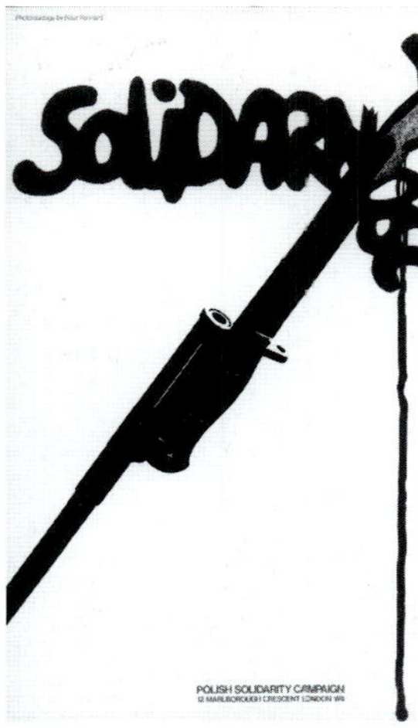

Above, left to right magazine covers:
New Statesman/23 October 1979
The Review/November 1984
New Society/11 October 1979
New Statesman/2 September 1983

Below far left
Production still from the film *Moonlighting* (1982), directed by Jerzy Skolimowski. The film was a response to martial law being imposed in Poland in 1981. The still shows Jeremy Irons, who plays a Polish guest worker in London, pulling down one of the posters produced for the Polish Solidarity Campaign. In the poster the Solidarnosc symbol has been montaged with barbed wire

Below left
Polish Solidarity Campaign poster/1981/ photolithograph
The posters were produced to raise awareness of Solidarity in Europe, and to sell for fundraising

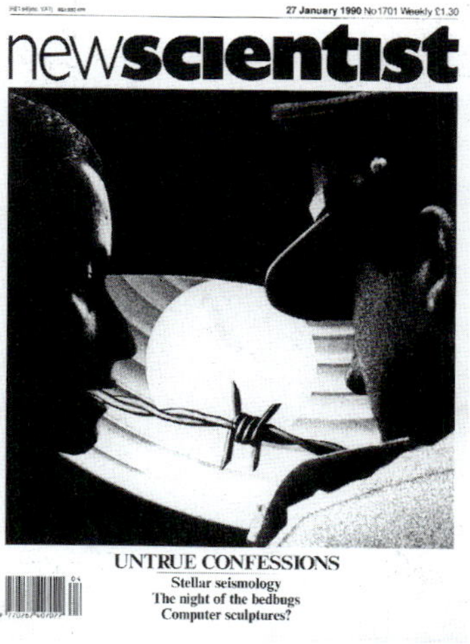

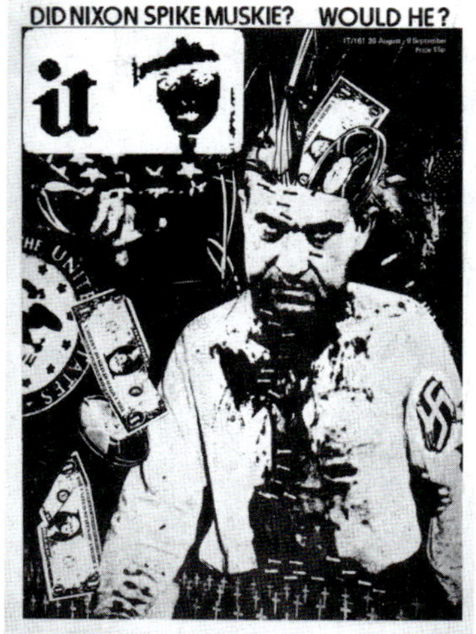

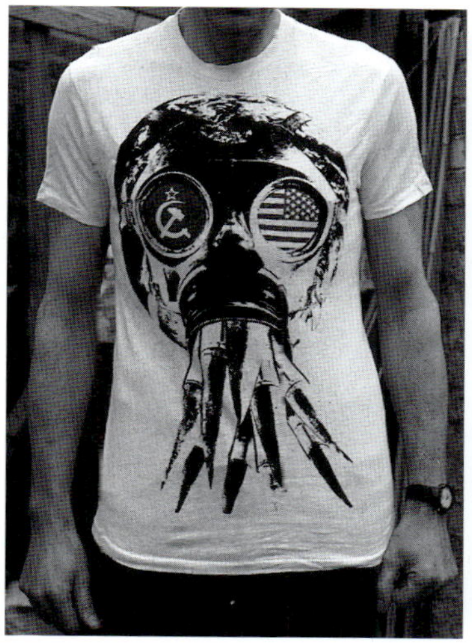

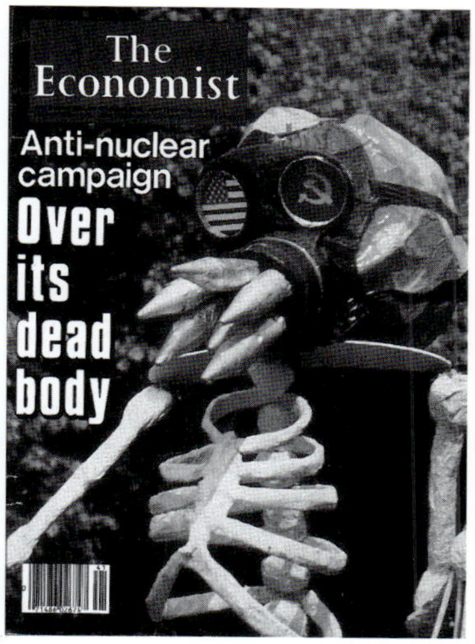

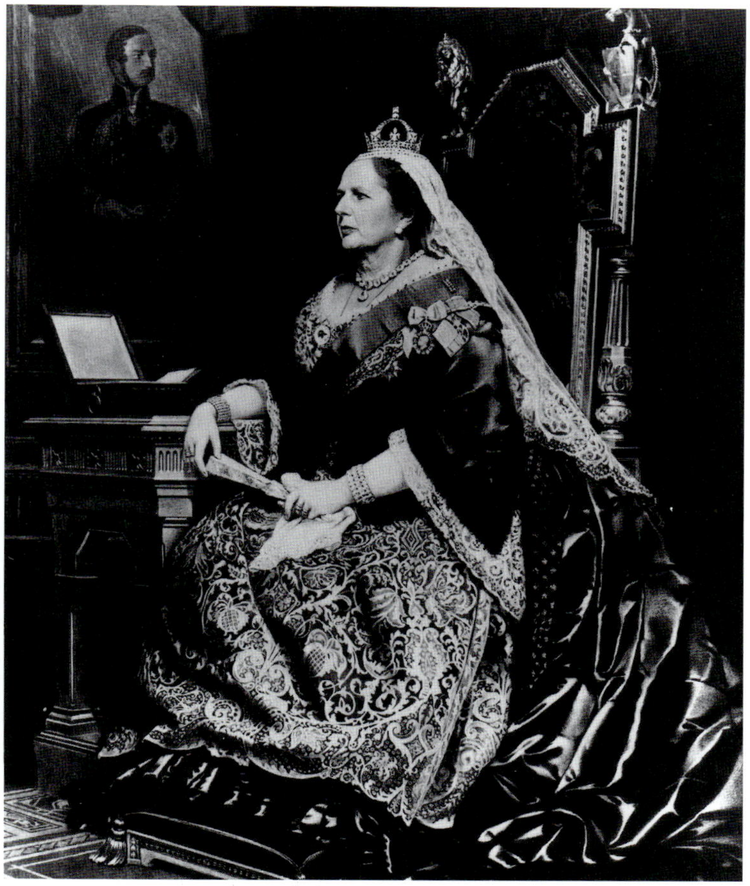

But usually the critical element in a photomontage is so integral that it is ideologically watertight and its meaning cannot be subverted by opposing interests. However, intention *can* be subverted by issues of context. An example is the *Economist* cover of 8 October 1983, which used a photograph by a freelance photographer of a sculptural version (made by anti-nuclear campaigners) of my montage *Defended to Death*. Originally this image was commissioned as a cover for a Penguin book but is used here with the headline 'Anti-Nuclear Campaign: over its dead body' within a magazine with an assiduously pro-nuclear stance. I have no control over this process.

There is no simple relationship of authorship to copyright when images are changed and different elements added or subtracted. In February 1983 CND asked me to go to the High Court to seek an injunction against the right-wing Coalition for Peace through Security who had taken one of my montages, *Disarming Britain*, showing Britain encircled in a CND symbol, from the cover of a CND pamphlet and added a hammer and sickle. They then produced their own version of the leaflet in which they claimed that CND were financed by Russian gold. I went to court, not on the issue of libel, which would have been a long and costly process, but merely on the flagrant abuse of copyright of my image. Because they had actually rephotographed my montage dot for dot, it appeared

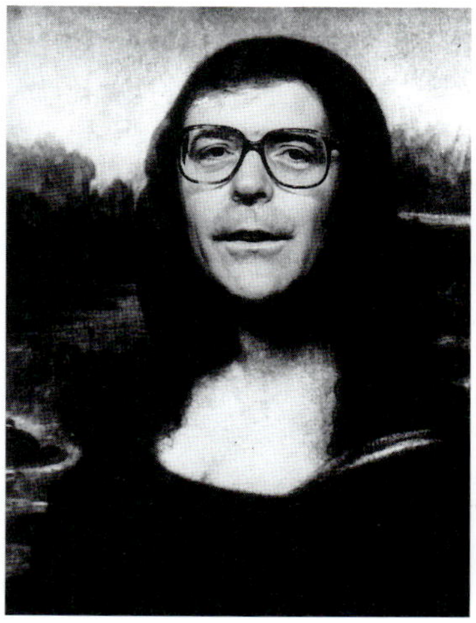

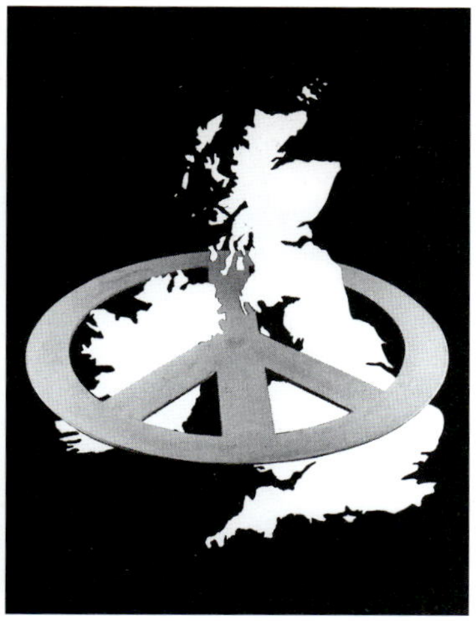

Above, magazine covers from left
New Scientist/27 January 1990
IT/26 August 1974

Above right
Defended to Death/photomontage/1983
Reprinted on a tee-shirt, 1985

Above far right
The Economist/8 October 1983
Magazine cover co-opting *Defended to Death*

Centre
Maggie Regina: Victorian Values/1983/ photomontage
First produced as a cover for a supplement of the *New Statesman* on Victorian values (27 May 1983) and later as a poster and postcard

Below far left
Major Mona/1991/photomontage

Below left
Disarming Britain/1982/photomontage

Below
Rubber Bullet/1985/oil and printers ink on canvas

Bottom
Posters of *Values 1* flyposted in Covent Garden to advertise solo exhibition *Values* at the Institute of Contemporary Arts, London, 1977

Opposite above left
Smashed/1978/photomontage

Opposite above right
Nelson Mandela/1990/photomontage
First published in the *Guardian*, 6 February 1990, four days before Nelson Mandela's release from prison. The photograph of him used was taken before he was imprisoned in 1963

Opposite below
Public Relations/1986/photomontage

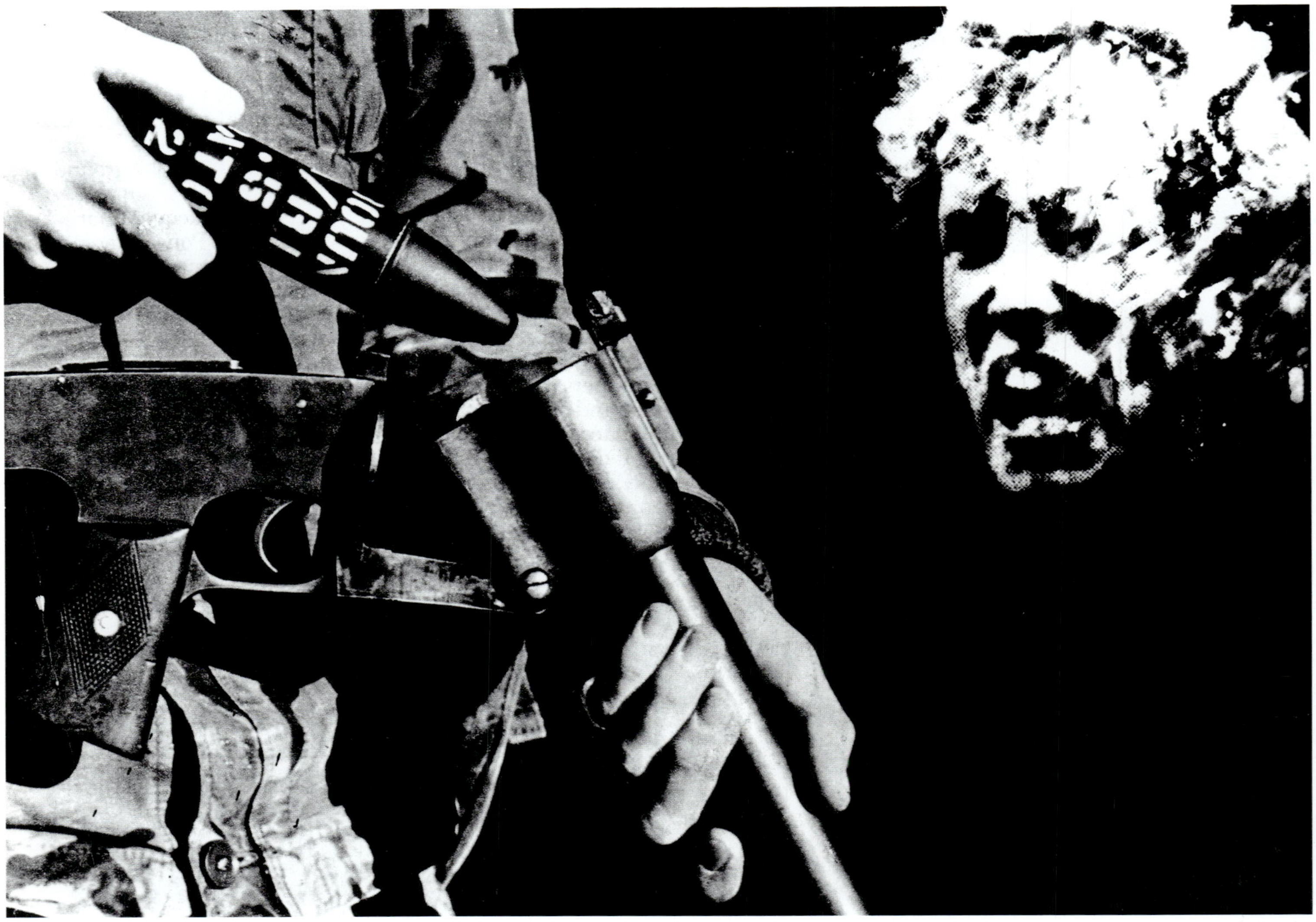

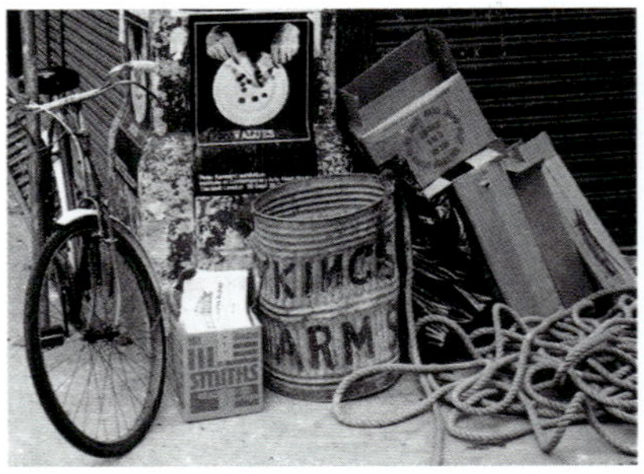

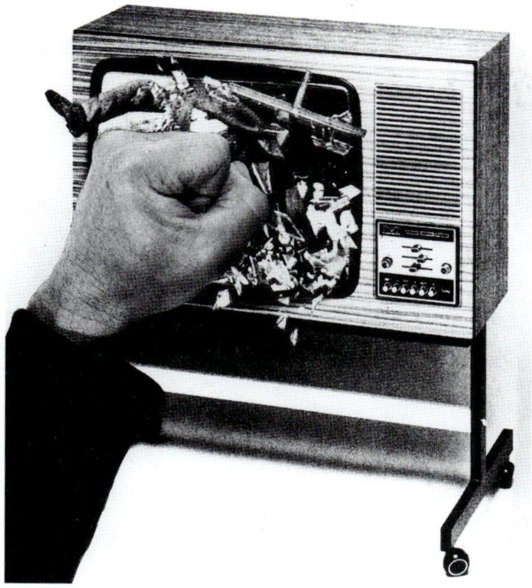

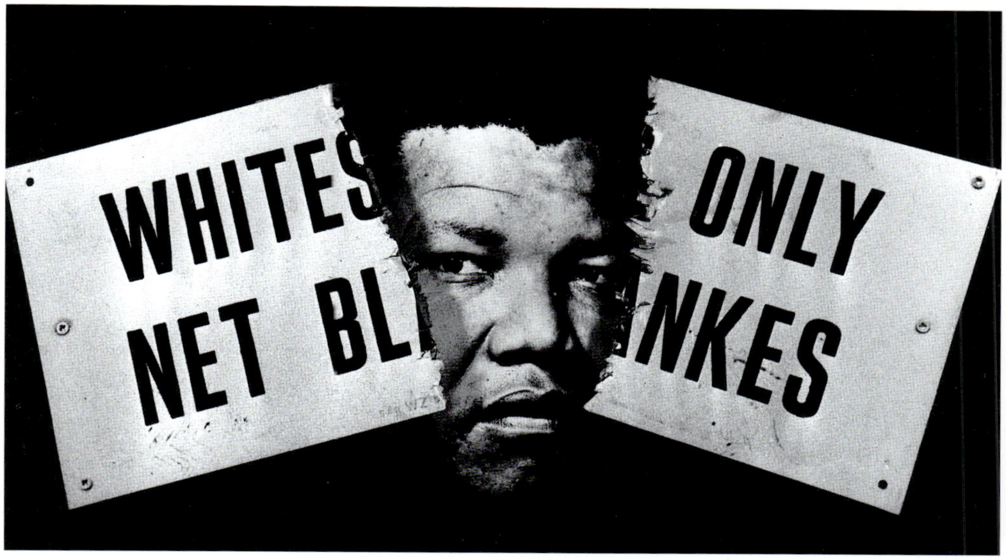
WHITES
ONLY
NET BL
NKES

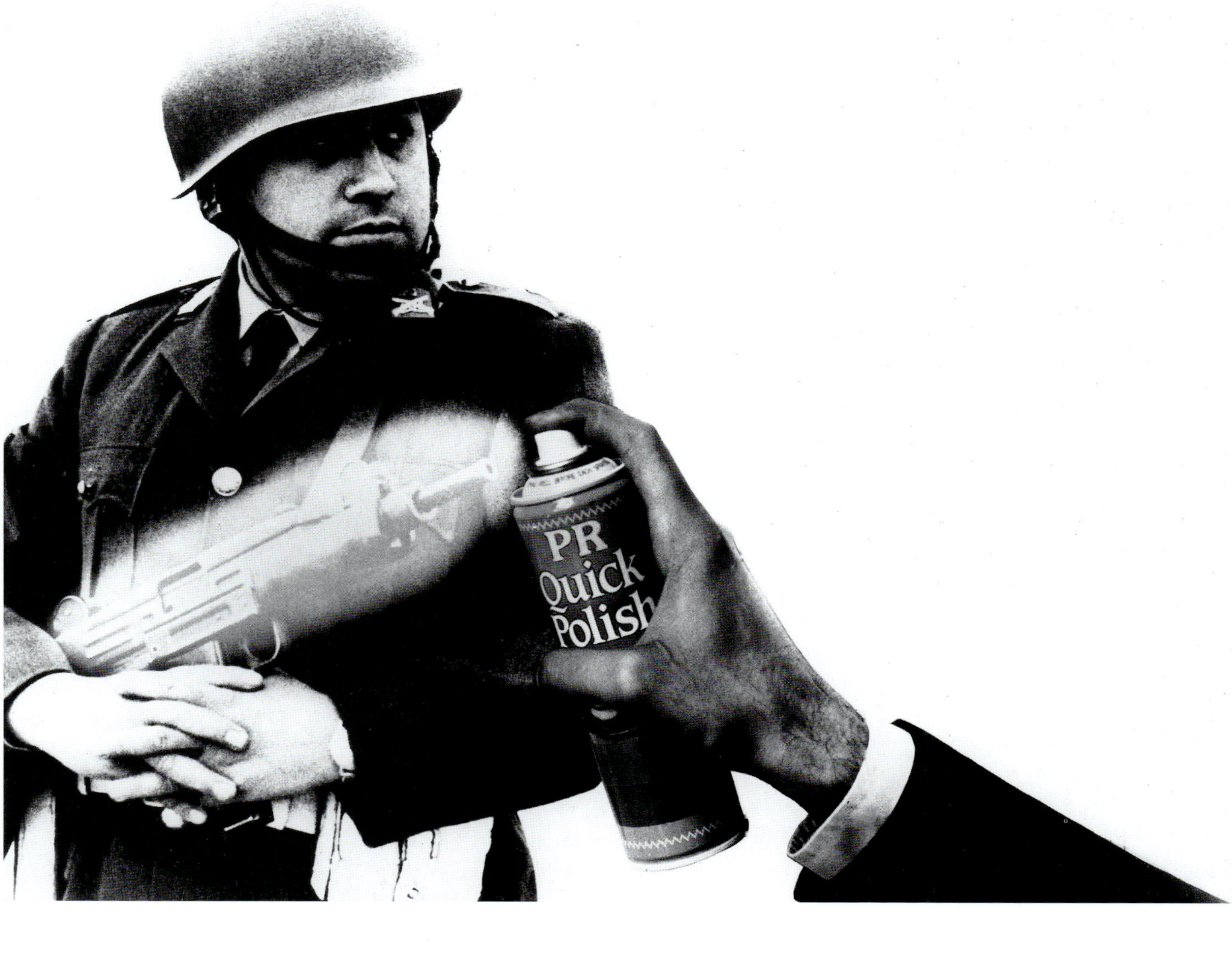
PR
Quick
Polish

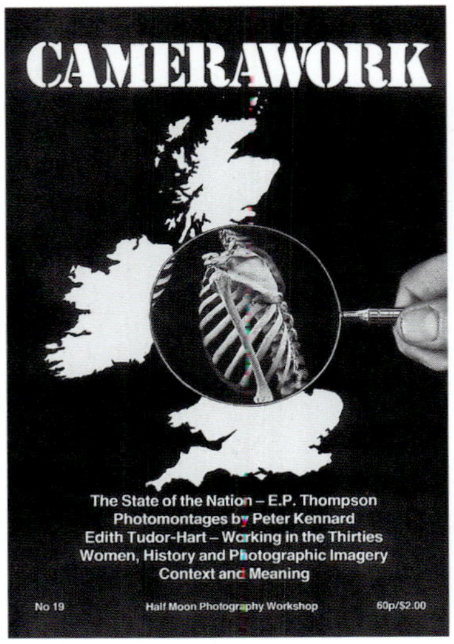

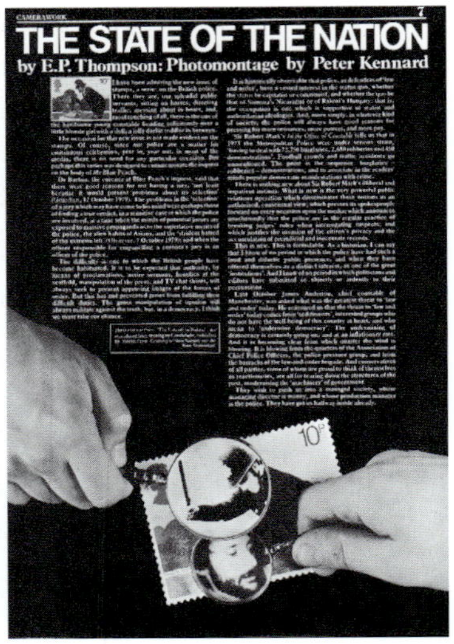
CAMERAWORK

THE STATE OF THE NATION

by E.P. Thompson: Photomontage by Peter Kennard

Right and opposite
Camerawork/July 1980
Cover and State of the Nation supplement, with text by historian E P Thompson. His text begins with a description of a newly issued postage stamp celebrating the British police which he then equates with the death of Blair Peach (seen in the lower magnifying glass under a police truncheon). He continues by discussing the imminent arrival of Cruise missiles in Britain and finally brings the strands together by saying that civil liberties are being eroded by the growth of the nuclear state: 'those thought susceptible to moral objection must be vigilantly watched; their letters opened and their telephones tapped ...' The photomontage was later made into a postcard to raise funds for the Friends of Blair Peach Committee

Opposite far right
E P Thompson addressing a European Nuclear Disarmanent (END) rally at Central Hall, Westminster, 1983. In front of him is a giant enlargement of *Haywain with Cruise Missiles*

to be an open and shut case. But it was not. Mr Douglas Hogg, the counsel for the Coalition, turned it into a learned debate about what constituted an original work of art. It became a farcical moment in the history of critical theory. As reported in the *Guardian* on 18 February 1983: 'Mr Douglas Hogg questioned whether Mr Kennard's art work could be described as original work within the meaning of the 1956 Copyright Act. But at the same time he said it could be argued that the Coalition's parody of the CND design was an original work.' A debate ensued in court about how much brain power was needed to make a work of art. In my case, in the eyes of the establishment, my brain was clearly not up to it. It was decided that my montage was not a work of art but the Coalition's appropriation was and we lost the case.

Archive A: Co-opting Constable
A yellowing page from the *Daily Mirror* Tuesday 17 October 1980. Under a reproduction of my montage *Haywain with Cruise missiles* it says:

> 'Protesters against nuclear warfare have recruited England's favourite landscape painter to their cause. In 1824 John Constable first exhibited his famous picture, *The Haywain*, showing a cart trundling through his native East Anglia. Now the government plans to allow huge trucks to rumble through the same landscape, each carrying some of the 160 American Cruise missiles with nuclear warheads which will be based in Britain. In protest at that decision artist Peter Kennard created a poster by mounting a cut-out of three Cruise missiles on a reproduction of Constable's famous painting.'

The Haywain was the only montage that I suceeded in getting into the *Daily Mirror* after having tried to get one printed there for years. Many was the morning I'd spent in the newsroom with a section editor telling me, 'Peter, we understand it but will the readers?' and that was as far as it got. This is a variation on a scenario that has recurred throughout my working life. The 'experts' arrogantly out-think the audience. I've shown images to many an editor or committee who want illusions rather than reality. I remember one disarmament committee where this happened. They thought my images were too hard and depressing and that we should use rainbows to depict a future with no nuclear weapons. This type of argument is always fallacious. Picturing the end of want and conflict in this way means a vision of the future is imposed. It robs people of the opportunity of imagining their own. My job is to make a critique of what we've got now, not to lay down a blueprint for what should follow. In reality, somewhere over the rainbow are nuclear silos. The beauty of nature doesn't erase the folly of humanity. It's the intractable stuff of human conflict and inequality that I try to deal with in my work, through sifting the endless stream of information and images. We might, in the west, feel we live in a post-modern simulacra, unable to act in the corporate narrative that bombards us and invades our dreams, but for most of humanity there is no such armchair speculation possible.

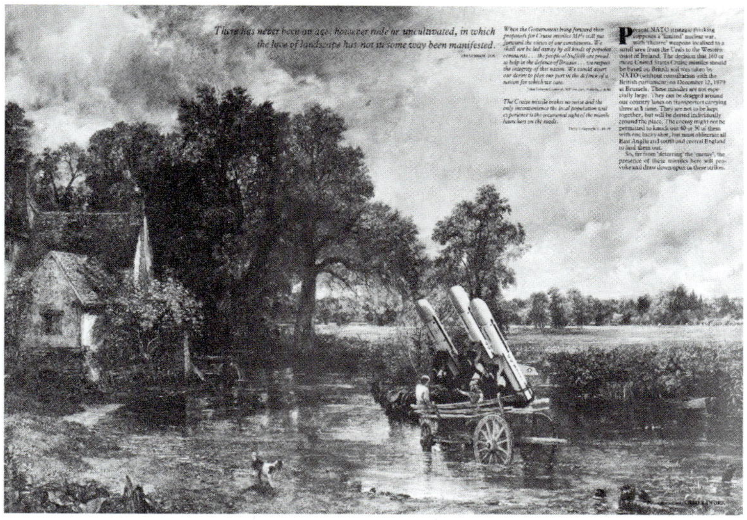

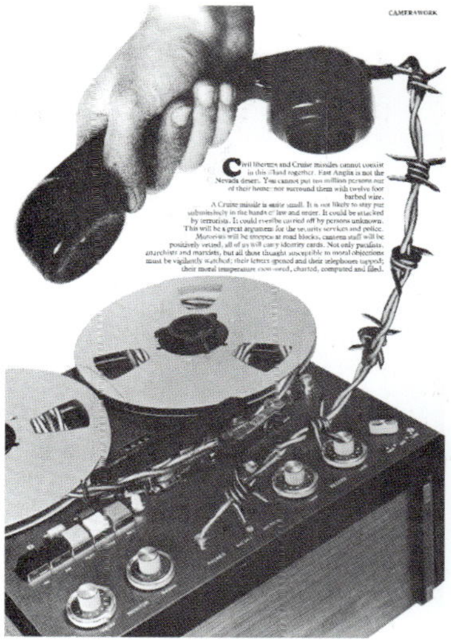

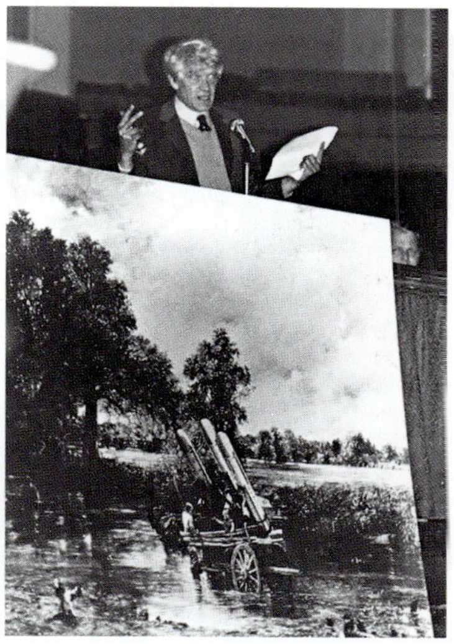

Archive A: The Haywain
My photomontage of 1980 whose full title finally became *The Haywain. Constable (1821) Cruise missiles. USA (1983–1988)* was first printed in a sequence of montages I made to illustrate a text by E P Thompson, 'The State of the Nation', in *Camerawork* July 1980. I also found a quote from Constable himself which I reproduced with the image: 'There has never been an age, however rude or uncultivated, in which the love of landscape has not in some way been manifested.' The image was quickly taken up by the Labour Party and made into a poster against the imminent arrival of the Cruise missiles. The Ministry of Defence had produced a leaflet for distribution to people living in the area where they were to be stationed. It was this leaflet that gave me the idea for the montage. Not only was the name Cruise an obscene euphemism for weapons (each of which contain the power of eighteen Hiroshima bombs) but the PR department of the Ministry of Defence had extended the euphemism to its use of imagery by putting a delicate watercolour of Cruise missiles sitting snugly in the rolling hills of the English countryside on the cover of their leaflet. Presumably painted by the chief Ministry of Defence watercolourist (a job of the utmost dialectical complexity) it fitted in with the words of their spokesman who said at the time that people shouldn't worry as Cruise missiles, 'will melt into the countryside'. An unspoken alternative scenario is that *we* would melt into the countryside if they were ever used.

When I first made the montage I included a number of elements, such as a gas mask on the dog and skeletons falling out of the window of Flatford Mill. I later simplified the image to allow only for the direct iconic conjunction of the farmworkers with gas masks and helmets and the missiles on the cart. It's often the case that, because photomontage is an additive form, one goes on adding and adding. The key is to subtract to the point where often only two main elements lock together. They can then interrupt and smash through the smooth veneer of government double talk, from whichever country their lies are emanating.

This montage became widely reproduced with the addition of different text in different languages by peace movements around the world. My favourite use of it is simply as a full-colour or black-and-white postcard with no text. Tens of thousands of these were printed over the years. This version infiltrated into the social fabric in unexpected ways. I was told by a number of shop owners that they had been bought from them by unsuspecting American tourists who hadn't noticed the missiles. The idea of these cards winging their way into middle-American households, is deeply pleasurable.

Many years later I got a 'phone call from the National Gallery who own the original *Haywain*. I thought that being a national museum and therefore an institution that operates very slowly they were

There are things I won't do. I won't use an air brush to 'soften the edges'; in fact it can be important that the cuts and joins are visible, that two or three things have been put together remains evident. Such images reveal how they're constructed, implying flux and the possibility of changing things in the world. I'm not trying to compete with advertising where the imagery is mainly smooth and seamless. Their aim is to create an alternative, carefree world in which to shop. My aim is to make images that are not a cover-up but an attempt to uncover a cover-up.

Cv/interview/November 1990

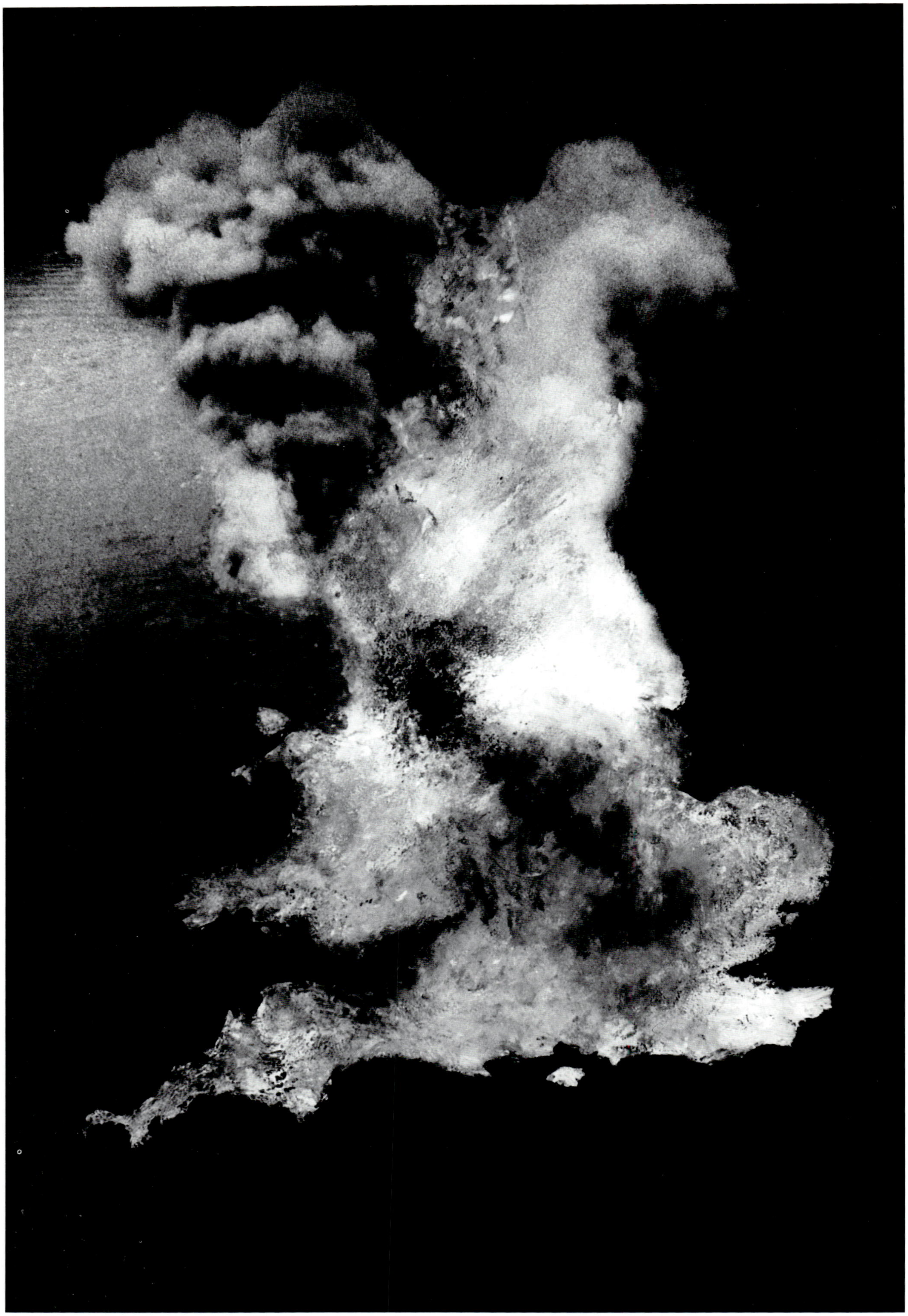

If you make art about the political world, an art that points a finger of blame, your situation is riddled with contradiction and compromise involving complex negotiation with authorities whose existence is conditional upon the maintainance of the status quo. We all live in the actual world as it is, we have no choice.

Art Monthly/April 2000

suddenly going to get stroppy about my use of the image. In fact they rang to ask my permission to use the montage in a lecture being given on Constable at the gallery. In this way the picture had wormed its way back into the gallery in its amended form. The original of the black-and-white version of the photomontage was later bought by the Victoria and Albert Museum long after the Cruise missiles had departed from English soil.

The most extraordinary montages of this period were the ones produced on the perimeter fence of Greenham Common. On specially designated days thousands of people went down to the women's peace camp and put up photos, mementoes, drawings, and leaves across the whole length of the fence. The inhumanity of the concrete silos was countered by human creativity weaving its way along the fence that guarded them.

Archive A: Greater London

Sorting through some of the many versions of the *Haywain* montage I come across one from a series of A3 peace posters I made for the Greater London Council (GLC) in 1983. Between 1982 and 1986 a radical political administration led by Ken Livingstone came to office in London and took over the running of the GLC. It was based in County Hall opposite the Houses of Parliament where one of the most right-wing governments in Britain since the 1930s was

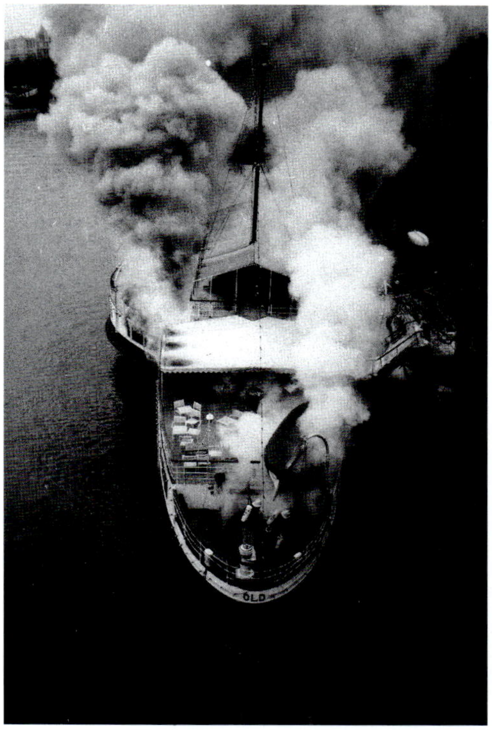

Opposite
Limited Nuclear War/1980/photomontage, oil and gouache
Based on President Reagan's comment that the USA could win a 'limited nuclear war', with the proviso that Europe would be wiped out. Also based on the line from page 19 of *Protect and Survive*: 'if you have a home fire extinguisher, keep it handy'

Above
Photograph of a boat on fire taken by chance when crossing a bridge over the River Thames in 1977. Later used as the basis for *Limited Nuclear War*, with the addition of paint

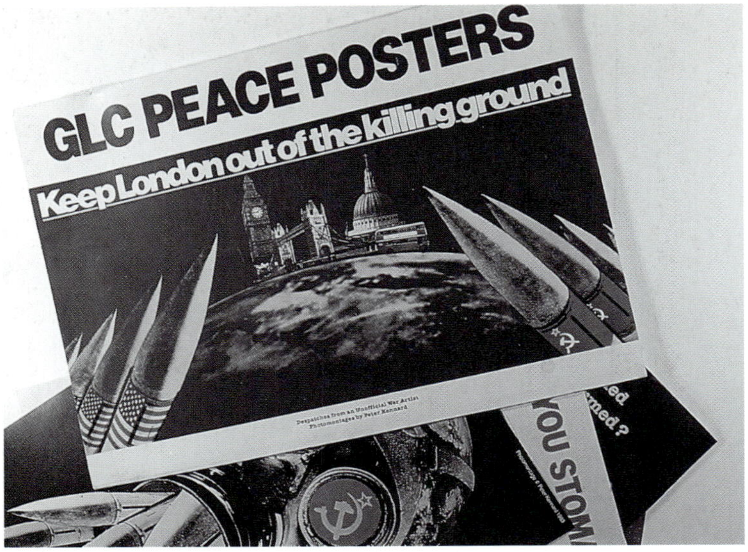

in power, led by Margaret Thatcher. The GLC had no statutory powers to intervene in the economy but developed into an extraordinary forum for women's organisations, anti-racist groups, trade unions and gay rights activists; the very people who were being attacked by Thatcher and her government over the river.

I got involved in a number of projects, firstly the *GLC Peace Posters Pack*. I remember collating thousands of my anti-nuclear posters into the packs with a group of sympathisers in an enormous wood-panelled room in County Hall. The pack, which consisted of 12 posters, was ordered by schools, youth clubs, community centres and trade unions. They were designed and printed by Peter Gladwin who I'd begun working with at *Camerawork*. My collaboration with him, which continues to this day, has been crucial to the development of my work. We worked together on another project for the GLC, *Target London*, an A3 box of 18 posters which, through the combination of text and image, elucidated the government's plan to protect Londoners in the event of a nuclear war. This was part of the GLC's remit. I took material from *Protect and Survive*, the pamphlet published by the government on what to do in times of nuclear war, and juxtaposed it with reports on nuclear war written by doctors, nurses and scientist's groups. It was this conjunction of the text with the images that pointed to the conclusion that the government had no actual plans to protect Londoners in the event

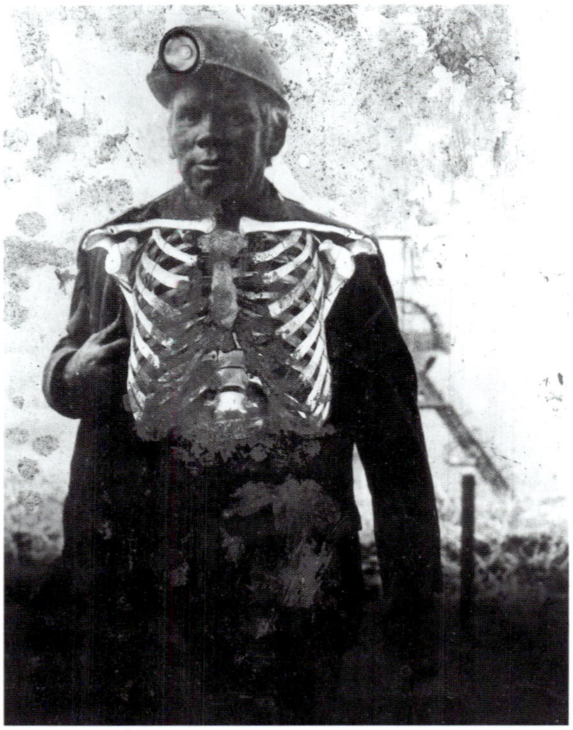

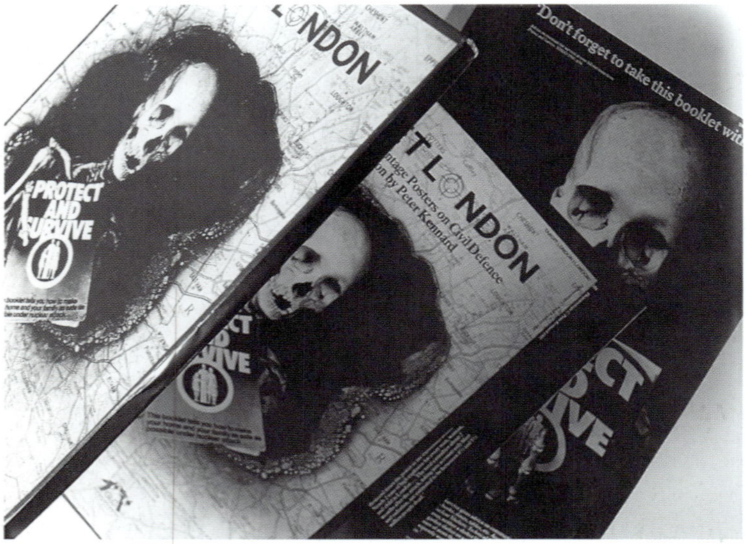

Above, left
GLC Peace Posters Pack/1983/photolithography
Twelve A3 posters in a folder

Centre
Miner/1976/photomontage, graphite and dust
The original workings are shown

Below left
Target London/1985/photolithography
A boxed set of 18 A3 text and image posters with a foreword by E P Thompson (Greater London Council [GLC], 1985)

Opposite
Decoration/1982/photomontage
Produced at the time of the Falklands War when Margaret Thatcher emerged from 10 Downing Street exhorting us to 'rejoice'

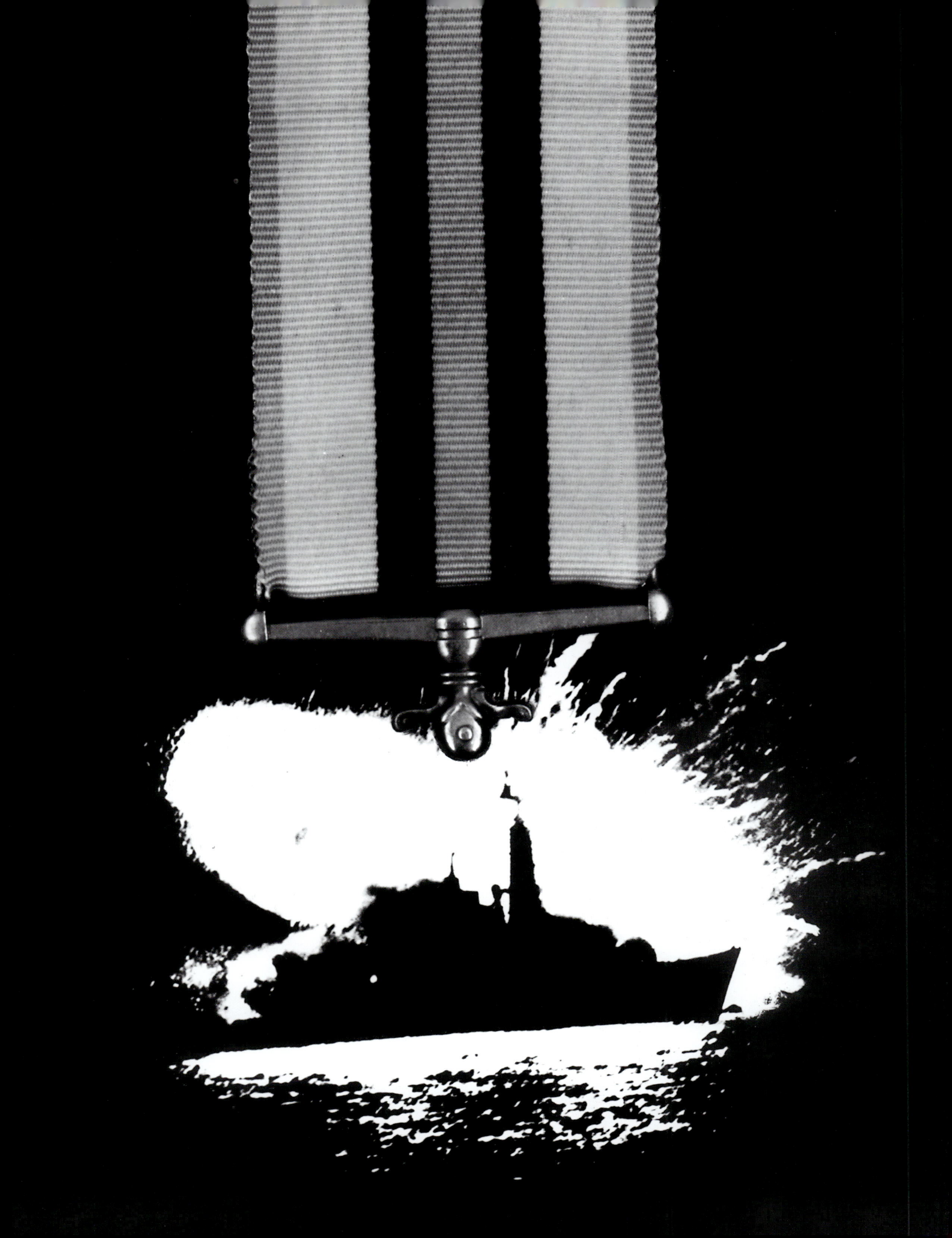

of nuclear war and in reality protection was impossible. The box of posters was a portable exhibition which was sent out to local councils and was available cheaply in bookshops. I heard that people had put it up in cafes, community centres, bus depots and launderettes, as well as more conventional spaces.

Two other collaborations followed at the GLC. One, with author Hilary Wainwright and designer John Finn, was the booklet *Jobs for a Change*. It tried to show an alternative to the waste of workers' skills that is unemployment. Using words, photomontage and photography it explored new ways of communicating possibilities for unlocking the economy from the lottery of the free market. I also collaborated with Bill Evans, a writer and industrial designer, (who had been involved with questions of arms conversion) and designer Roger Huddle on a book called *About Turn* which described possible alternative uses of defence workers' skills. I remember the first copies arriving from the printer a few hours before the end of the GLC in 1986. The first half of the book described the situation of defence workers, the second, possible alternatives using existing plant, such as the plans of Lucas Aerospace workers who had actually made prototypes of socially useful products and thereby shown that the concept of arms conversion could be a reality. For the second half of the book I made montages that symbolically acted out this possibility: tanks into tractors, Trident missiles into

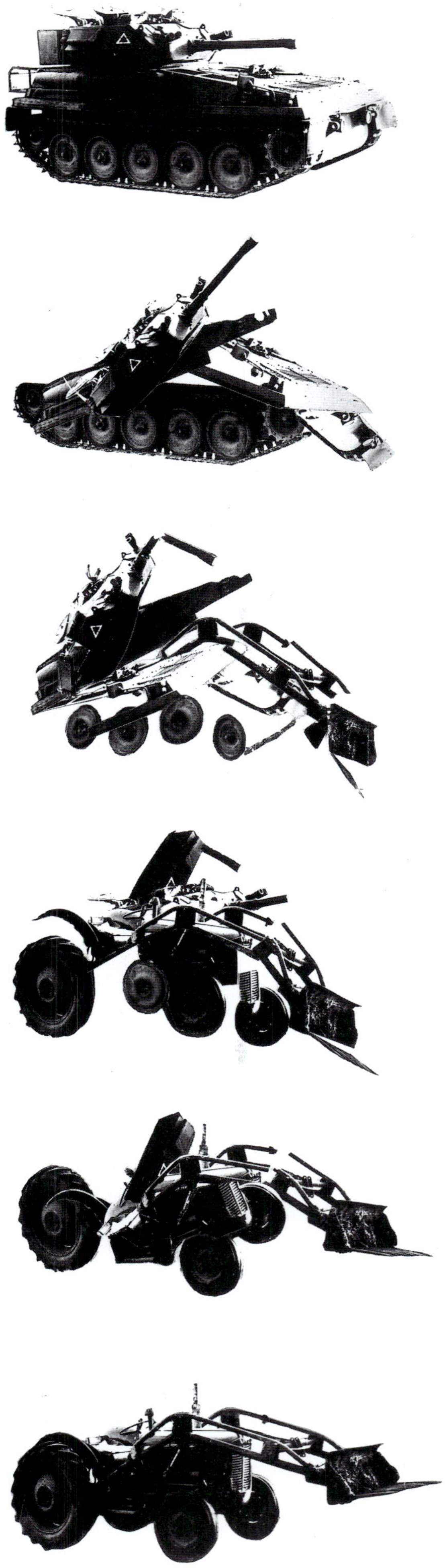

Right
Conversion 1 (Swords into Plowshares)/ 1982/photomontage
First produced for an educational display pack, The Socially Useful Show (CAITS, 1982), explaining the work of the Lucas Aerospace Combined Shop Stewards Committee on the possible conversion of arms industries to peaceful production. It led to many further photomontages on arms conversion

Opposite above left
Jobs for a Change (GLC Economic Policy Group, 1983)/photomontage for book cover

Opposite above right
About Turn (Pluto Press in association with the Greater London Conversion Council, 1986)/photomontage for book cover

Opposite below
Conversion 6 (Trident into Wheat)/1985/ photomontage

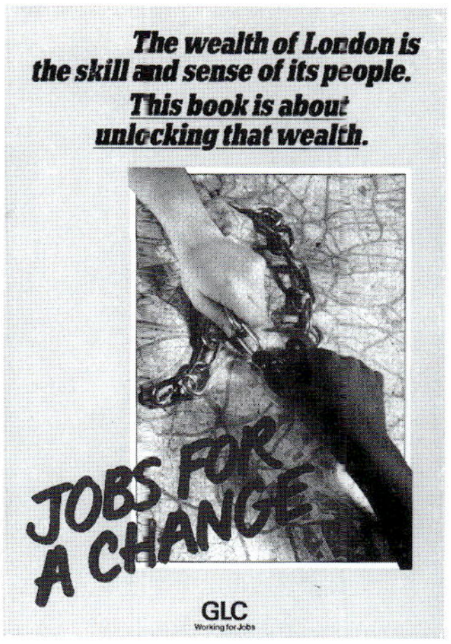
The wealth of London is
the skill and sense of its people.
This book is about
unlocking that wealth.
JOBS FOR
A CHANGE
GLC
Working for Jobs

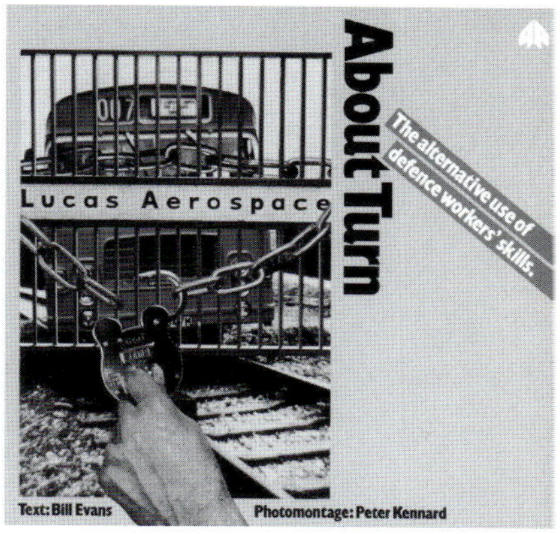
About Turn
The alternative use of
defence workers' skills.
Lucas Aerospace
Text: Bill Evans
Photomontage: Peter Kennard

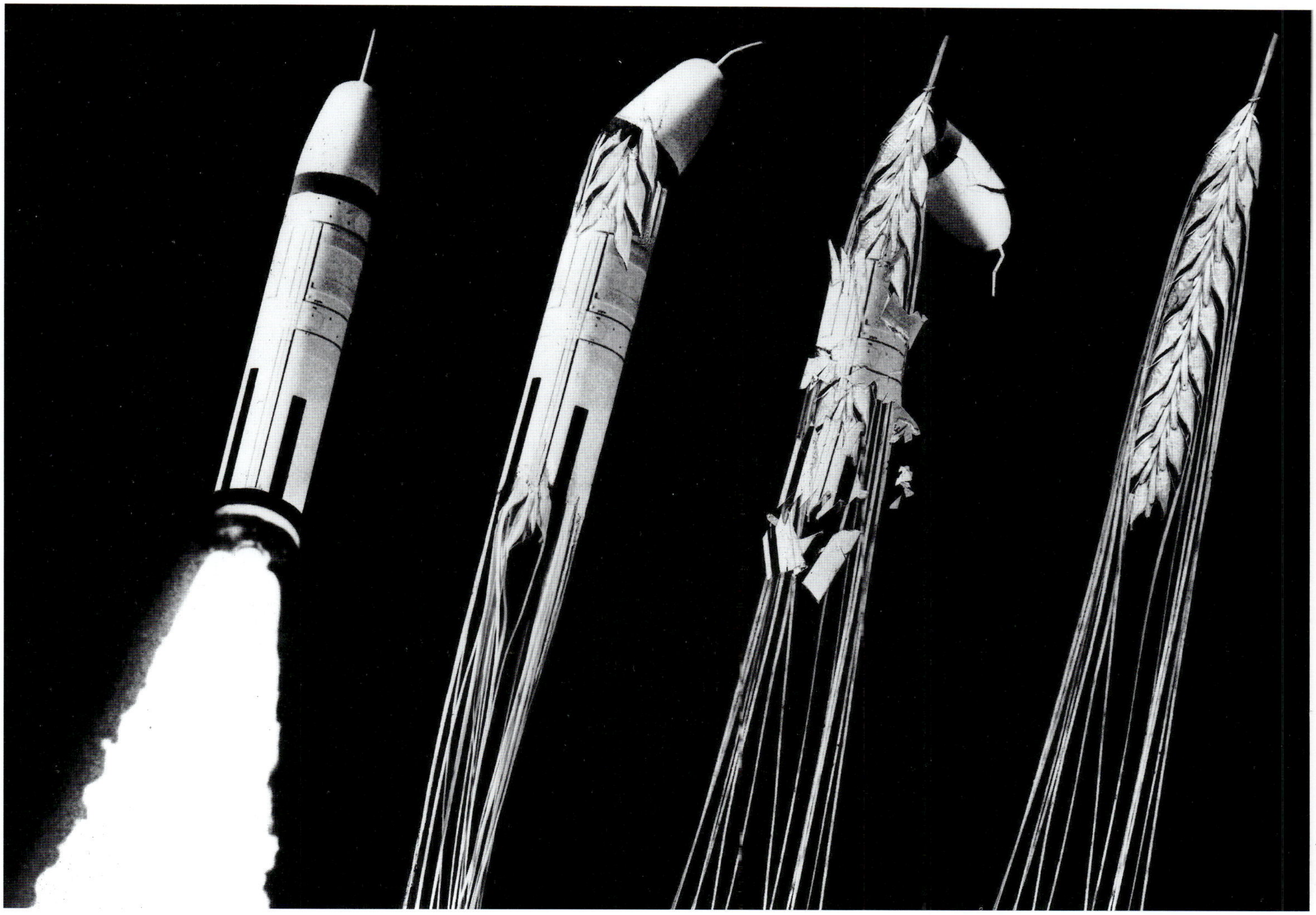

I want to put down urgent subject matter that is not only an image of the event portrayed but an image of the experience of the person in the event portrayed, without formal distortion. To be a go-between-a-news-vendor.

Art and Artists/December 1973

My work is becoming more informal, it spills out into the space. I'm still using montage, I've just increased the number of elements and use real objects rather than their representation in a photograph.

Creative Camera/interview/June–July 1995

corn, bombs into food sacks. Trying through images to make concrete the old dream of swords into ploughshares. These images were influenced by watching my young sons playing with transformer toys in which they grappled for what seemed like hours with transforming one war-like object into another war-like object. At one point I contacted a company that made transformer toys suggesting to them the possibility of making a tank that could be transformed into a tractor. They blanked me out, filed under 'nutter'.

Archive B: Ken Livingstone

I come across a photograph of Ken Livingstone in a pile of old GLC pamphlets. I had met Ken at the GLC and we had stayed friendly, so that on the last day of my exhibition *Welcome to Britain* at the Royal Festival Hall in 1994 I had the idea of inviting him to come back into a building once controlled by the GLC and speak about how he saw the current state of things in the capital. Standing on pallets in the middle of placards, an apparent shipwreck of debris, he appeared to be arguing with the materials around him. He was lit by a portable traffic-light set on red which was an integral part of the installation. His presence changed the work. He became an element in the montage of materials and his speech, which took up questions of homelessness, nailed the installation to specific issues.

For my next solo show, at Gimpel Fils, *Our Financial Times* in 1995, I asked Ken if he would speak again. He agreed to do four separate performances. The exhibition consisted of a number of battered placards stretched out along the gallery, held up by vices on plinths. Four of the plinths were wired for sound and had long wires attached to microphones hanging on nails. On the walls were a number of international newspapers turned to the financial pages, these were being ripped by hands printed and drawn on them. For his performance Ken walked down the length of the gallery talking about the issues of third world debt, the International Monetary Fund and the World Bank. He didn't discuss the work as art or discuss art and politics, he just talked about the issues that the work raised in his mind. He walked around the placards, changing microphones as he went. At the end, he picked up the last placard and carried it outside the gallery. He walked off down the road in the direction of Claridges – a lone demonstrator in Mayfair – still talking into the microphone, relaying his message about third world debt back into the gallery. Many of the people who came to see these events told me that there came a moment for them during his performance when they forgot they were in an art gallery. The jolting of the placards caused by the large number of people moving around the space combined with Ken's powerful words created the atmosphere of a demonstration, albeit in the unusual surroundings of a west end art gallery.

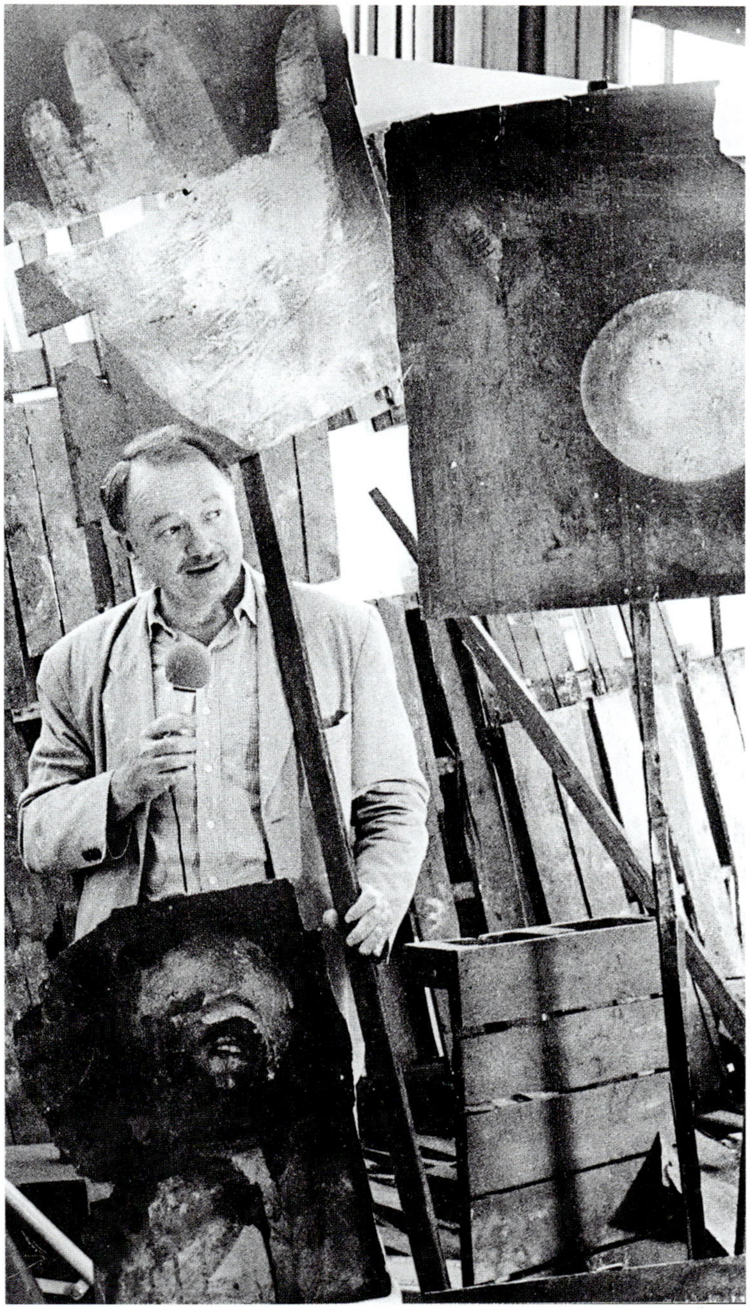

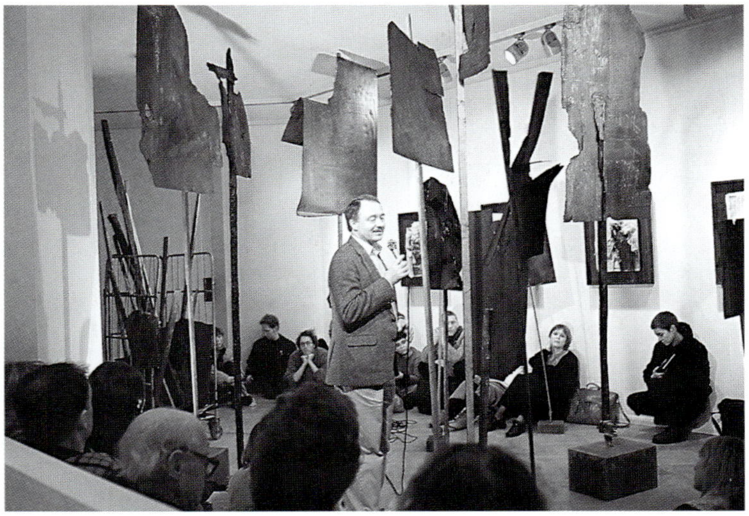

Above
Ken Livingstone performing as part of the installation *Welcome to Britain*, the Royal Festival Hall, London, 1994

Below
Ken Livingstone performing as part of the installation *Our Financial Times*, Gimpel Fils, London, 1995

Ken collaborated with me on a number of exhibitions in London, Liverpool, Cambridge and Folkestone. His performances turned into a debate with the audience and throughout the length of the exhibitions the microphones remained live so that people coming into the gallery could talk into them and their voices would become the voice of the placards.

Archive A: Welcome to Britain
The exhibition at the Royal Festival Hall had begun life at the Towner Art Gallery, Eastbourne where I tried out the idea of extending the installation of pallets. I use the exhibitions as laboratories for developing my work. Archive B – my own space – is not big enough so I use the gallery space in which to experiment. Over the last ten years I have had five solo exhibitions at Gimpel Fils, London, each being an installation. Through the commitment of René Gimpel to my work, I have been able to use a gallery to develop new projects. It also gives me the opportunity to develop new economic terms for selling work in a private gallery. In my 1992 show *Our 999* at Gimpel Fils, each print was on sale for £29.99 or £19.99 for students, OAPs and the unemployed. In 1998 for the group show *Accrochage* also at Gimpel Fils, the price list reads: 'Carl Andre £22,000.00; Art and Language £12,000.00; Jenny Holtzer N.F.S.; Peter Kennard £39.99, OAPs, students and unemployed £29.99, Yves Klein £25,000.00.'

Below
Box/1992/dust, oil, acrylic and photograph on cardboard packing case

Opposite above left
Home News/1992/mixed media
Installation, Towner Art Gallery, Eastbourne

Opposite above right
Home News/1992/mixed media (detail)
Installation, Towner Art Gallery, Eastbourne as part of solo show *Welcome to Britain*,1992

Opposite below
Our 999/1972–92/30 dyeline prints (edition of 500)
Installation, Gimpel Fils, London, 1992. The price of prints, with a reduction for OAPs, students and unemployed, was shown prominently on the wall. The exhibition went back over 20 years work to take stock of the new political situation since the destruction of the Berlin Wall in 1989

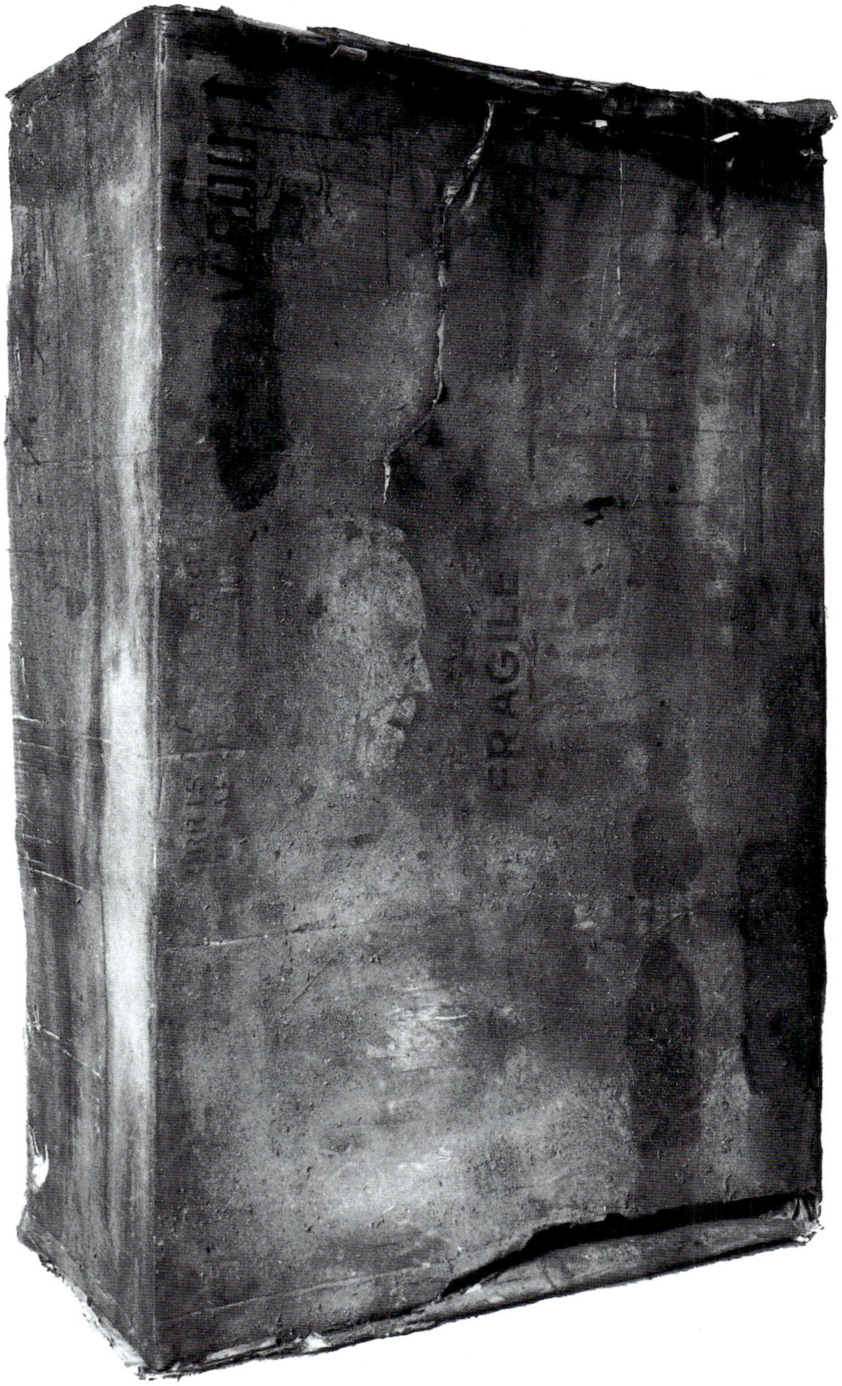

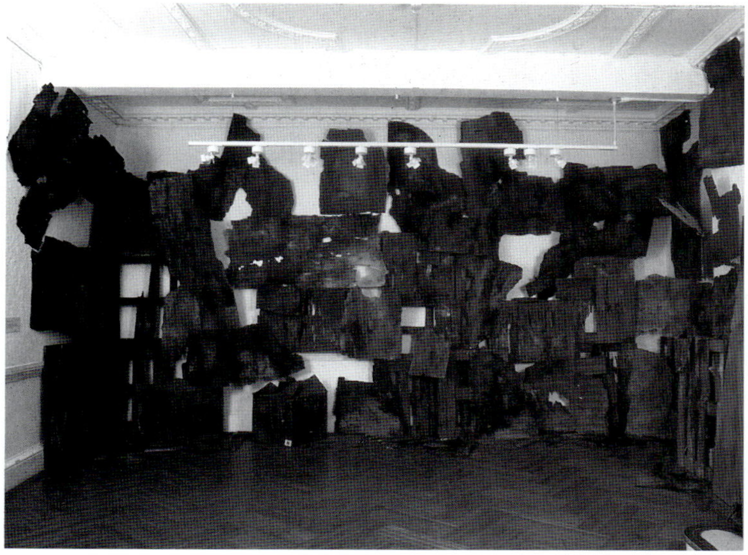

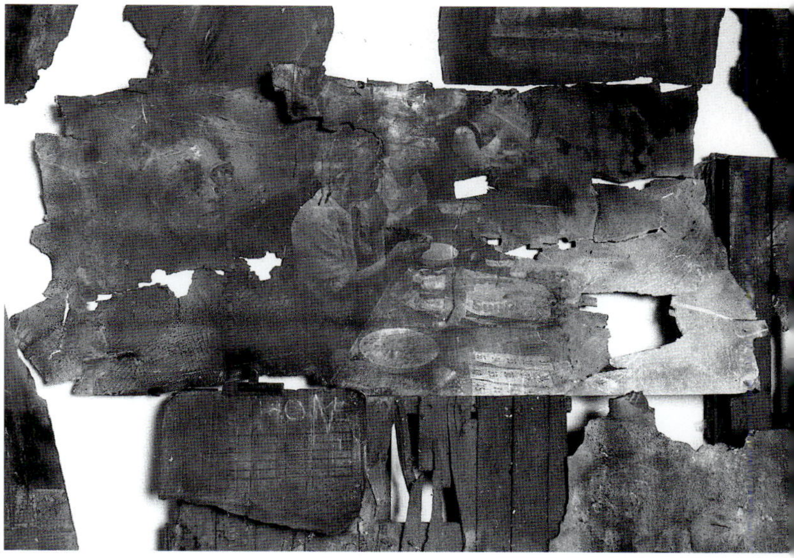

Gimpel Fils is unusual. The primacy of commercial interests is usually a central consideration for private gallery owners. Recently I showed my current work to a gallery owner in New York with whom I had had dealings in the past. He took one quick look at the work and delivered a homily on the fact that America was experiencing an economic boom and that his collectors would be put off if his gallery showed work critical of the free market.

The Towner show was the result of the Cross Channel Photographic Mission (CCPM) commissioning photographers to record the changes that the Channel Tunnel would bring to Europe. My work tried to show what the French would find when they came to the light at the end of the tunnel. Because of this commission I managed to get the work in a much expanded form into the Royal Festival Hall. A very public space where the location became a key element in the installation's narrative meaning. I wanted to put a version of what was outside the Festival Hall inside. One of the most awful contradictions I'd become aware of at that time was that when I went to get my culture on the South Bank I had to manœuvre my way round scores of homeless people of all ages who were trying to survive living on the concrete of the South Bank. To feast my eyes on the art at the Hayward Gallery I had to avert my eyes, look away, on the journey to its entrance.

The poet, Peter Reading, who I greatly admired, had written a long poem, *Perduta Gente*, which explored homelessness in relation to the celebration of culture on the South Bank. I invited Peter to collaborate on this show and we printed up a number of pages from the poem on placards and interspersed them throughout the installation. In this way the usual use of the placard as a site to demand change became instead a site of poetic description of the surrounding debris. We also recorded Peter standing on a traffic island in Newington Green, north London, reading his poem amidst the sound of traffic and police sirens. The recording played during the course of the exhibition through headphones. *Welcome to Britain* had only been allowed to be shown in the Festival Hall because it was part of the CCPM initiative. The management were deeply unhappy with what they perceived to be a load of old rotting wood. They demanded that it was cordoned off with rope to deter potential arsonists! They were further dismayed when it was reported in the *Guardian* that mice had taken up residence in the installation and dishes of rodent poison became another unforeseen element in the piece.

Through the efforts of Shân Maclennan, a very committed education officer at the Festival Hall, Peter and I were able to work together for a week with people who had lived on the streets in the area and now attended a day centre at St Botolph's church, Aldgate, in the east end of London. We were provided with a large working

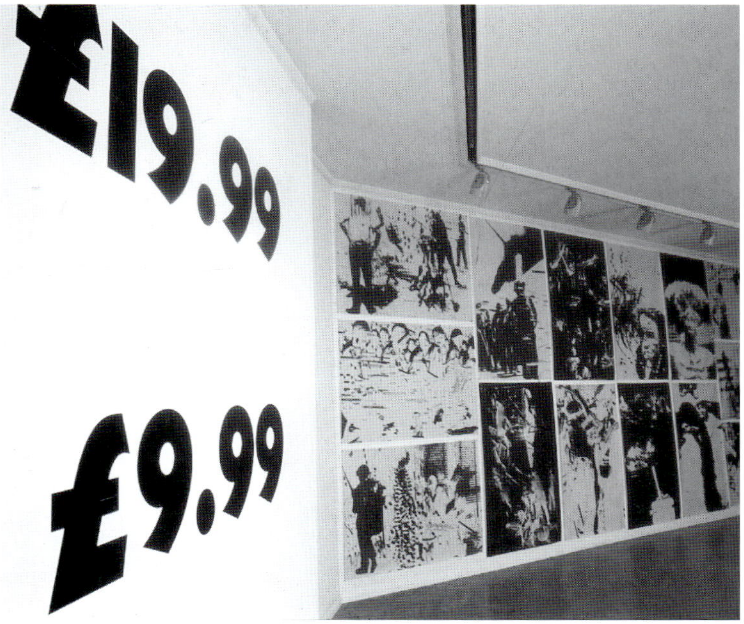

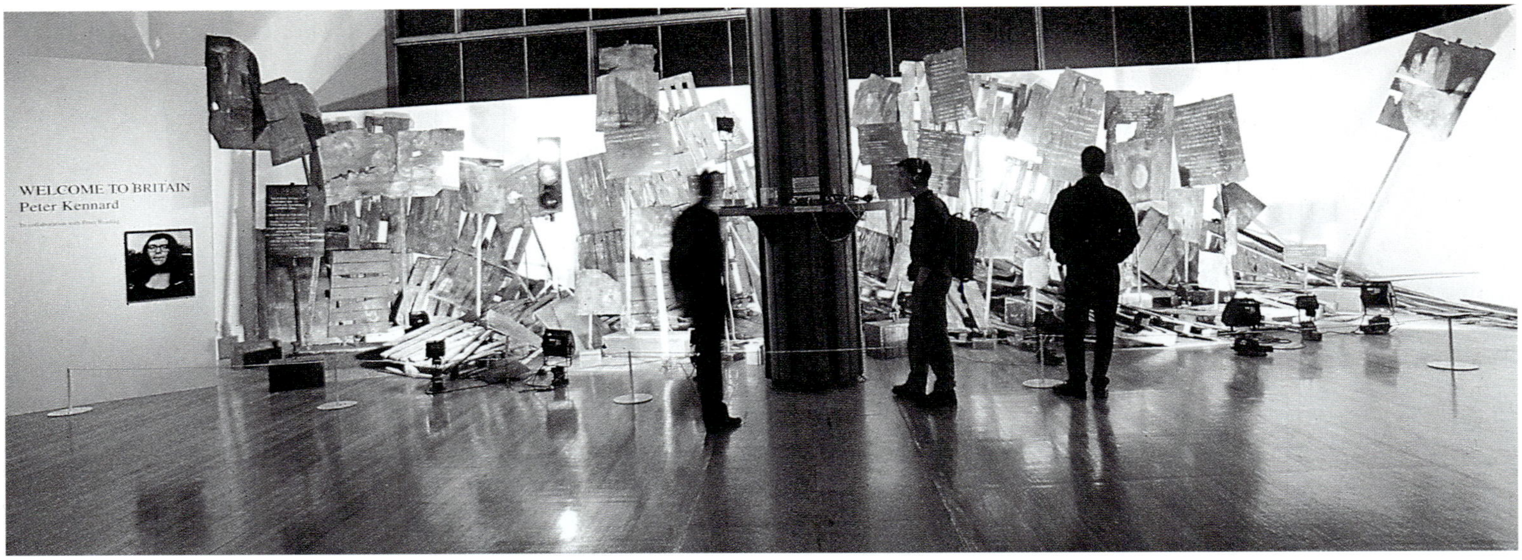

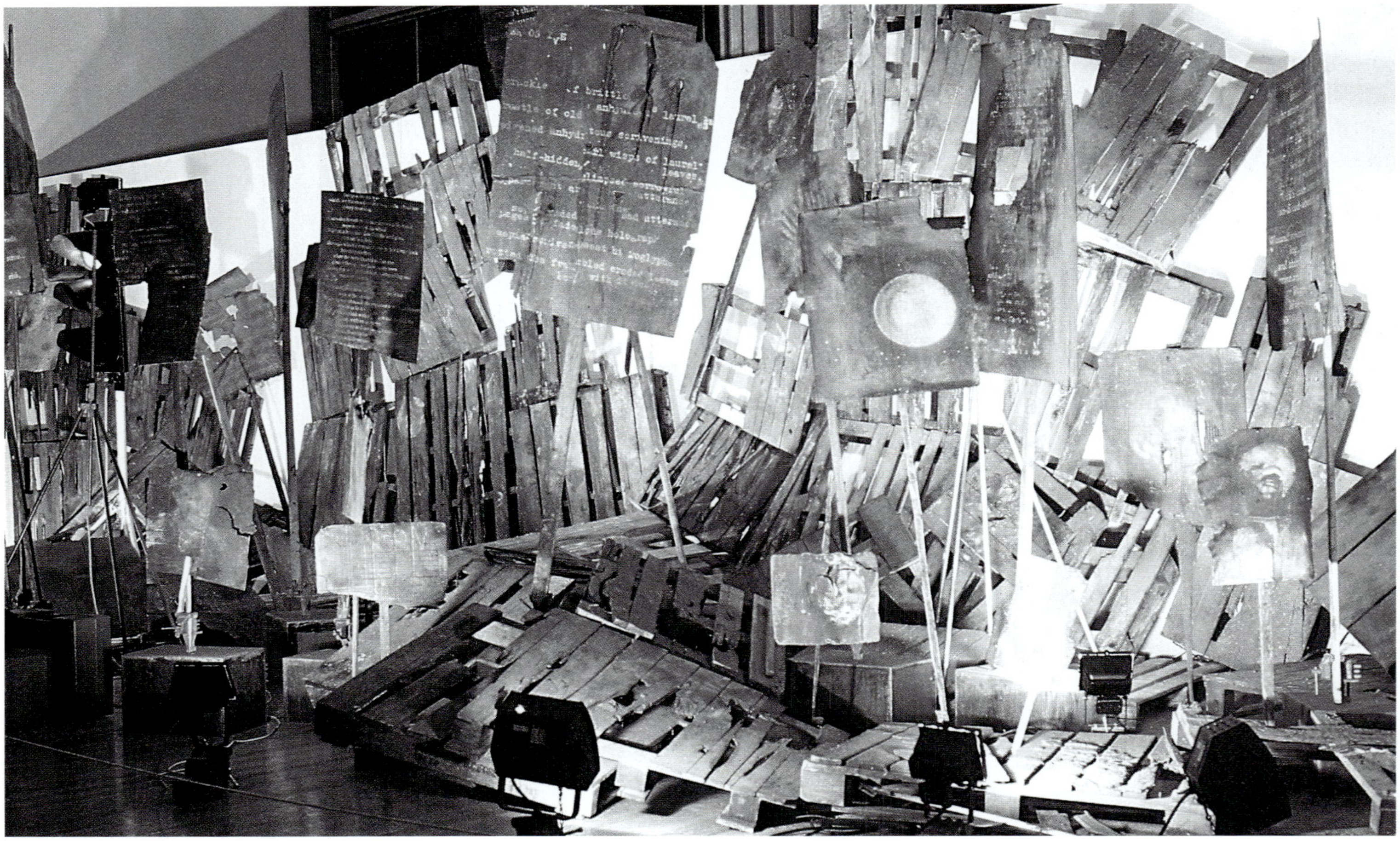

Above and centre
Welcome to Britain/1995/mixed media
Installation, the Royal Festival Hall, London

Right
A vote being taken by participants of the *Welcome to Britain* workshop held in the Royal Festival Hall, 1995, concerning the cover design of *Voice of the Unheard*

Far right
Voice of the Unheard/1995/photocopy

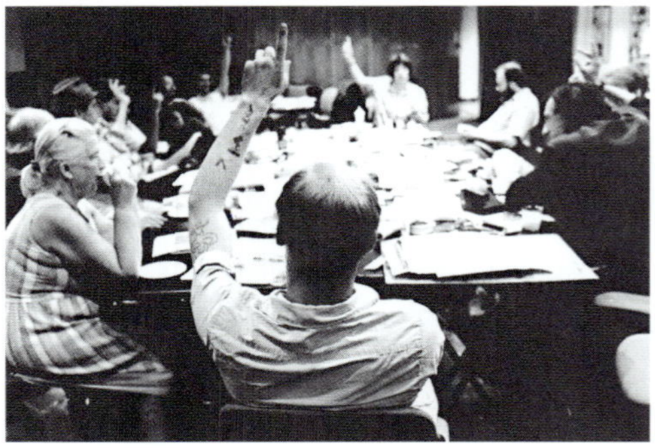

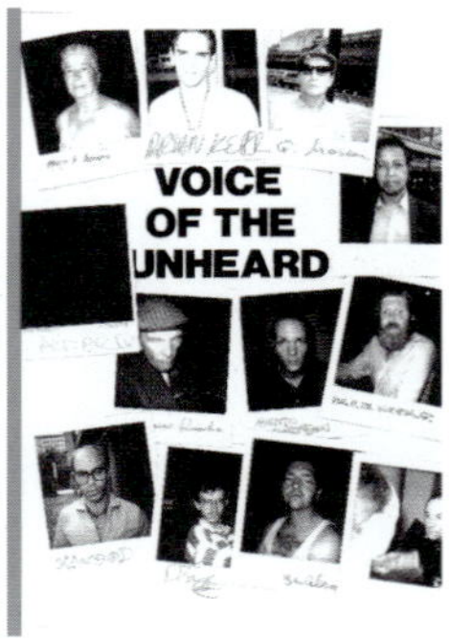

My work has not become part of the art system even though I show in galleries. It crosses categories. It can be seen as illustration; it works in newspapers; it is sculptural installation. To many people it appears not to be art at all. And a bloody good thing too. I like the sense that it can't be catalogued; that I'm a nebulous figure who turns up in funny places.

Creative Camera/interview/June–July 1995

space and the people who came to work with us were provided with free meals and materials. They produced extraordinary work in a variety of media and a photocopied book of all their work was produced at the end of the week. They, as the authors, decided to call it *Voice of the Unheard*. It opened with a prose piece by Abdul Hye, which began: 'Somebody of no home is homeless. This talk is not all that easy. The bit of cloth what he had has completely finished because of his rolling against the floor in the tube station, railway station and so on...'

Archive A: Workshops

I always try to hold practical workshops when I have exhibitions in public galleries, often with young people who have had difficult lives. I try and work towards a group production that becomes a photocopied book that people can take away. The workshops start with stacks of magazines and newspapers from which people clip images and headlines and gradually begin to make work about their experiences. Most people say they can't do art, that they've never done it since school, but through cutting, pasting, tearing, ripping, drawing and photocopying, the mystique surrounding art can break down very quickly. People surprise themselves with what they can produce. Images seen for years in a set order in a newspaper or magazine are ripped from their context and can suddenly become elements that can be used to document their own lives. Drawing from their own experiences, those who don't have the money to participate in consumerism, can subvert the intended messages of advertisements. The hierarchy of image production is broken down and the images are used as a language with which to answer back. The excitement generated in practical workshops can be exhilarating, as people who are robbed of any creative outlet have the opportunity to use the media of everyday life to begin to tell their own stories.

Archive A: Teaching

A blue file thick with material about education surfaces from the pile. The first piece of paper is a West Surrey College of Art and Design memo, my favourite from 20 years as a part-time lecturer in various art schools. I think it exemplifies the way in which the managerial culture of Thatcherism tried to take over the art schools but often collapsed in desperation as it came into conflict with the natural messiness and exuberance of a creative art college. I think of it as a found poem and quote it in full:

> QUALITY TARGETS NO 3 DMG
> ITEM
> Litter, throughout the Department
> TARGET OBJECTIVE
> 100% of all litter removed on day of deposition (litter to include drinks cans, plastic cups, miscellaneous unwanted work, unwanted furniture, etc)
> MONITORED
> All staff
> TARGET COMMENCEMENT
> Immediate from formal announcement
> DELIVERED BY
> All staff
> All students
> REVIEWED WHEN
> Weekly
> REVIEWED BY
> DMG

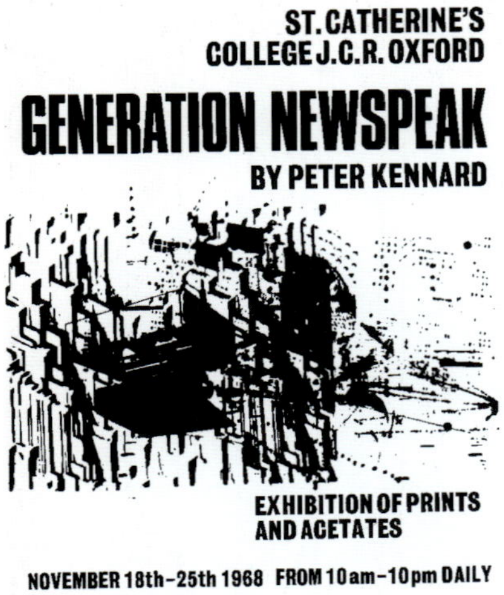

I was lucky as my first experience as an art student was at the Byam Shaw School of Art. Its principal was Maurice de Sausmarez who was one of the most inspiring teachers I have known. When talking about a student's work he never fixated on a particular bit of painting and discussed whether green should be red. He attempted to get to the underlying idea – the why of one's work. He was never prescriptive. He gave amazing lectures on Friday afternoons at the college which still reverberate in my mind. I can remember one, where he played Stravinsky's *Rite of Spring* on a gramophone while showing slides of Picasso's cubist paintings from that period. He made connections across disciplines, totally believing in the importance of art for the creation of a humane society.

I began teaching part-time in 1979 and have taught in a number of colleges up to the present. I am currently teaching at the Royal College of Art and the Byam Shaw. Teaching has been my main source of income, allowing me to make the work I choose to make. I made the choice to teach rather than use photomontage in the commercial world. I tried it a few times, making adverts under the guidance (*sic*) of an art director but the conflict of interests left a bad taste in my mouth. I found it very difficult to put less effort into an advert than my own work and though the money was good, to what ends? I was using the same skills that I had developed to expose advertising to make advertising. I couldn't stomach it. I also found that teaching could be incredibly involving and energising in relation to my own work. While I was working at West Surrey College from 1990–1995 the course director was Peter Hall who had developed, out of what often seemed insuperable odds (lack of funding, lack of management support), a really vibrant course. Lecturers coming from very different areas within photography worked as a team and encouraged a vast number of students from very different backgrounds to produce outstanding work.

You can't legislate for inspiring educationalists like Maurice and Peter, but you can learn by their example, which I've tried to do. I now work as a tutor at the Royal College of Art on the photography course where, as a team, we try to encourage work across the vast area that goes under the umbrella term 'photography'. I also work part-time at the Byam Shaw which is a continuing link to my own beginnings.

To me, art schools are vital places in society. They are valves that open up an endless flow of ideas. As well as producing artists, they create a space where those that can't or won't fit in society can develop their thoughts and work out their relationship to the world. The more the colleges become institutionalised and run on grid-like lines the less they are able to be responsive to student's needs. I was lucky to get a grant through my years at college and my student life was much easier than that of students today, many of whom

Above
Generation Newspeak/1968/photo-lithograph
Poster for first solo exhibition, St Catherine's College, Oxford, 1968

Opposite
Generation Newspeak 3/1968/printers ink on acetate with glass and wood (destroyed)
Work for exhibition that was made while a student at Slade School of Art, London

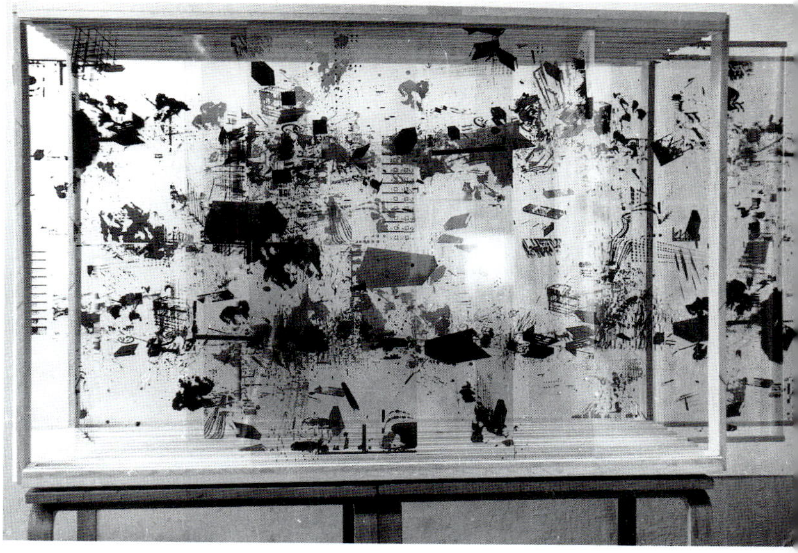

have to work their way through college and struggle to get materials to make work. It becomes more and more difficult for working-class students to go to college and for this New Labour should be ashamed.

I well remember a weird meeting at West Surrey College when an educational consultant was brought in to explain to us the new modular system that was going to be introduced to the art school. As the acetates built up on the overhead projector, with what appeared to be thousands of arrows indicating pathways and avenues, my mind went back to those unlegislated moments in my own art education, maybe in a nearby cafe or a studio, where some alchemy happened which felt like real knowledge was being imparted. Something you'd never be able to find amongst the cost-cutting arrows and terminologies of bureaucracy.

My father went to art school for a year after the war, but because my grandmother was widowed, he had to leave and find a job in order to support her and his sister. Then as now there were no grants. He went into commercial art and though he never said it to me directly, I think he never got over the curtailing of his art education. After retirement he started many evening classes in art and then aborted them through being too self-critical. In a sense, this over-developed critical faculty, which he turned on the work of others as well as himself, was a reaction to never having had the opportunity to make his own work in his youth. I think it also explains why my brother Christopher and I are both slightly obsessive workaholics. I remember when I was in my teens painting away in the larder while he was down the other end of the passage dissecting dog fish. He is now Professor of Clinical Neurology at Imperial College, London. I always felt my father was constricted by his job, first as a typographer and later when his eyesight worsened as a machine minder in a repro department in an advertising agency. If he'd finished art school his life might have been different.

This background has reinforced my belief in the importance of art schools. I believe that whatever their shortcomings, both ideologically and in terms of funding, they should be defended against all encroachments. I still find it a great feeling when a student, after grappling with their work for some time, suddenly comes through with something that really speaks, something that is rooted both in their personal experience and in their understanding of art. I've also worked in art therapy and taught in evening classes and in each place there comes that moment when the hand produces what the mind cannot explain. It's a tragedy that art has been downgraded in the national curriculum although it came as something of a surprise to find that my work was cited in a Department of Education and Science document the *National Curriculum in Art for ages 5–14*. It states: 'explore the techniques

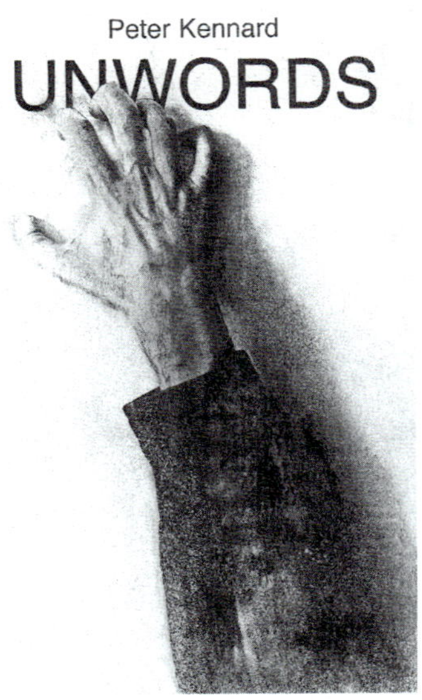

Left
Unwords (Bluecoat, 1996)
Book cover

Centre
Unwords 24/1996/carbon toner, charcoal and pastel on paper
The sequence of images in *Unwords* which begins with text from the Universal Declaration of Human Rights has, by *Unwords 24*, been overtaken by the prices on the Futures market

Below
Unwords 27/1996/carbon toner, charcoal and pastel on paper
By *Unwords 27* the hand turns to face us, its palm imprinted with both stock market prices and resolutions from the United Nations

Opposite above
A United Nations security guard at the solo exhibition *Images for Disarmament*, United Nations Palais des Nations, Geneva, 1989

Opposite below
Newspaper 2/1995/carbon toner, charcoal and pastel on newspaper

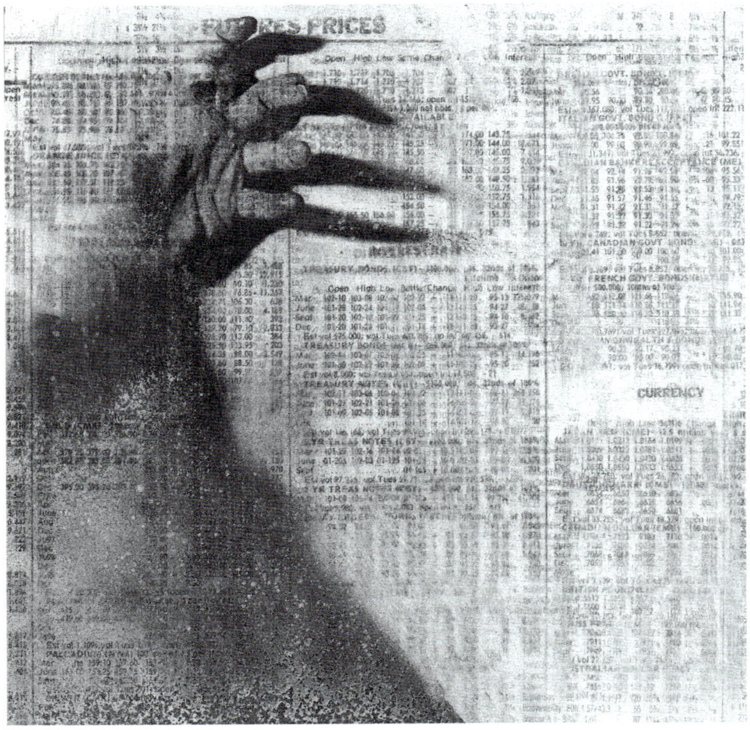

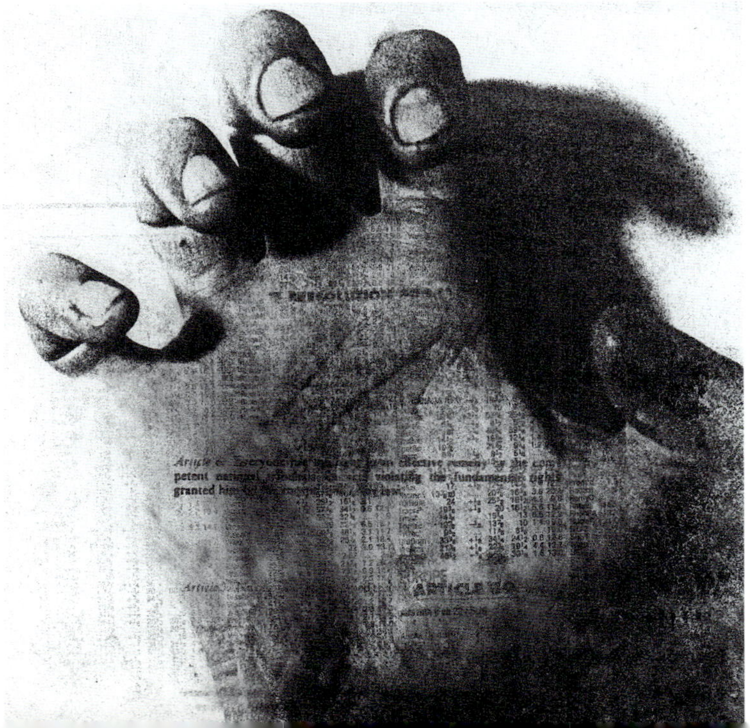

of photomontage on the theme of "Protest". Refer to artists such as Alexander Rodchenko, John Heartfield, George Grosz and Peter Kennard to inform this work' (Welsh Office, August 1991).

Archive A: UN to Unwords
Some copies of *Unwords* come to the top of the pile. In 1989 I was invited to show my exhibition *Images for Disarmament* at the United Nations Headquarters in the Palais des Nations, Geneva. The invitation had come from the UN Staff Movement for Disarmament, a group of United Nations' workers who were trying to put pressure on the UN to fight for nuclear disarmament. The work was shown in the main hall of the UN building and numerous delegations passed through the area enabling me to debate, through interpreters, with an international audience. The exhibition culminated in an international conference at which I spoke on issues concerning art and disarmament. The conference was daunting, in that, every time I cleared my throat and mumbled a few ill-chosen words, it was simultaneously translated into nine languages. But it developed into a debate on the role of culture as a public force and the idea of the artist as witness. Because the audience were mainly politicians and diplomats, their response was ambiguous. They were aware of the potential of art to deal with big issues but I felt that they were also fearful of what they rightly

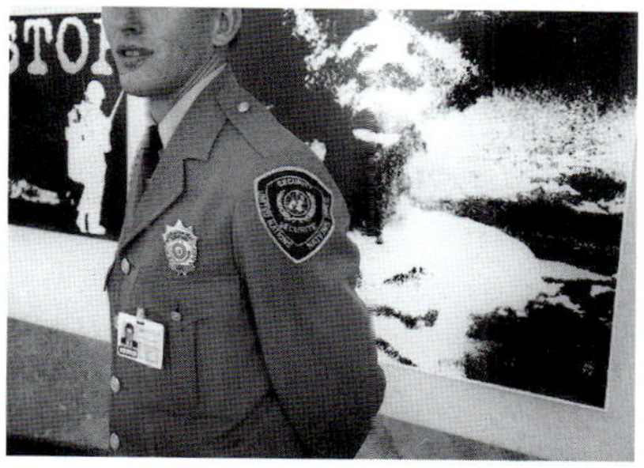

perceived to be their inability to control it. Artists and writers continue to be silenced, locked up and tortured all over the world because of their work, and that fact must inform any debate on the role of art in the international arena.

The UN and its role in the international community continues to influence my work. I have made a great deal of work concerning the distance between the language of the UN and the reality of actual events. Work that questions whether barbarism can be addressed in any way by the aspirations expressed in the UN declarations on democracy and freedom, or conversely, if their words are simply empty rhetoric entirely determined by the imperatives of price indexes and market reports. In 1996 I made a book, *Unwords*, and a touring exhibition of the same name which began at the Bluecoat Gallery, Liverpool. In the book, the struggle for human rights, exemplified in the United Nations Declaration of Human Rights, leads into the resolutions of the UN Security Council on the former Yugoslavia and finally becomes buried in the numbers of the *Wall Street Journal* financial pages. In the book I refer to four events which happened during the period of its creation and try to connect them. It begins with the UN celebrating 50 years of the UN Charter, then goes on to the fall of the UN 'safe area' of Srebrenica, where thousands were massacred. It continues with the execution, by the Nigerian government, of Ken Saro-Wiwa for campaigning against the destruction of Ogoni land by Shell Oil. It ends in December 1995 with Wei Jingsheng, a Chinese pro-democracy activist being jailed after a show trial and the fact that a few days later a large US trade delegation arrived in China eager to do business.

I later made a set of large photo-drawings on paper, *Resolutions*, that showed the horrors perpetuated in former Yugoslavia. The images were overlaid with words taken from the hundreds of UN Security Council resolutions on Yugoslavia which were made between 1991 and 1995. The images of what actually happened reveal the uselessness of the words. This conflict between weasel words from the UN and from politicians, added to the continuous flow of market reports and the growing power of multinational corporations, fuels the anger which is at the root of all my work. The language of human aspirations has been debased, grabbed by the powerful and spat out over the people it pretends to protect. Hence *Unwords*.

The hands in *Unwords*, *Our Financial Times* and *Domesday Book*, try to grab something back, to resist and tear at these words and numbers. The hand has become a key image for me in portraying the essence of this struggle. I think the hand also represents my own relationship to the possibility of making images. The paper becomes torn up in a frenzy. I tear at the paper in frustration at the impossibility of being able to show through images what's really

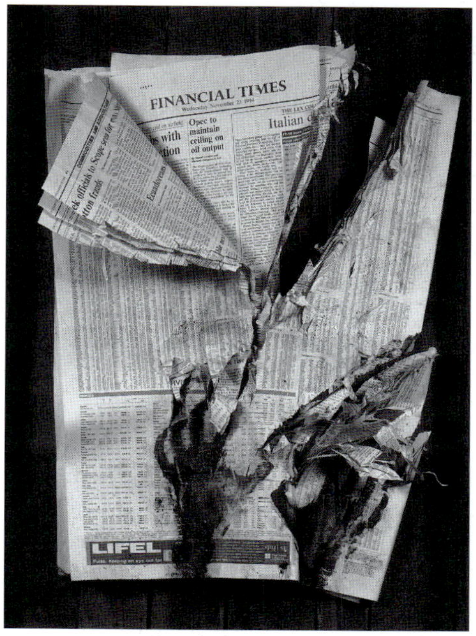

My work attempts to rip apart the smooth, apparently seamless surface of official deceit to expose the conflict underneath.

Images for the End of the Century/1990

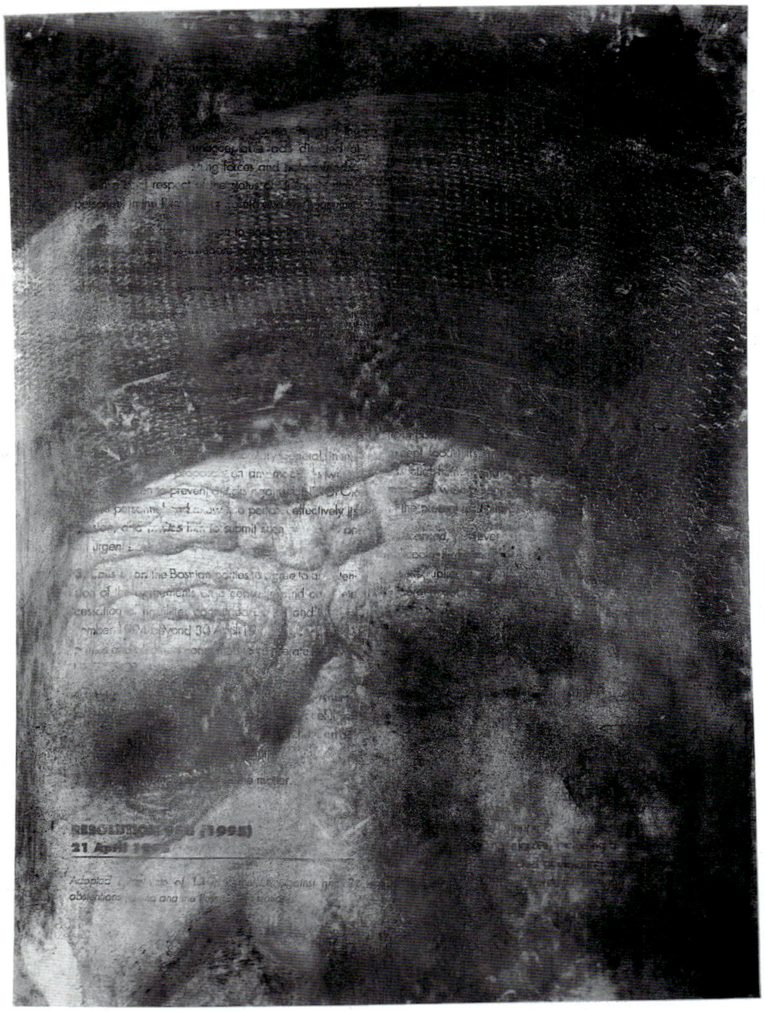

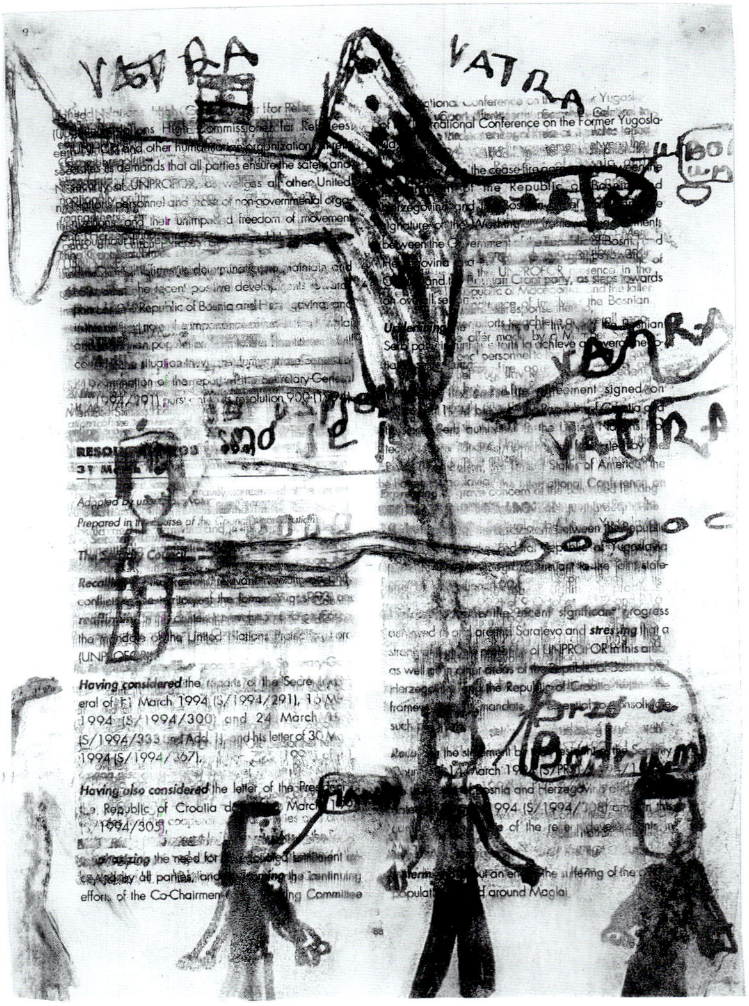

Above left
Resolutions 3/1995/carbon toner, charcoal and pastel on paper

Above right
Resolutions 8/1995/carbon toner, charcoal and pastel on paper

Opposite above
Keep London Out of the Killing Ground/1984
GLC poster on 80 sites in London during 1984

Opposite below
Tory Tax Squeeze/1996
Poster for the inception of the Labour Party general election campaign used on many sites in Britain

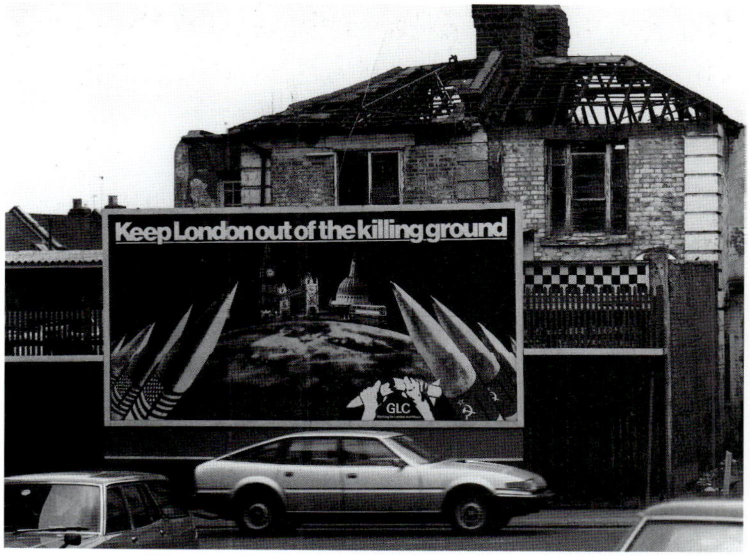

happening. I use photos of my own hands as that seems more honest, but through drawing over them with charcoal and toner they come to represent the hands of others, white or black. They tear at newspapers, UN reports and corporate messages in a fury. They tear at the intractibility of the wall of words and numbers. The shape of the tears becomes the image, the action becomes the montage. The physical assault on the page is my way of answering back.

Between Archive A and Archive B: 15 February 2000
It's four in the afternoon. Over the last few months memories have been caught in moments and written down when the imperatives of the present haven't demanded my time. Now I'm walking from Archive A to Archive B, down Balls Pond Road, over Kingsland Road. The everyday, the streets I know so well are soaked in correspondences. My memory has been switched on. Arrested moments are flashing up into my consciousness. It begins to rain. I go and sit in a cafe and write this. I've just passed a broken-down wall in Balls Pond Road and immediately it's as if I'm back eleven years to 1989. I was doing a lot of photomontages for the *Guardian* at the time and on Friday 9 November 1989, as the Berlin wall began to be dismantled, I suggested that I did a montage for Monday's paper. It had to be done by Sunday at 2pm. I got some prints of the Berlin wall from the *Guardian* picture files. As yet there were no photos of the wall actually coming down so I went to Balls Pond Road and photographed the end of a collapsing wall. I montaged the photo of the wall onto a photo of the Berlin wall and Jenny Matthews took photographs of us shaking hands. On Monday 12 November 1989 *Germany Shakes* was published in the *Guardian*.

As the rain comes down I look out of the window at the hoardings and I remember the few times my own work became posters on hoardings on the street, and also the hoardings and adverts I refused. The time an advertising agency saw my work in a magazine and invited me along to a meeting to discuss a campaign. I went into the conference room and spread out all over the table were images of gleaming missiles. It turned out that they had seen my anti-nuclear work, decided I must be a hired hand, and thought I might like to work on a campaign for one of their clients, an arms manufacturer. I made my excuses and left.

A man comes into the cafe with a young boy who must be his son. They look wet and bedraggled and must have decided to take shelter from the rain. I am reminded of the times when, as a child, I used to walk to Paddington library on Saturday afternoons with my father. We went almost every week as he was a great reader. We often went into a cafe on the way to break the journey. The library used to have a row of lecterns at the far end with a selection of that day's papers on display. The lecterns were made of heavy

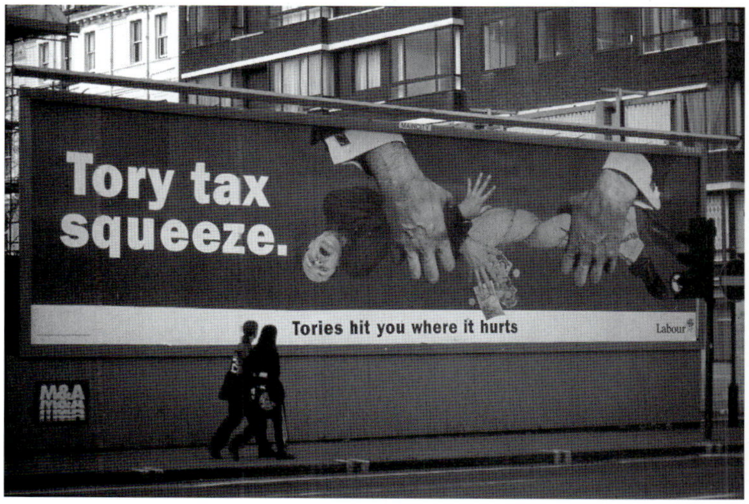

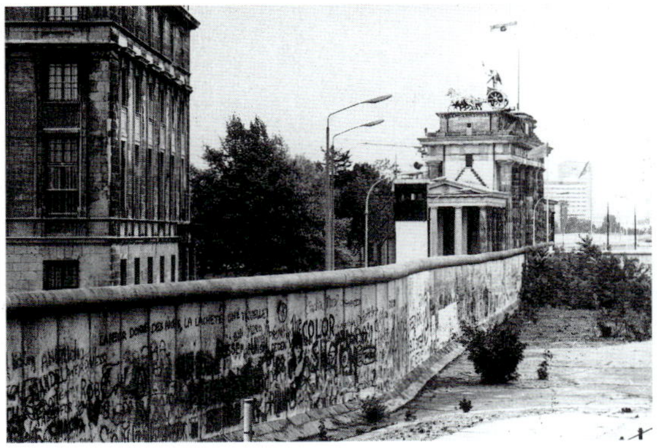

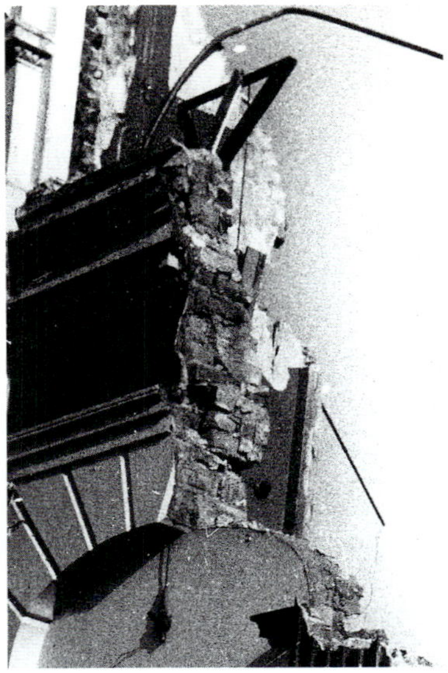

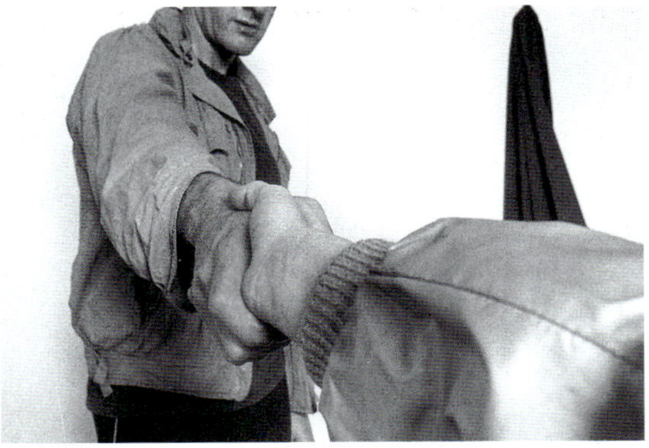

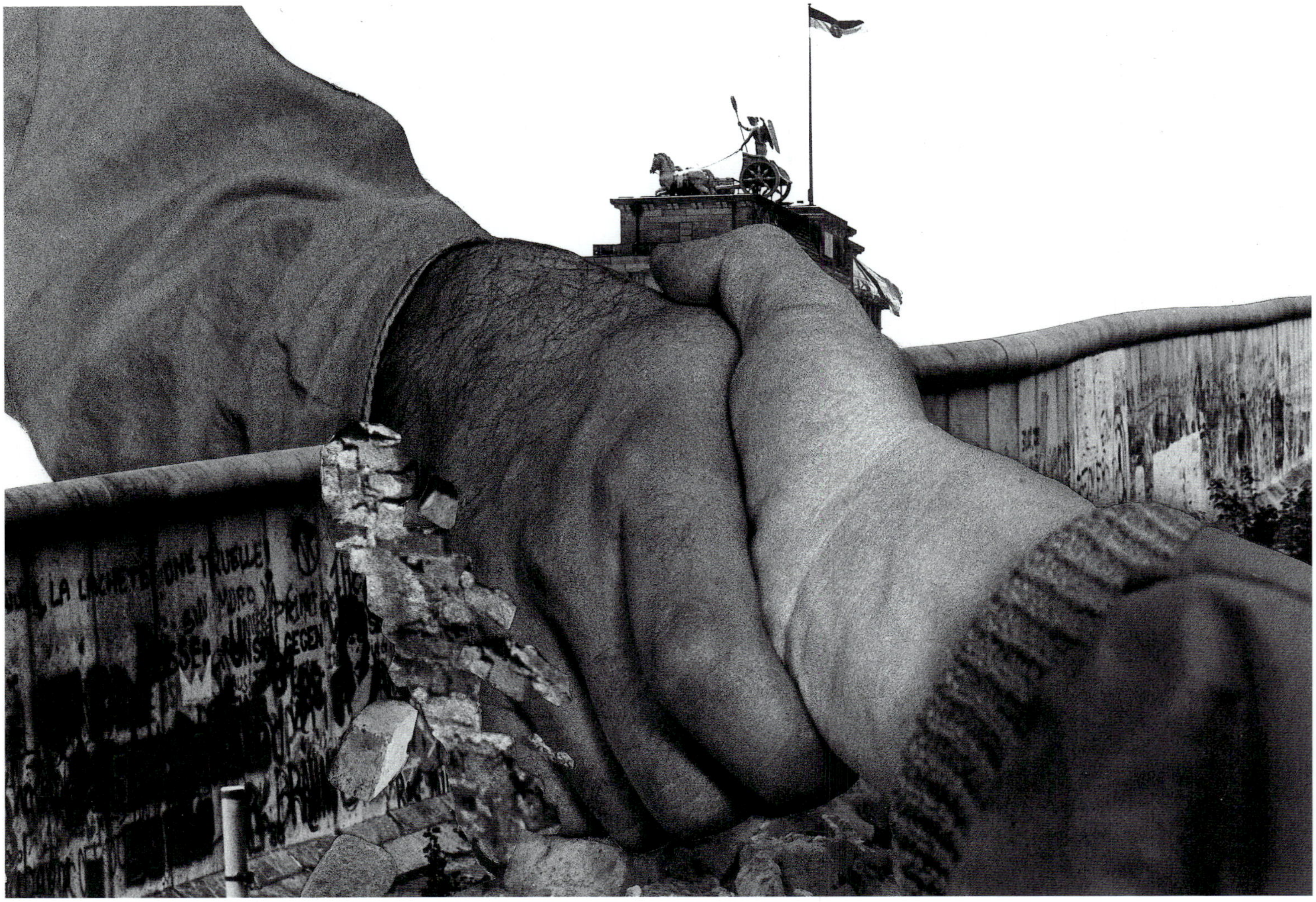

Above left
Photograph of the Berlin Wall (date unknown)

Above middle
Photograph taken in Balls Pond Road, London, 1989 for *Germany Shakes*

Above right
Photograph taken for *Germany Shakes*, 1989

Centre
Germany Shakes/1989/photomontage

Opposite
The Guardian/12 November 1989

My photomontages are constructed to show that events are not as natural and inexorable as they often appear to be in photographs, but the result of a set of choices and decisions. They aim to subject photographic images to human criticism.

Image for the End of the Century/1990

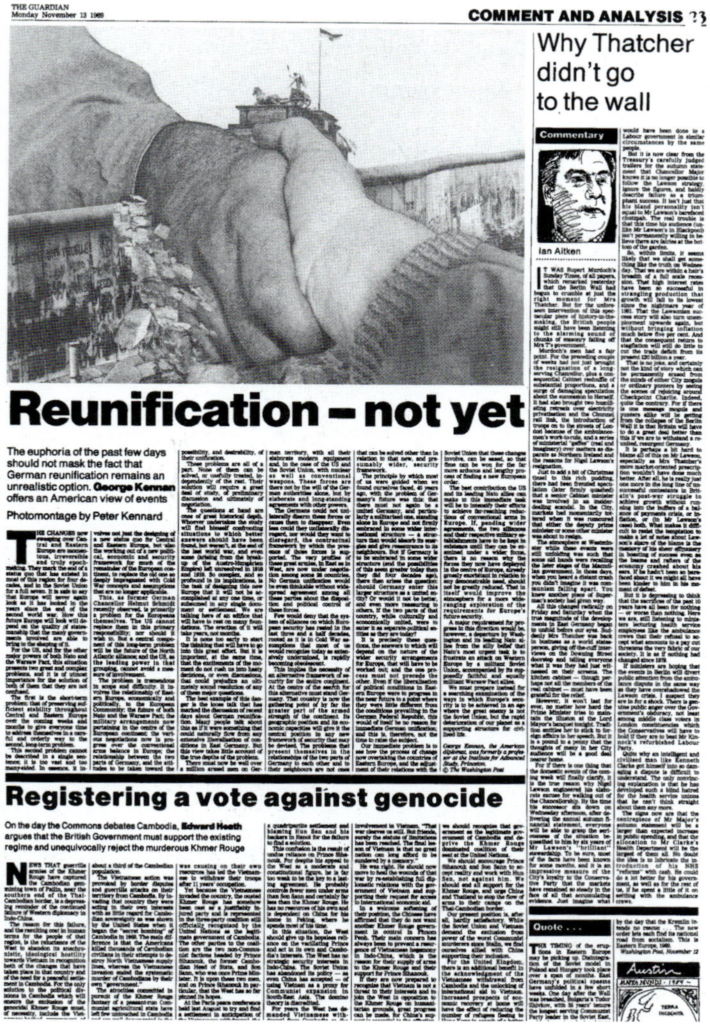

polished wood and gave the newspapers a weight and importance I found strange and fascinating. There was often a man, sitting near the lecterns, who wrote obsessively across sheets of paper which he kept in bundles in plastic bags. He would jump up from his table and go to a lectern, underline a sentence or a word in the newspaper, and go back to his tabmle and write. It was as if he was developing some private code based on that day's news. I never saw anyone interrupt his fearsome concentration. Today I connect those Saturdays in the library with my own obsessions with newspapers, originally by using their space for the reproduction of my photo-montages and, more recently, by trying to find a way to merge a drawn and photocopied image with the page of a newspaper, so that the very texture of the image is infused with the grit and grime of newsprint. This resulted, in 1997, in my installation *Reading Room*, in which 21 lecterns made with the help of Sylvie Borel and Peter Longfellow filled a dark space lit only by the lights attached to each lectern. On the lecterns are the financial pages of newspapers from many different countries. I add faces onto the pages. All their eyes stare back. The faces are based on photos that I have taken in London or Jenny Matthews has taken from around the world. To make them I found a way to photocopy the images of the faces directly onto the newspaper leaving the photocopy unfixed. Then I rub, scratch and draw with charcoal directly onto it, so that the

Newspapers (Reading Room)/1996–97/ carbon toner, charcoal and pastel on newspaper

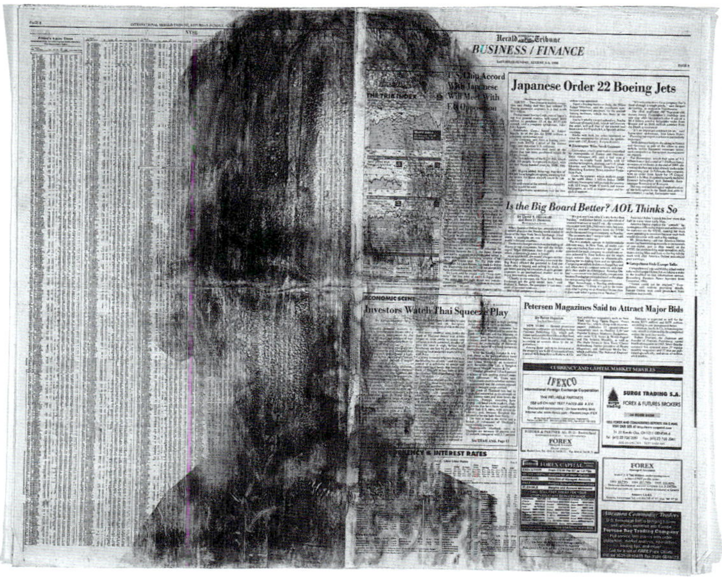

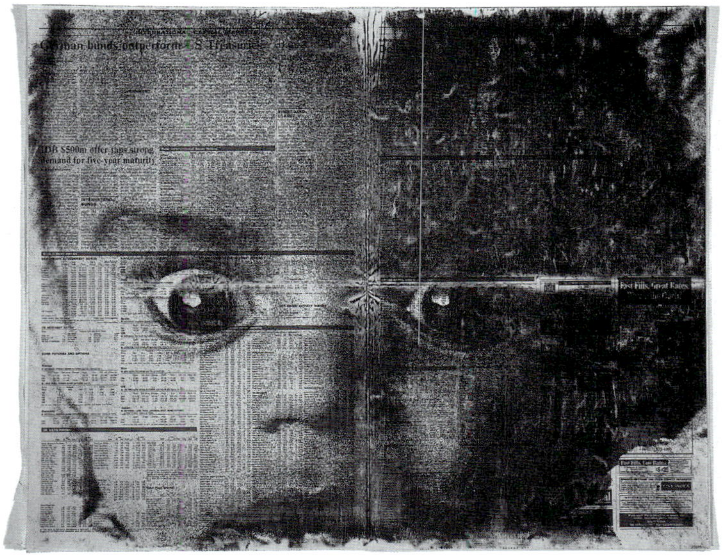

photograph and the drawing become totally locked together and seamless. I try to connect the expressiveness of the hand-made mark to the material fact of the photo. The images of the faces are injured, smeared and blurred, dissolving in the grain of charcoal and unfixed toner. They appear to emanate from the actual substance of the newspaper. The faces contradict the bland columns of numbers from the market reports on which they are overlaid. These numbers become like tiny pieces of shrapnel piercing their skin. But the faces continue to stare back and implicate us as we stare at them.

I've also used this method of making images in *Unwords* and in *Resolutions*. In all this work I've tried to develop the physicality of the image through the connection of the photographic and the autographic mark. I've tried to move away from the flat photographic print, to get under the surface, and through bonding the photograph with the drawing, produce an image which appears to be disintegrating into the shards of charcoal and carbon that have formed it. In *Reading Room* I want you to feel the dirt of the image on your hands, like ink coming off today's paper.

Sitting here in the cafe, the memory of images flash connections I'd never imagined. As if the thousands of images I've put together have become one. From the paintings of faces dissolving into

I think all the stuff I do is pretty accessible. It tries to give voice to those who are increasingly marginalised and silent. It's not art about art, it's art about the world. It's trying to bring the outside in – the world into the gallery.

Creative Camera/interview/June–July 1995

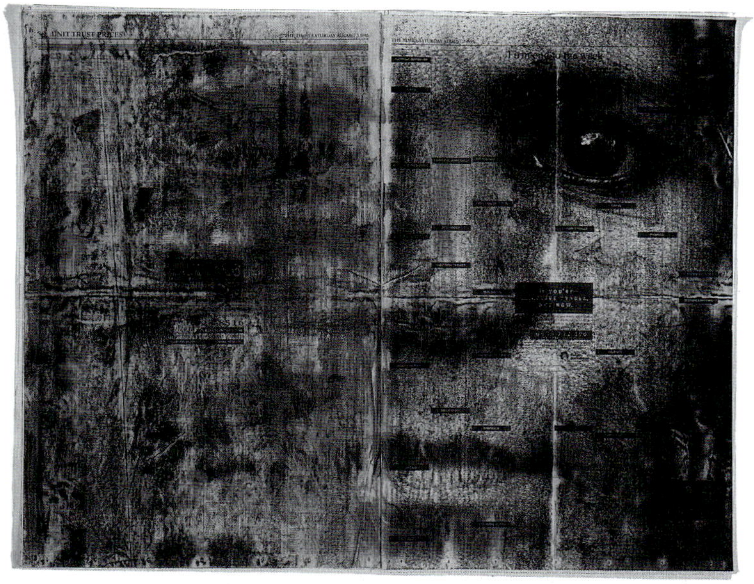

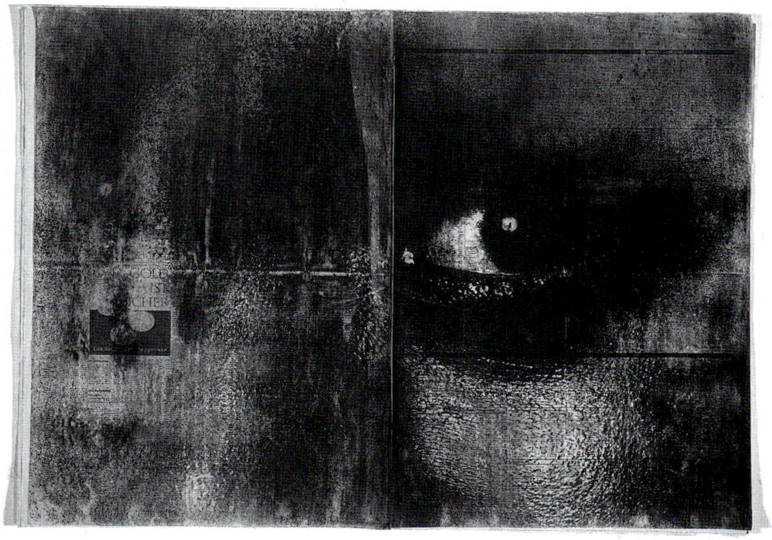

crosses, through to the faces on the pages dissolving into stock market numbers. It's the fluidity that connects it all. Each image that I have made is just a minute attempt to halt the flow for that precise moment. Stop the flux. Pin something down and pummel it into some sort of sense. To give a reason. To show a reason for what happens. To break into fragments what appears inexorable. To ground the grip of oppression to its roots and thereby show human causation. To house the fragments in a project for that time ... this time. Mark out a moment in history as a moment of becoming ... a moment that can change. Turn pictures inside out into their opposite. Make still images, heavy with their own history, join into a new configuration, a new history. A history of another possibility. Dismantle the screen, or maybe just scratch, tear, cut or scumble its logos. An action against ... a demolition contractor ... an image brickie ...

The stuff piles up. There is nowhere else for it to go. The images flash by, temporarily confined in a pamphlet, poster, catalogue, book, and then reconfigured into another form to be put out again. They circulate and then come back to the pits, retuned they go out again. Their effect cannot be measured and is not worth worrying about. I do. I work with others, knowing we can only dent the surface of things together. Alone we slide down the smooth corporate surfaces, unable to gain a foothold on their stranglehold.

The problem is to make the invisible visible. It is increasingly necessary for artists to ring visual alarm bells.

Images for the End of the Century/1990

Below
Reading Room/1996–97/carbon toner, charcoal and pastel on newspaper with wood and metal
Installation, Gimpel Fils, London, 1997

Opposite
Skin 6/1999/silver print

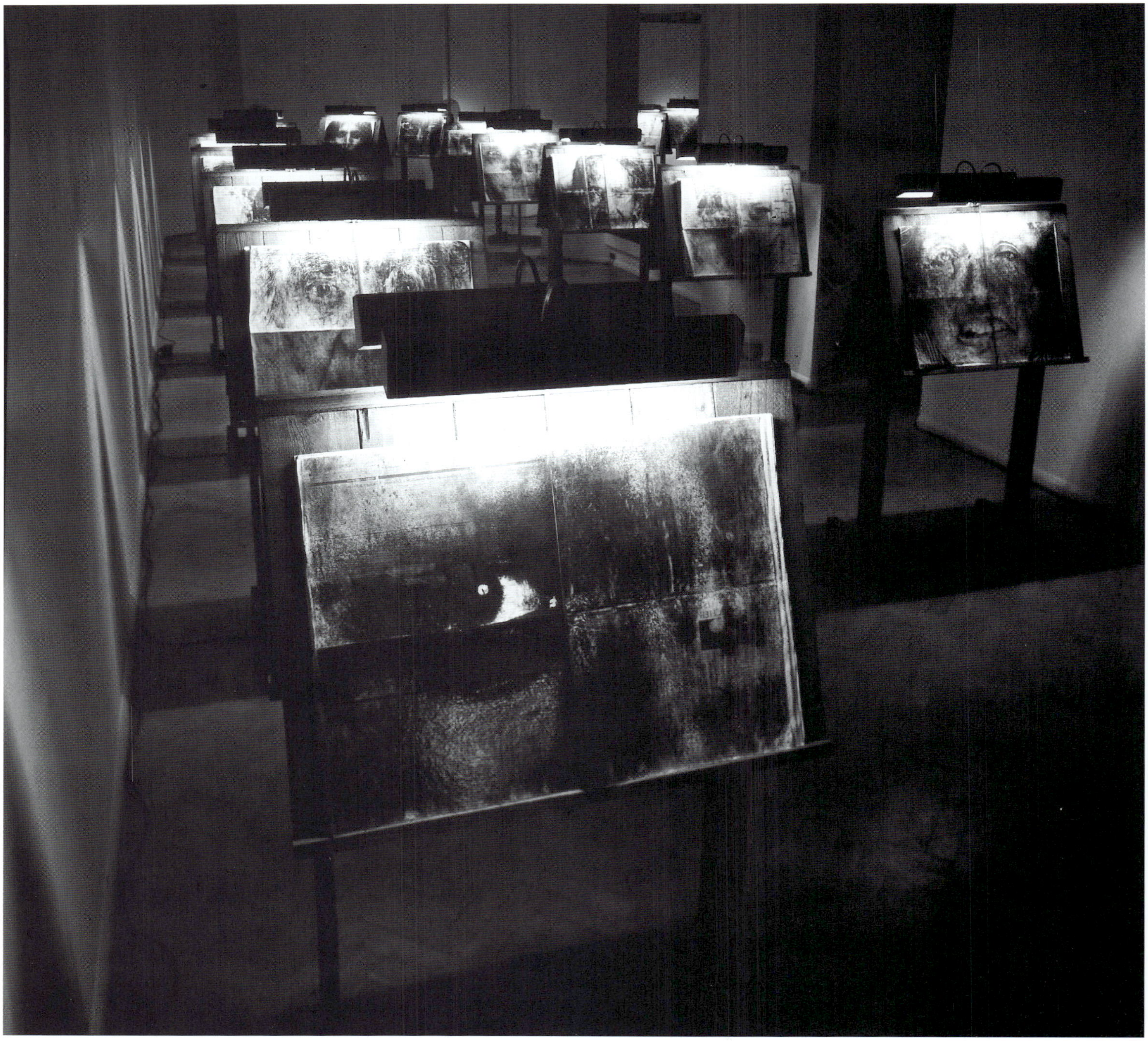

Our world contains terrible equations. A fraction of the billions of dollars spent annually on weapons equals the cost of alleviating infant mortality in the developing world. The single click of a camera shutter cannot picture this connection, cannot equate the one with the other. But two clicks can be brought together to create a third meaning.

Images for the End of the Century/1990

The stuff piles up. And now after having put a probe into the flow and taken some readings, I have made some connections and reached no conclusions. When I make an image of a current event, a war, a struggle for human rights, I walk back into the past, keeping my eyes fixed on the present, imagining a possible future. The closing prices are the only international news that appear everywhere whatever the local headlines. Their numbers crawl like tanks over skin. They appear unstoppable, but in Tiananmen Square a student stopped a column of tanks by standing in front of them ...

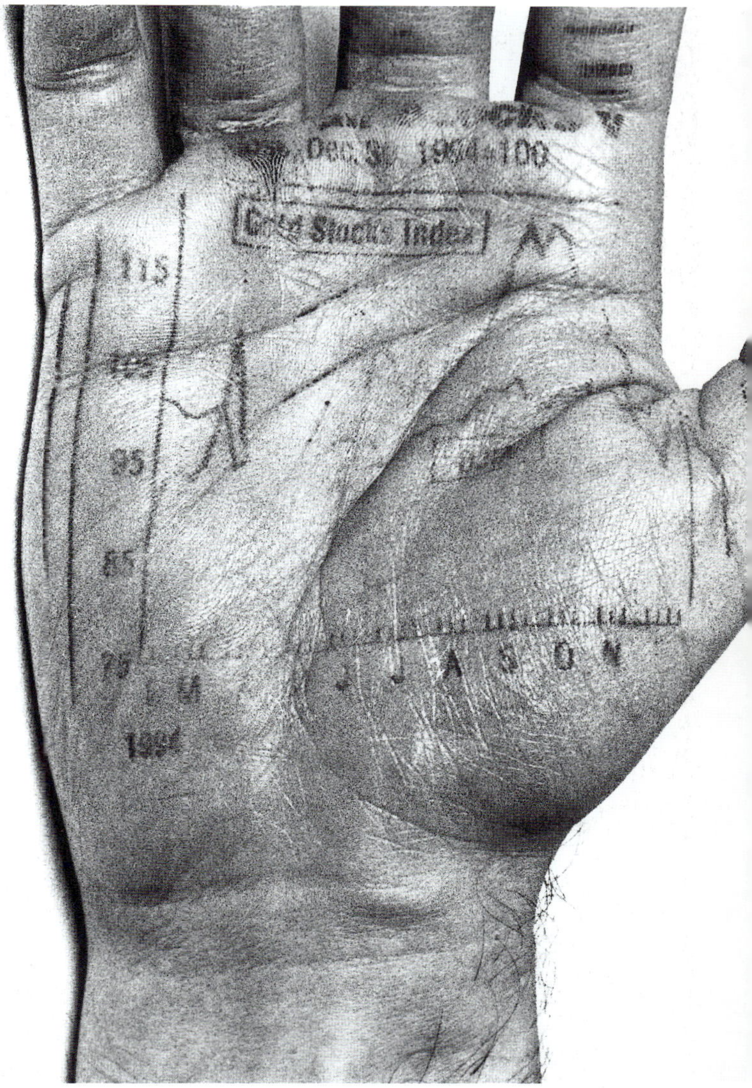

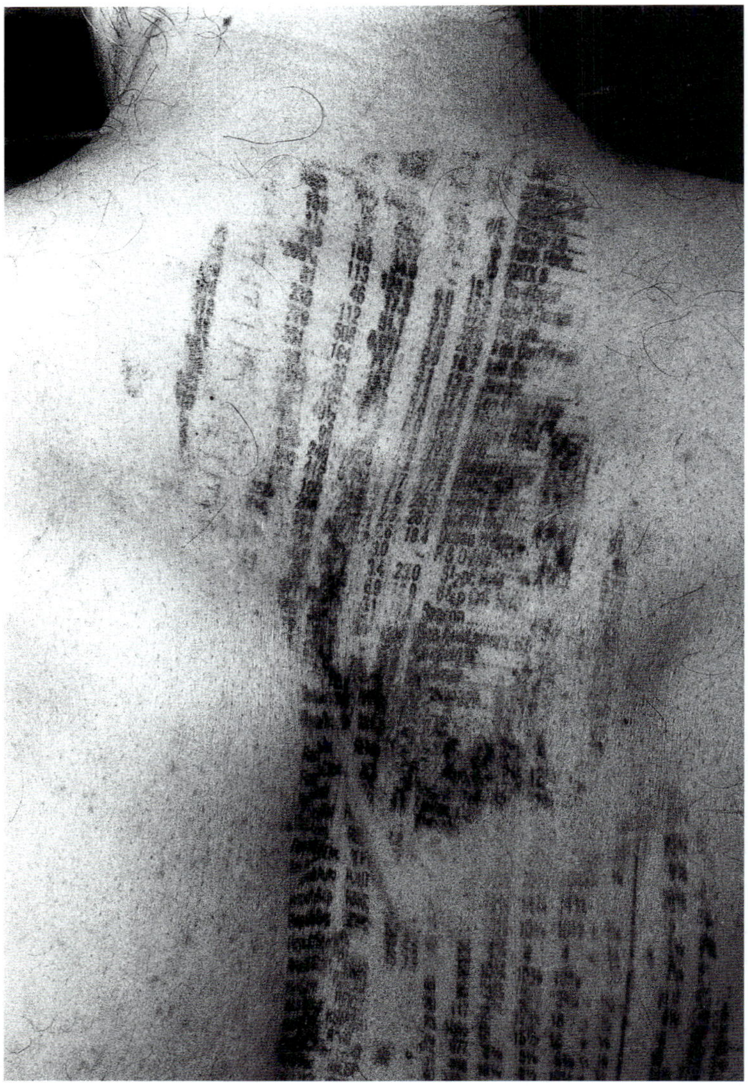

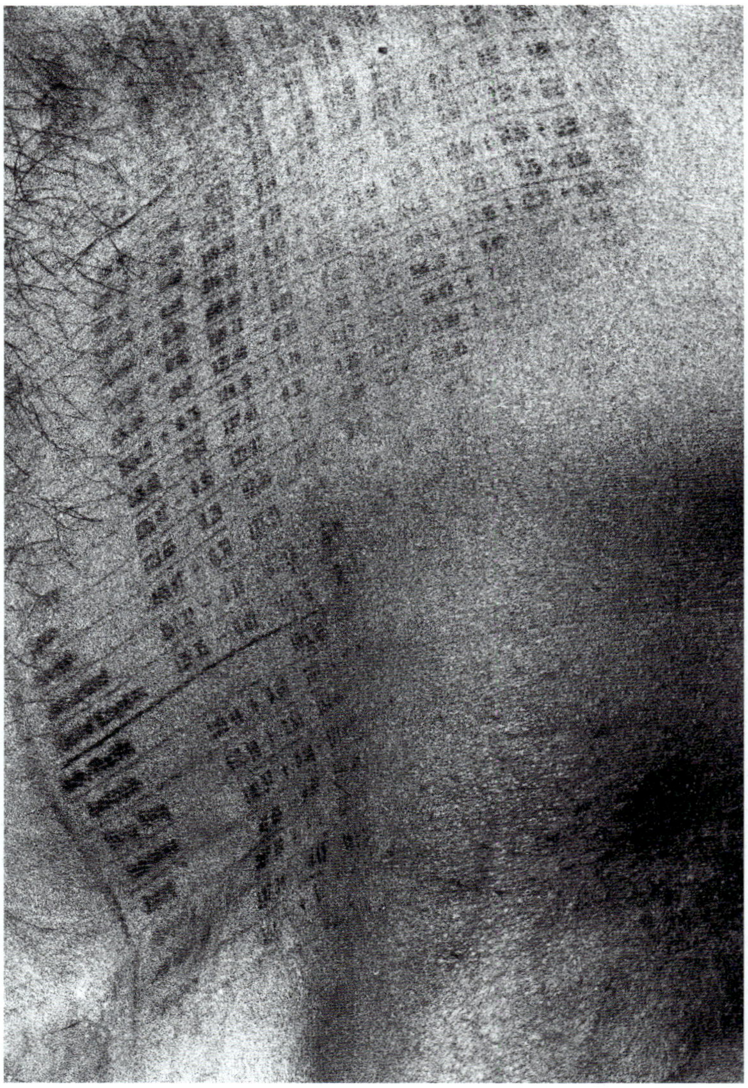

Left
Skin 1/1999/silver print

Right
Skin 10/1999/silver print

Opposite
Skin 15/1999/silver print

Chronology of work

Selected solo exhibitions

1968 *Generation Newspeak Phase 1* St Catherine's College, Oxford
1970 *Generation Newspeak Phase 2* Zees Arts, London
News You Missed Institute of Contemporary Arts, London
1971 *Printevents* (artist in residence) Gardner Arts Centre, Sussex University
1973 *Photomontages* Photographic Study Centre, University of Southampton
1977 *Values* Institute of Contemporay Arts, London
1978 *A Document on Chile* Half Moon Gallery, London (touring)
1980 *No Nuclear Weapons* Camerawork, London (touring)
1981 *Images for Disarmament* Institute of Contemporary Art, London; Arnolfini Gallery, Bristol
1982–3 *Dispatches from an Unofficial War Artist* County Hall, London; Museum of Modern Art, Oxford; Southampton City Art Gallery
1984 *Data 1984* The Pit, Barbican Centre, London (touring UK and Germany)
1985 *Peter Kennard: Images Against War 1965–85* The Pit, Barbican Centre, London
1987 *In a Right State* Aspex Gallery, Portsmouth; Camerawork, London; Bluecoat Gallery, Liverpool
1989 *Images for Disarmament: Photomontages for Peace* United Nations, Palais des Nations, Geneva
1990 *Images for the End of the Century* (installation) Gimpel Fils, London
Images for the End of the Century (photomontages) Imperial War Museum, London; Fruitmarket Gallery, Edinburgh
1992 *Break up – Eastern Europe* Laing Gallery, Newcastle-upon-Tyne
Stop: Paintings and Photomontages 1973–1991 Kent Gallery, New York
Our 999 Gimpel Fils Gallery, London
Welcome to Britain Towner Art Gallery, Eastbourne
Out of Order Zone Gallery, Newcastle-upon-Tyne
1994 *Welcome to Britain* Royal Festival Hall, London
1995 *Our Financial Times* with Ken Livingstone MP Gimpel Fils, London
Welcome to Britain Sassoon Gallery, Folkestone
From an Abandoned Alley Cambridge Darkroom
1996 *Unwords* Bluecoat Gallery, Liverpool; Mead Gallery, Warwick Arts Centre, Coventry; Gateway Galleries, Old St Chad's; Rowley's House Museum, Shrewsbury
1997 *Photomontages – a 20 year retrospective* Zelda Cheatle Gallery, London
Reading Room Gimpel Fils, London; Edinburgh College of Art
Home Dazed and Confused Gallery, London
Unwords Millais Gallery, Southampton Institute
1999 *Domesday* Gimpel Fils, London
2000 *Reading Room* Royal College of Art, London

Selected group exhibitions

1985–8 *Whitechapel Open* Whitechapel Art Gallery, London
1986 *Art Meets Science* Smith's Gallery, Covent Garden, London
1989 *Through the Looking Glass: Photographic Art in Britain 1945–89* Barbican Art Gallery, London
Invention d'un Art Pompidou Centre, Paris
1991 *Shocks to the System* Royal Festival Hall, London (touring)
Photomontage Now Manchester City Art Gallery
Come and See Kufa Gallery, London
1992 *The Cutting Edge* Barbican Art Gallery, London
1993 *Do You Speak English?* International Artists' Centre, Poznan, Poland
1994 *Where is Home?* Kent Gallery, New York
1995 *No More Hiroshimas* Phœnix Gallery, Brighton
Pretext: Heteronyms Clink Street Studios, London
Foto Biennale Enschede Rijksmuseum Twenthe, Holland
Canvas and Camera II Association Gallery, London
Paste-Up Past and Present Kent Gallery, New York
1996 *50th Anniversary Exhibition* Gimpel Fils, London
1998 *Eye Witness* Tom Blau Gallery, London
Inventory Shoreditch Photo Biennale, London
Sur les pouvoirs et les incertitudes Representing UK at the *Rencontres Internationales de la Photographie*, Arles, France
Accrochage Gimpel Fils, London
The Power of the Poster Victoria and Albert Museum, London
1999 *Art in Exile* Brixton Art Gallery, London
Housing and Homelessness Candid Gallery, London
2000–1 *Look Out* Curated by Peter Kennard, Wolverhampton City Art Gallery; Ipswich Museum and Art Gallery; Pitshanger Art Gallery, London

Selected public collections

Antwerp Art Gallery
Arts Council of England
Gallery of Modern Art, Glasgow
Imperial War Museum, London
National Museum of Photography, Film and Television, Bradford
Science Museum, London
University College, London
Victoria and Albert Museum, London

Film and video

1982 Photomontages for Labour Party political broadcast against nuclear weapons

1983 *Photomontage Today: Peter Kennard*, directed by Chris Rodrigues and Rod Stoneman, 35 minutes, Arts Council of Britain

Photomontages for Labour Party election broadcast

1984 Animated sequences for *Unstable Elements*, newsreel for Channel 4

1986 *State of Emergency – South Africa*, Bandung File, Channel 4

1987 Animated montage sequence for *The People's Flag*, Platform Films for Channel 4

1991 *Heartfield the Father of Photomontage* (sequence on Peter Kennard's photomontages), Granada Television

1992 *Welcome to Britain*, The Late Show, BBC2

Publications

Evans, Bill and Kennard, Peter, *About Turn*, Pluto Press, 1986
Greater London Council Economic Policy Group, *Jobs for a Change*, GLC/Pluto Press, 1983
Kennard, Peter and Sissons, Ric, *No Nuclear Weapons*, CND/Pluto Press, 1981
Kennard, Peter, *GLC Peace Posters Pack*, GLC, 1983
Kennard, Peter, *Target London*, GLC, 1985
Kennard, Peter, *Images for the End of the Century*, Journeyman/Pluto Press, 1990
Kennard, Peter, and Livingstone, Ken, *Our Financial Times*, Gimpel Fils, 1995
Kennard, Peter, *Unwords*, Bluecoat, 1996
Kennard, Peter, *Domesday Book*, Foreword by Harold Pinter, Manchester University Press, 1999

Limited editions

1992 *Peter Kennard: Photomontages 1973–1991*. Boxed portfolio of 12 signed and dated silver prints. Edition of 30. Introductory text by John Berger. Kent Gallery, New York

Selected articles on Peter Kennard

Berger, John, 'Seeing Through Lies', *Sanity*, December 1981
Berger, John, 'Global Warning', The *Guardian*, 15 June 1990
Brett, Guy, 'News You Missed', *The Times*, 17 June 1972
Clark, Robert 'The Wrinkles of War' The *Guardian*, 21 May 1996
Cork, Richard, 'Danger Signs', The *Listener*, 8 August 1985
Cork, Richard, 'The Problems of Idealism in Modern Art', *Evening Standard*, 23 September 1970
Courtney, Cathy, 'Wordless', *Art Monthly*, July–August 1996
Cumming, Laura, 'See the Dome from a Different Angle', The *Observer*, 12 December 1999
Fuller, Peter, 'Aesthetics and Nuclear Anæsthesia', *The Naked Artist,* Writers and Readers, 1983
Lubbock, Tom, 'Rip It Up and Start Again?', The *Independent*, 7 December 1999
McCabe, Eamonn and Vullliamy, Ed, 'Image Makers: Peter Kennard', The *Guardian*, 4 November 1989
Pilger, John, 'Giving a Voice to the Silent Majority', The *Guardian*, 25 February 1997
Potts, Robert, 'Tunnel Vision', *The Times Literary Supplement*, 1 July 1994
Reid, Shirley, 'New Labour', *Creative Camera: 30 Years of Writing*, Manchester University Press, 1999
Roberts, John, 'Peter Kennard at the Museum of Modern Art', *Art in America*, December 1983
Rye, Jane, 'Toxic Celebration', *London Magazine*, February/March 2000
Sanders, Mark, 'No More Mr Nice Guy', *Dazed and Confused*, June 1994
Slyce, John, 'Through the Smokescreen', *Red Pepper*, July 1997
Slyce, John, 'Art and Activism for a Broken World', *Red Pepper*, June 2000
Tisdall, Caroline, 'Future Shock', The *Guardian*, 25 October 1980
Tisdall, Caroline, 'Peter Kennard', *Art and Artists*, December 1973
Williams, Val, 'Over in Two Clicks', *Creative Camera*, December 1991
Worpole, Ken, 'Do You Ever Wish You Were Better Informed?', *New Statesman*, 19–26 December 1980